THE SHIA REVIVAL

VALI NASR

THE SHIA REVIVAL

How Conflicts within Islam Will Shape the Future

W. W. Norton & Company

New York • London

For information about permission to reproduce selections from this book, write to
Permissions, W. W. Norton & Company, Inc., 500 Fifth Avenue, New York, NY 10110

Manufacturing by Courier Westford
Book design by Chris Welch
Production manager: Anna Oler

Library of Congress Cataloging-in-Publication Data

Nasr, Seyyed Vali Reza, 1960–
The Shia revival : how conflicts within Islam will shape the future / Vali Nasr. — 1st ed.
p. cm.
Includes bibliographical references and index.
ISBN-13: 978-0-393-06211-3 (hardcover)
ISBN-10: 0-393-06211-2 (hardcover)
1. Shī 'ah—Political aspects—Middle East. 2. Islam and politics—Middle East—
History—20th century. 3. Middle East—Politics and government—1979– .
4. Shī 'ah—Relations—Sunnites. 5. Sunnites—Relations—Shī 'ah. I. Title.
BP194.185.N37 2006
297.8'209045—dc22

2006012361

W. W. Norton & Company, Inc., 500 Fifth Avenue, New York, N.Y. 10110
www.wwnorton.com

W. W. Norton & Company Ltd., Castle House, 75/76 Wells Street, London W1T 3QT

2 3 4 5 6 7 8 9 0

FOR

AMIR, HOSSEIN, AND DONIA

CONTENTS

AUTHOR'S NOTE

This book is not a work of historical scholarship. Its contribution is in the new ideas and arguments that it brings to an understanding of the Islamic world and Middle East history and politics. I have written this book with a general audience in mind, and I have therefore avoided the usual method of transliteration or citation of notes seen in scholarly works. In referring to foreign names or terms, I have used a simplified phonetic pattern closer to the Arabic, Persian, or Urdu pronunciation, depending on the context of the discussion. The notes are meant for the most part to provide references for a striking piece of information or a quotation. Finally, all translations are mine unless otherwise stated.

Heed not the blind eye, the echoing ear, nor yet the tongue, but bring to this great debate the test of reason.

—*Parmenides*

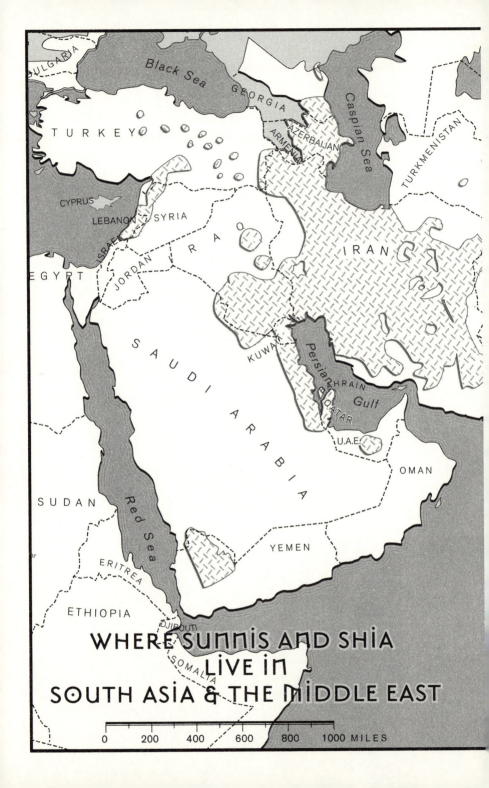

WHERE SUNNIS AND SHIA
LIVE IN
SOUTH ASIA & THE MIDDLE EAST

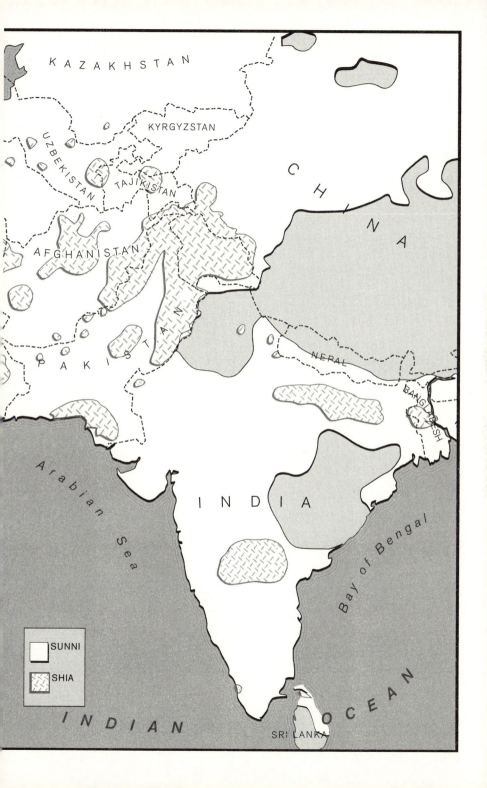

THE SHIA REVIVAL

INTRODUCTION

I n early 2003, right around the start of the war in Iraq, I was visiting an old Shia friend in Pakistan. We talked about the
changes that were beginning to sweep the Middle East. For my
friend there was a twist of irony to all the talk of Shias and Sunnis
that was beginning to fill the airwaves, clearly confusing those in the
West who thought that all that mattered in Iraq and the Middle East
was the fight for democracy. It made him think of an exchange he
had had with a high-ranking U.S. official.

My friend had been a senior Pakistani government official in the
1980s, the liaison with the Pentagon in managing the war against the
Soviets in Afghanistan. He reminisced that back in those days, when
Iran and Hezbollah were waging an active terror war against the
United States and the Afghan mujahideen were the "good guys," his
American counterpart, a senior official at the Pentagon, often teased
him by saying that Shias were "bloodthirsty, baby-eating monsters."

My friend would retort that Americans had got it wrong. "Just wait and see," he would tell his colleague from the States. "The real problem will be the Sunnis. They are the bullies; the Shias are the underdogs." Time passed, and my friend retired from government service. One sleepy afternoon in the fall of 2001, after September 11, his slumber was disturbed by the noise of sirens as a caravan of black SUVs descended on his house in Islamabad. His old American friend, now an important man in Washington, had come back to Pakistan to manage another war in Afghanistan, and he had decided to drop by. The American asked my friend, "Do you remember our discussions all those years ago about Shias and Sunnis? I want you to explain to me what you meant when you said that the Sunnis would be the real problem." So my friend explained the difference between the two sects of Islam, and who had dominated whom and when and why, and what all that would mean today.

What my friend told his American visitor took on greater importance as the Iraq war added a layer of complexity to the already difficult problems facing the United States after 9/11. There were now also the implications of the Shia-Sunni conflict to consider as American leaders looked for ways to contain the threat of Islamic extremism, grapple with the challenges of Iran and Hezbollah in Lebanon, and bring reform to the Middle East.

I was on a research trip in Pakistan in April 2003 when two million Shias gathered in the Iraqi city of Karbala to mark the Arbaeen, the commemoration of the fortieth day after the martyrdom of the Shia saint Imam Husayn at Karbala in 680 C.E. Saddam Hussein had banned such gatherings for years. The last thing he wanted was that many Shias together in one place, in a state of high religious excitement, venerating a hero of their faith who was a close relative of the Prophet Muhammad himself and who—so the Shia believe—had died resisting tyranny to the last.

On that particular "fortieth day," so soon after the one on which U.S. Marines and jubilant Iraqis had pulled down Saddam's hollow image in Baghdad's Firdous Square, I happened to be on the outskirts of Lahore, visiting the headquarters of a Sunni fundamentalist political group known as the Jamaat-e Islami (Islamic Party). The office television set was tuned to CNN, as everyone was following news from Iraq. The coverage turned to scenes of young Shia men standing densely packed in the shadow of the golden dome of Imam Husayn's shrine at Karbala. They all wore black shirts and had scarves of green (the universal color of Islam) wrapped around their heads. They chanted a threnody in Arabic for their beloved saint as they raised their empty hands as if in prayer toward heaven and in unison brought them down to thump on their chests in a rhythmic gesture of mourning, solidarity, and mortification. The image was magnetic, at once jubilant and defiant. The Shia were in the streets, and they were holding their faith and their identity high for all to see. We stared at the television screen. My Sunni hosts were aghast at what they were seeing. A pall descended on the room.

Iraq had not seen such scenes in a generation or more, and now the world was bearing witness to the Shia awakening. The CNN commentator was gleefully boasting that Iraqis were free at last—they were performing a ritual that the audience in the West did not understand but that had been forbidden to the Shia for decades. What Americans saw as Iraqi freedom, my hosts saw as the blatant display of heretical rites that are anathema to orthodox Sunnis. Iraqis were free—free to be Shias, free to challenge Sunni power and the Sunni conception of what it means to be a true Muslim; free to reclaim their millennium-old faith. "These actions are not right," said one of my hosts. Iraqis—by which he meant the Shia—"do not know the proper practice of Islam." The Shia-Sunni debates over the truth of the Islamic message and how to practice it would continue, he added, not just peacefully and symbolically but with bombs and bullets. He was talking not about Iraq but about Pakistan.

My hosts at the Jamaat said forlornly that the situation in Iraq would open sectarian wounds in Pakistan and that the struggles certain to ensue in Iraq would be played out in the mosques and on the streets of Karachi and Lahore, too. Later that year bomb blasts during the Shia festival of Ashoura (the main commemoration of Husayn's martyrdom) killed scores, in Baghdad and Najaf and in Quetta, Pakistan. A common thread had already begun to weave together sectarian conflict in the two countries. That thread has long run through the fabric of social and political life across the broader Middle East—at times invisible within a regional politics that can be more intricate and colorful than the pattern on an Isfahan carpet, but at other times as obvious as the stripe running down the middle of a highway.

The Shia-Sunni conflict is at once a struggle for the soul of Islam—a great war of competing theologies and conceptions of sacred history—and a manifestation of the kind of tribal wars of ethnicities and identities, so seemingly archaic at times, yet so surprisingly vital, with which humanity has become wearily familiar. Faith and identity converge in this conflict, and their combined power goes a long way toward explaining why, despite the periods of coexistence, the struggle has lasted so long and retains such urgency and significance. It is not just a hoary religious dispute, a fossilized set piece from the early years of Islam's unfolding, but a contemporary clash of identities. Theological and historical disagreements fuel it, but so do today's concerns with power, subjugation, freedom, and equality, not to mention regional conflicts and foreign intrigues. It is, paradoxically, a very old, very modern conflict.

For the quarter century between the Iranian revolution in 1979 and September 11, 2001, the United States saw the Middle East far too often through the eyes of the authoritarian Sunni elites in Islamabad, Amman, Cairo, and Riyadh, who were America's major local allies. Even in Western scholarly tomes on Islam, the Shia received only cursory treatment. As the Middle East changes and the Sunni ascendancy continues to come under challenge, the U.S. perspective on the region must change as well. Responding to European objections to the war in Iraq, Secretary of Defense Donald Rumsfeld famously distinguished the "old Europe," which opposed the war, from the "new Europe," which was more likely to support it. The war has also drawn a line (albeit in a different way) between an "old" and a "new" Middle East. The old Middle East lived under the domination of its Arab component and looked to Cairo, Baghdad, and Damascus—those ancient seats of Sunni caliphs—as its "power towns." The region's problems, ambitions, identity, and self-image were primarily, if not exclusively, those of the Arabs. The dominant political values of the old Middle East are a decades-old vintage of Arab nationalism.

This Middle East, now passing uneasily away, was at its core a place by, for, and about the Sunni ruling establishment. The new Middle East coming fitfully into being—its birth pangs punctuated by car bombs but also by peaceful protests and elections—is defined in equal part by the identity of Shias, whose cultural ties and relations of faith, political alliances, and commercial links cut across the divide between Arab and non-Arab. Consider that Iraq, together with Egypt and Syria one of the three most important Arab countries and a serious contender for Arab-world leadership during the Arab nationalist heyday, elected a Kurd as its first postwar president and has been cultivating far closer relations with Iran than with its Arab neighbors. Iraq's Shia and Kurdish majority even chose to omit the customary pledge of allegiance to Arab identity in the country's first attempt at a new constitution in the summer of 2005, declaring Iraq to be not an "Arab republic" but a "federal republic" instead.

The elected officials of Iraq's fledgling postwar government are the first Shia leaders that the United States has had any direct and meaningful contact with since the Iranian revolution. When American leaders spoke of changing the region's politics for the better after the Iraq war, they were in effect talking about democratizing the old Sunni-dominated Middle East. They gave little thought to the new Middle East that is emerging, and have yet to grasp its potential. This Middle East will not be defined by the Arab identity or by any particular form of national government. Ultimately, the character of the region will be decided in the crucible of Shia revival and the Sunni response to it.

The Middle East today is more vulnerable to instability and extremism than at any time since Iran's Islamic revolution swept a U.S. ally off the throne of that country and brought Shia radicals to power there. America's call for democracy in the region has rattled its friends while failing to placate its enemies. The conflict in Iraq has brought to power a Shia religious coalition and created an Islamic-cum-nationalist insurgency that is strengthening jihadi extremism.

Thus the Shia-Sunni conflict has captured world attention, but to Arabs and Iranians, Afghans and Pakistanis living in the region, it is an age-old scourge that has flared up from time to time to mold Islamic history, theology, law, and politics. It has been far more important in shaping the Middle East than many realize or acknowledge. And it has become deeply embedded in popular prejudice, as stereotypes of the plebeian Shias and their wrongheaded view of Islam have defined how many Sunnis have seen their kinsmen. In Lebanon, popular lore has held that Shias have tails; they reproduce too prolifically, are too loud in expressing their religiosity, and, given

Lebanon's debonair self-image, are ridiculed for their low-class, tasteless and vulgar ways.[1] Despite the political popularity of Hezbollah, Shias face discrimination and are dismissed as provincial, uncouth, and unfit for their lofty pretension of representing Lebanon. In Saudi Arabia, it is said that Shias spit in their food—a slander no doubt meant to discourage even socialization over meals between Sunnis and Shias—and that shaking hands with a Shia is polluting, necessitating ablutions.[2] In Pakistan, Shias are tagged with derogatory nicknames such as "mosquitoes."

The West, too, has had its wars of religion: the Thirty Years' War, the conflict in Northern Ireland, and the quieter but real prejudices and forms of discrimination that Westerners have applied against one another over religious differences. These conflicts and rivalries have not always been over matters of theological principle but more often have reflected competing claims to power made by rival communities with roots in differing religious identities. Religion is not just about God and salvation; it decides the boundaries of communities. Different readings of history, theology, and religious law perform the same role as language or race in defining what makes each identity unique and in saying who belongs to it and who does not.

We live in an age of globalization, but also one of identity politics. It is as if our world is expanding and contracting at the same time. Diverse peoples embrace universal values, and once insular communities engage in unprecedented levels of commerce and communication with the outside world. Yet at the same time the primordial or near-primordial ties of race, language, ethnicity, and religion make their presence felt with dogged determination. This is the reality of our time, and the Muslim world cannot escape it. Its conflicts of identity ebb and flow alongside those struggles that more often draw the world's gaze—between fundamentalism and modernism, or authoritarianism and democracy—as shapers of Muslims' futures.

As war, democracy, and globalization force the Middle East to open itself up to a number of long-resisted forms of change—conflicts such as the Shia-Sunni rift will become both more frequent and more intense. Before the Middle East can arrive at democracy and prosperity, it will have to settle these conflicts—those between ethnic groups such as Kurds, Turks, Arabs, and Persians, and, more importantly, the broader one between Shias and Sunnis. Just as the settlement of religious conflicts marked Europe's passage to modernity, so the Middle East will have to achieve sectarian peace before it can begin living up to its potential.

In the coming years Shias and Sunnis will compete over power, first in Iraq but ultimately across the entire region. Beyond Iraq, other countries will (even as they embrace reform) have to cope with intensifying rivalries between Shias and Sunnis. The overall Sunni-Shia conflict will play a large role in defining the Middle East as a whole and shaping its relations with the outside world. Sectarian conflict will make Sunni extremists more extreme and will likely rekindle revolutionary zeal among the Shia. At times the conflict will be bloody, as it strengthens the extremists, swelling their ranks, popularizing their causes, and amplifying their voices in politics, thus complicating the broader effort to contain Islamic radicalism. Even those who will attempt to douse the flames of sectarian conflict will not always do so in the name of moderation. They will, rather, seek to build a common front between Shias and Sunnis in a larger struggle against the United States and Israel.

Shias and Sunnis are not monolithic communities, and this book does not begin from that premise. The followers of each sect are divided by language, ethnicity, geography, and class. There are also disagreements within each group over politics, theology, and religious law, not to mention the divide between the pious and the less vigilant or even the outright secular. The Shia world and the Sunni world overlap and intermingle geographically. They also spread across a variety of cultural zones and myriad smaller ethnic communities. There are Arab, Persian, and South Asian cultural zones, to name a few, and then within these zones there are further linguistic and ethnic divisions. In Iraq, for instance, there are broad differences between Arab, Kurdish, and Turkoman Shias, as well as between city folk, tribespeople, peasants, and marsh dwellers. Yet no matter how much we may focus on the diversity of opinions, customs, attitudes, and interests within each community, in the end it is not the diversity that defines the conflict but the conflict that defines social attitudes that are widely shared.

Like many populations that have lived uneasily near each other for a long time, Shias and Sunnis have their stories of common struggles, communal harmony, friendship, and intermarriage. There are clerics, such as Ayatollahs Muhammad Asef Mohseni of Afghanistan and Kalb-e Sadeq of India, who preach sectarian peace. In Iraq, major tribes like the al-Jubouri, Shammar, and Tamimi all in varying proportions have both Shia and Sunni members. Across the Middle East Shias and Sunnis have often rallied around the same political causes and even fought together in the same trenches, most notably against foreign occupation, as in Iraq against the British in 1920 and in Lebanon against Israel in the late 1980s. In fact, no cause in modern times has brought the two sides together more than the fight against Israel. But none of this makes the Shia-Sunni conflict imaginary or irrelevant. The social and political attitudes that sustain it have strong roots in religion, history, and the recent experiences of both communities. The Iran-Iraq war of the 1980s, Saddam's brutal suppression of the Shia uprising in 1991, the Iranian-Saudi rivalry since 1979, the Saudi-Pakistani-Taliban alliance in the 1990s, and Saudi Arabia's enormous financial investment in the infrastructure of Sunni extremism in South and Central Asia in the 1990s have all been expressions of the sectarian substructure that runs beneath Middle East politics and continues to affect events, even if it is not always obvious to outside observers.

Many commentators have pointed out that even in Iraq, where Shia-Sunni conflict is most intense, the hostility between the two communities does not run as deep as that between Protestants and Roman Catholics in Northern Ireland or Christians and Muslims in Lebanon. Hatred is less visceral, and Shias blame Saddam, not their Sunni neighbors, for their poverty and suffering. There are more mixed communities, and there has been frequent intermarriage. But the growing intensity of sectarian conflict in Iraq is corroding these bonds.[3] As Rwandans and residents of the Balkans can sadly testify, mixed marriages and a history of communal coexistence are no guarantee against fratricide. Even Sarajevo's cosmopolitan blend of Muslim, Croat, and Serbian communities, with its hybrid culture and mixed families, did not protect it from the violence of Yugoslavia's genocidal wars.

In Iraq, rage against suicide bombings by Sunni extremists (many of whom, it should be noted, are non-Iraqis) has led to vigilante Shia reprisals, including kidnapping, torture, executions, and assassinations, even as senior Shia leaders continue to urge restraint.[4] Moreover, what amounts to ethnic cleansing by both sides is changing the human landscape of the country by force. Al-Daura, an anti-coalition stronghold in southern Baghdad, had been three quarters Sunni and a quarter Shia, but Shias recently began to leave the neighborhood in droves.[5] In Ramadi, a jihadi and ex-Ba'thist hotbed in the restless Sunni province of al-Anbar, the local Sunni population could not stop insurgents from pushing the city's Shia inhabitants to leave.[6] In Basra, the violence has been flowing the other way as Shia extremists murder Sunni clerics, other leaders, and even ordinary people, sparking a Sunni exodus from the largest city of the Iraqi south.[7]

What makes sectarian conflict particularly relevant to the future of the Middle East is that it is surfacing at a time when anti-Americanism, religious conservatism, and extremism are on the rise. Sunni extremism feeds on anti-Shia bias and even violence. The spasms of sectarian rivalries strengthen Sunni extremism and sanction the violence, which—at least in places where the Shia can fight back—leads to a vicious cycle of provocation and revenge followed by more of the same.

Sectarian politics is also making its mark at a time of intense and wider-than-ever debates about the future of democracy in the region. Those debates are not only about the rights of individuals, the reform of unrepresentative governments, and the rule of law, but also about the relative power of Shias and Sunnis in defining and running governments and controlling state resources. For the United States to bring stability to its relations with the Middle East, it will have to invest in democracy, but that investment can bear fruit only if it broadens and deepens its ties within the region and goes beyond a small clique of authoritarian rulers to engage a broader segment of the region's population. This will have to mean broader and deeper engagement with the Shia, a lesson that was writ large after the fall of the Taliban in Afghanistan. Building democracy in that country cannot happen without including Shias in the political process. A fifth of the population but traditionally marginalized by the dominant Sunni Pashtuns, the Shias have most to benefit from democracy. Not only did the fall of the Taliban free them from the yoke of religious tyranny, but changes that followed the war gave them a say in Afghanistan's future, as their existence and rights were for the first time recognized in the country's new constitution.

The Middle East's sectarian pains are not divorced from the larger political and economic and security problems that ail the region. Dictatorships have failed to build inclusive political systems that share power and give a place at the table to all. Economic stagnation and mismanagement have made things worse. The resurgence of the Shia-Sunni conflict feeds on the malaise at the heart of the Middle East's political and economic life, so much of which is marred by a persistent inability or unwillingness to negotiate over power peacefully and through regular channels. When change comes, it is abrupt and violent; what engineers call "graceful," as opposed to "cataclysmic," system transformation is a difficult thing to bring about in the Middle East. History and theology may establish the identities of rival groups; but the actual bones of contention are far less likely to be religious ideas than matters of concrete power and wealth doled out along communal lines.

Peace and stability will come to the Middle East only when the distribution of power and wealth reflects the balance between the communities and the political system includes all and provides for peaceful ways of resolving disputes. Once the conflicts that have already been set in motion are exhausted, the majority of Shias and Sunnis will settle for a political order that they can share—not dominated by one or the other, theologically or politically—and that represents everyone's social, economic, and political aspirations.

This book is not about the war in Iraq but about the conflicts that the war and its aftermath have unleashed and how those conflicts will shape the future. My aim is to explain why there is a Shia-Sunni conflict, why has it become more salient of late, and what it will mean for both the future of the Middle East and the Muslim world's relations with the West. There is much here about Islam and Islamic history and more about what it means to those who follow that faith. It is not possible to write on these issues without also writing about a topic of great interest to the West in recent decades: Islam's complex and seemingly unbreakable ties to politics.

To Western eyes, Muslim politics is defined by Islamic values. Politics may look for truth in religious texts, but it will always do so from within a context that is not purely religious. People read, understand, and interpret their sources of sacred meaning in relation to the hopes and fears that define their daily lives. It is therefore not always possible to talk of one Islamic reality, and less so of one Shia or one Sunni reality. Piety and politics for Shias and Sunnis alike are shaped by the particularities of life in societies as varied as those of India, Iran, and Saudi Arabia. As different as such contexts are, the Iraq war has changed them all.

Chapter 1

THE OTHER ISLAM
Who Are the Shia?

E very year on the tenth day of the holy month of Muharram, the first on the Islamic lunar calendar, Shia Muslims show a distinctive face of Islam, one that sees spirituality in passion and rituals rather than in law and the familiar practices that punctuate Muslim lives. Open spaces and narrow alleys in cities, towns, and villages take over from mosques and seminaries as Shias individually and collectively make a show of their piety and their identity. No observer of this day, the festival of Ashoura, will remain unaffected by the Shias' display of fealty to their faith. None will fail to see the uniqueness of Shia Islam or the values and spirituality that define it.

Every year on this day—whose date on the Western calendar changes from year to year because of differences between the Gregorian solar reckoning and the lunar months of the traditional Muslim calendar—the Shia mark the anniversary of the death of their most vividly recalled saint, the grandson of Prophet Muhammad known among the Shia as the Imam Husayn. The day is called Ashoura, from the Arabic word for "tenth." It is an occasion for collective atonement through lamentation and self-flagellation. It is a distinctly Shia practice and has no parallel in Sunnism. In those areas of the Muslim world where Shias and Sunnis live side by side, Ashoura underscores Shia distinctiveness and often draws Sunni opprobrium. Ashoura is a day when the Shias announce who they are—often going to great extremes to do so—and when the Sunnis, by condemning and protesting, in equal measure may announce their objection to Shia practices.

When Ashoura falls on a warm day late in the spring, throngs of Shia women and children line the narrow byways of the old city of Lahore, a medieval village now surrounded by the sprawling bustle of modern urban Pakistan. Old Lahore's meandering streets (too small for cars), its antique villas with their high ceilings, graceful courtyards, and jutting verandas, and its ornate mosques and tower-ing gates take a visitor back centuries, to the days when the Mughal emperors ruled these lands. On one side of the old city sits the grand Badshahi (Royal) Mosque. Arching gates mark each of the four main passages into the old city's humming bazaars. To the dis-cerning eye of the knowing pedestrian, the old city reveals itself to be a Shia settlement, dotted with small shrines and places of wor-ship dedicated to Imam Husayn.

Each quarter of the old city has its own Ashoura procession. They compete and converge as they wend their way through the streets, visiting every one of those mosques and places of worship. At the head of each procession marches a group of young men car-rying a tall metal staff ornately decked with thin strips of red, green, and white cloth that flutter and snap in the breeze. High on the staff sits a triangular black pennant. Above it, at the very top, is the elaborately carved shape of a human hand. The hand represents the five holy people whom the Shia hold in highest regard: the Prophet Muhammad, his daughter Fatima al-Zahra, his son-in-law and cousin Ali, and his grandsons Hasan and Husayn. The hand and the black flag mark Shia houses, mosques, and processions from India to the Middle East.

Young boys offer water to the watching crowd. Everyone drinks and says a prayer for the martyred Husayn. Behind the men carrying the staff comes a riderless white horse with a beautiful saddle on its back and white feathers on its drooping head. The horse is the center of attention. Its empty saddle reminds watchers of its fallen master, the object of the crowd's adulation. Several women, their heads covered with scarves, trail the horse, gently beating their chests and chanting "O Husayn!" They are praying for forgiveness, for on this day, the Shia believe, God answers prayers and forgives the repentant more readily than on any other day—regardless of either the nature and number of the sins committed or the penitent's degree of adherence to the daily practices that characterize Muslim piety.

Some of the women are weeping. The atmosphere is charged with anticipation. From around a bend in the street comes a rhythmic thudding interspersed with chanting. Then the bulk of the procession, a long line of men, heaves into view. Dressed in black, they walk four abreast and fill the narrow alleyway. Following the lead of an older, white-bearded man up front, they beat their chests with both hands as they chant and call in unison, "Ya Husayn!" As the procession passes, the sounds of the voices and the thumping echo from the old city's ancient walls.

The sights and sounds of Ashoura are gripping. This is a ritual filled with symbolism and passion. It is deeply spiritual and communal. It defines Shias and renews their bond to their faith and community. It reminds believers that the essence of their religion is not works but faith. With some local variations, the same ritual will be taking place on this day in the Indian city of Lucknow, the Iranian capital of Tehran, Karbala in southern Iraq, the island country of Bahrain in the Persian Gulf, and the town of Nabatiye in southern Lebanon. Ashoura is an act of piety, but not one that is recognized as an obligatory practice of the faith. It has no foundation in the Quran and was not practiced at the time of the Prophet. Yet this is also Islam, even if not in a guise that most Westerners readily associate with the religion.[1]

So what is Shiism? And what separates the Shia from the Sunni? Most Western discussions of Islamic matters or the Arab world tend to focus, often implicitly, on Sunnism. This is perhaps to be expected, since the overwhelming majority of the world's 1.3 billion Muslims are Sunnis. Shias number from 130 million to 195 million people, or 10 to 15 percent of the total.[2] In the Islamic heartland, from Lebanon to Pakistan, however, there are roughly as many Shias as there are Sunnis, and around the economically and geostrategically sensitive rim of the Persian Gulf, Shias constitute 80 percent of the population.

The divide between Shiism and Sunnism is the most important in Islam. The two sects parted ways early in Muslim history, and each views itself as the original orthodoxy. Their split somewhat parallels the Protestant-Catholic difference in Western Christianity. Just as past intra-Christian conflicts shaped European politics, so the Sunni-Shia conflict continues to shape the history of the Islamic world and the broader Middle East.

Shiism and Sunnism not only understand Islamic history, theology, and law differently, but each breathes a distinct ethos of faith and piety that nurtures a particular temperament and a unique approach to the question of what it means to be Muslim. The rivalry goes back to the early days of Islam and the succession crisis that followed the Prophet Muhammad's death in 632 C.E. Most Muslims at the time (the forebears of the Sunnis) followed the tribal tradition according to which a council of elders would choose the most senior and respected elder to become the head of the Islamic community, or *umma*. Early Muslims found justification for this practice in the Prophet's declaration that "my community will never agree in error." For the Sunnis, the successor to the Prophet would need no exceptional spiritual qualities but would merely have to be an exemplary Muslim who could ably and virtuously direct the religious and political affairs of the community. The Sunnis chose Abu Bakr, the Prophet's close friend and father-in-law, as his successor or caliph. A small group of the Prophet's companions believed that the Prophet's cousin and son-in-law, Ali ibn Abi Talib, was more qualified for the job and that it had been the wish of the Prophet that he lead the Muslim community. In the end consensus prevailed and all dissenters, Ali included, accepted Abu Bakr's leadership.

Abu Bakr was succeeded by Umar, Uthman, and finally Ali. Sunnis call these four men, whose successive terms spanned the three decades from 632 to 661, the Rightly Guided, or *Rashidun*, Caliphs. They had all been close companions of the Prophet and were knowledgeable in matters of religion. For Sunnis, the time of these caliphs was Islam's golden age, an era when political authority continued to be informed by the pristine values of the faith and when Muslim society remained close to its spiritual roots.

Even the era of the Rightly Guided Caliphs, however, proved to be far from harmonious. Umar was killed by an Iranian prisoner of war, but most notably, Uthman was murdered in 656 by mutinous Muslim soldiers, his blood spilling onto the Quran that he was reading. The young Muslim community was in shock at the spectacle of Muslims murdering the successor to the Prophet. The aftereffects of

Uthman's murder plagued the caliphate of Ali. He faced mutinies—including one that included Abu Bakr's daughter and the Prophet's wife, Ayesha—and was hard-pressed to restore calm, and soon confronted a strong challenge from Uthman's cousin Muawiya, the governor of Damascus, who demanded that Ali avenge Uthman's murder. The tribal demand for justice soon took on the quality of a power struggle between the new caliph and the governor. A civil war between the caliph's army and Muawiya's forces ensued, further miring the Muslim community in conflict and confusion. That war ended only when Ali was assassinated by angry extremists who blamed both him and Muawiya for the crisis. Muawiya survived their wrath to assume the caliphate. The nearly century-long reign of the Umayyad dynasty (661–750) had begun, and Damascus would be its center.

Sunni Muslims accepted Muawiya's rise. He lacked religious authority, but he guaranteed the basic order that the faith was thought to need. Under the Umayyads the caliphs became both pope and caesar, delegating authority over religious matters to professional religious scholars and functionaries, the ulama. The Sunnis were well on their way to embracing their traditional stance of accepting a regime's legitimacy so long as it provided order, protected Islam, and left religious matters to the ulama.[3] The famous saying "Better sixty years of tyranny than a single day of civil strife" captures the spirit of the Sunni position.

Not all Muslims were content with this formula, and Shiism arose in part on the foundation of their dissent. Ali's murder, the transformation of the caliphate into a monarchy, and the de facto separation of religious and political authorities under the Umayyads led a minority of Muslims to argue that what had come to pass was the fruit not of God's mandate but of man's folly. They saw the roots of the problem going back to the choice of the first successor to the Prophet. Muslims had erred in choosing their leaders, and that error had mired their faith in violence and confusion. The dissenting voices rejected the legitimacy of the first three Rightly Guided Caliphs, arguing that God would not entrust his religion to ordinary mortals chosen by the vote of the community and that Muhammad's family—popularly known as the *ahl al-Bayt* (people of the household)—were the true leaders of the Muslim community, for the blood of the Prophet ran in their veins and they bore his charisma and the spiritual qualities that God had vested in him.[4] Abu Bakr and Umar were particularly at fault for ignoring the Prophet's wishes about how his authority should be handed on and convening a gathering at Saqifah Bani Saeda to elect his successor. This view would become foundational to Shiism.[5]

After a chaotic period, dissenters and foes of the Umayyads began to identify Ali, the Prophet's cousin, virtual adoptive son, and son-in-law, as the one who should have been the Prophet's successor all along. According to some accounts the first convert to Islam, while still in his teens, Ali was the hero of many of the early Muslim battles and was known for his chivalry and heroism, symbolized by his legendary forked-tongued sword (*zulfiqar*). In one tale, Ali risks death by sleeping in the Prophet's bed in order to fool assassins as Muhammad escapes from Mecca to Medina. Ali is the font of spirituality for the Shia.[6] They apostrophize Ali as "Lord of the Faithful" (*amir al-mu'minin*), "Lion of God" (*asadollah*), and "King of Men" (*shah-e mardan*). "There is no hero but Ali," they cry, "and no sword but his *zulfiqar*" (*La fata illa Ali, la saif illa zulfiqar*). It is common for Shias to invoke Ali's aid by saying *Ya Ali madad!* (O Ali, help me!)

The early Shias argued that the Prophet had chosen Ali as his successor and had made a testament to that effect, telling a congregation of Muslims at Ghadir Khumm, during his last pilgrimage to Mecca, that "whoever recognizes me as his master will recognize Ali

as his master." Ali was thus chosen by Muhammad's testament. The
Festival of Ghadir Khumm, marking the date when the Prophet
anointed Ali as his successor, is an important date on the Shia calendar. For Shias, the profession of faith is "There is no god but God
and Muhammad is his Prophet, and Ali is the executor of God's
will" (la ilaha illalah, Muahammadan rasul allah wa Alian waliullah).
For Shias, therefore, Ali was always the rightful caliph.[7] Though he
was eventually elected caliph, his partisans (literally, Shiite-Ali)
believe that the initial usurpation of his right to rule by Abu Bakr,
Umar, and Uthman gravely occluded the ideal Islamic authority.

The Shias disagree with the Sunnis not only over who should
have succeeded the Prophet but also over the function that his successor was to play. Sunnis, whose familiar name is short for ahl al-
sunnah wa'l-jama'ah (people of tradition and consensus), believe
that the Prophet's successor was succeeding only to his role as
leader of the Islamic community and not to his special relationship
with God or prophetic calling, and that the consensus of the
Muslim community that selected Abu Bakr and the succeeding
Rightly Guided Caliphs reflected the truth of the Islamic message.
Underlying these views is the spiritually egalitarian notion—which
in the West would be identified with the "low church" Protestant
variant of Christianity—that all believers are capable of understanding religious truth in a way and to a degree that renders special
intermediaries between man and God unnecessary.

Shiism is based on a more pessimistic assessment of human falli-
bility. Just as humans could not find salvation until the Prophet took
up the task of guiding them toward it, so after him people need the
help of exceptionally holy and divinely favored people in order to
live in accord with the inner truths of religion.[8] The descendants of
Ali, known collectively as the imams (not to be confused with ordinary prayer leaders in mosques) provide that continual help, renew-

as Catholic priests!

ing and strengthening the bond between man and God. The ulama, or clergy, carry on the project of the imams in safeguarding and sustaining the faith. Without the right leadership, Shias insist, the true meaning and intent of Islam will be lost. The differences between Shias and Sunnis are thus not only political but also theological and even anthropological.

Shias believe that the Prophet possessed special spiritual qualities, was immaculate from sin (*ma'soum*), and could penetrate to the hidden meaning of religious teachings. Shias further believe that Ali and his descendants had these special spiritual qualities too. They bore the light of Muhammad (*nur-e Muhammadi*). They were his "trustees" (*wasi*) and were privy to his esoteric and religious knowledge. They could understand and interpret the inner meaning of Islam, as opposed to merely implementing its outward manifestations.[9] Since it was the Prophet's will for Ali to succeed him as caliph, loyalty to the Prophet has to mean refusing to accept any other outcome. The caliphate of the Sunnis encompassed far less of the prophetic function than the imamate of the Shias.

The Sunni conception of authority has centered on a preoccupation with order. Religion does not depend on the quality of political authority but only on its ability to help the faith survive and grow. Medieval Sunni jurists developed a theory of government according to which clerics would uphold the government's authority so long as the rulers provided stability and order and protected the Muslim community.[10] Sultans did not have to be spiritual leaders or pretend to create a perfect Islamic order. One might even say that their main job was to protect Islam's values and interests rather than realize its spiritual ideals. This distinguished the Sunni attitude toward power from that of the Shia, who denied such legitimacy to the caliphs and sultans.

By the ninth century of the Common Era, Sunni law had defined

the proper practice of the faith as the ulama and the caliphs established a balance between religious and political domains. The four
Sunni jurisprudential schools—the Hanafi, Maliki, Shafi'i, and
Hanbali—differed in their methodologies and philosophies of law,
but not on the larger issues that defined Sunnism. Sunni theology
evolved around debates on the nature of God and the scope of
rational explanation of the manifestations of his will.

Shiism took a different path. After Ali's death, the caliphate
became the possession of dynasties—first the Umayyads and later
the Abbasids. The Shia rejected the authority of the caliphs in
Damascus and Baghdad and continued to argue that the rightful
leaders of Islam could come only from the marriage between Ali
and Fatima, Muhammad's daughter. The Shias' insistence on the
Prophet's progeny as the only legitimate holders of authority obviously posed a grave challenge to the caliphs. The resulting conflict
profoundly shaped both Sunnism and Shiism.

The Shia view became crystallized at the siege and battle of
Karbala in 680 C.E., when soldiers of the second Umayyad caliph,
Yazid I, massacred Ali's son Husayn along with seventy-two of his
companions and family members (that number has since symbolized martyrdom). Husayn's refusal to admit the legitimacy of the
Umayyad caliphate had been a stance that he shared with the people of Kufa, Ali's capital. Many Kufans were liberated slaves and
Persian prisoners of war who had risen in revolt against the distinctly Arab character of Umayyad rule. Since that time, this town
near Najaf has had a special emotional resonance for Shias. In 2004,
when the firebrand Shia cleric Muqtada al-Sadr symbolically moved
from Baghdad to Kufa to deliver his sermons dressed in a white
funeral shroud, he was signaling his resolve to sponsor an armed
challenge to U.S., coalition, and Iraqi government authority.

Having decided to crush Husayn and the Kufan revolt by force,

Yazid sent an army of thousands to the area. They laid siege to Husayn's caravan, whose male members (except for Husayn's ailing son, Ali) put up a valiant resistance. Among Shias, the gallantry of Husayn and his brother and standard-bearer Abbas are legendary. Dug in with their backs to a range of hills, Husayn and his men held off the Syrian army for six grueling days. Then the Umayyad general Shimr, a figure forever damned in Shia lore, managed to cut off Husayn's troops from their source of water, thereby forcing a fight in the open. Nerved by a courage born of desperation and a steadfast belief in the rightness of their cause, Husayn and his parched, outnumbered men bravely charged the much larger Umayyad army, only to be cut down and massacred. The fallen were beheaded; their bodies were left to rot in the scorching heat of the desert, and their heads were mounted on staffs to be paraded in Kufa before being sent to the caliph in Damascus. Husayn's body, along with those of his companions, was buried on the battlefield by local villagers. Shia legend has it that an artist drew Husayn's noble countenance as it awaited display at Yazid's court. That image of Husayn, in a majestic pose with arched eyebrows and piercing eyes, the Shia believe, is the same that adorns shop windows in Karbala and is carried in Shia processions. Egyptians claim that Husayn's head was buried in Cairo, where today the Sayyidina Husayn (Our Lord Husayn) Mosque stands at the mouth of the Khan Khalili bazaar.

Husayn's sister, Zaynab, accompanied her brother's head to Damascus. There she valiantly and successfully defended the life of the lone surviving male member of the family, Husayn's son, Ali, who would succeed his father as the fourth Shia imam, thereby ensuring the continuity of Shiism. Zaynab bore witness to Karbala and lived to tell the tale. That Husayn's heroism became legendary and gave form to Shiism is very much her doing: Shiism owes its existence to a woman. It celebrates the strong characters and brav-

ery of female figures in a way that has no parallel in Sunnism.[11]
Women like Zaynab and her mother, Fatima, played major parts in
Shia history and fill a role in Shia piety not unlike the one that the
Virgin Mary plays in the popular devotionalism of Catholic and
Orthodox Christianity. Zaynab lived most of her life in Cairo, and a
mosque popular with women sits where her home once stood. She
is buried in Damascus; her shrine, the mosque of Sayyida Zaynab
(Lady Zaynab), is a popular place for Shia pilgrims to visit.

As recounted by Zaynab, the bloody murder of the Prophet's
grandson served to galvanize the Shia faith. Husayn had been the
Prophet's favorite. The Shia recount the Prophet saying "I am of
Husayn and Husayn is of me" not only to emphasize the gravity of
Husayn's murder but to underscore that Husayn and his actions represented the Prophet's wishes. The brutality of the Umayyad army
shocked the Muslim world at the time. Whatever people may have
thought of the merits of Husayn's rebellion, the manner in which
the progeny of the Prophet had been slaughtered repulsed many
and underscored the tyranny of the caliph's rule. There were revolts
and open displays of sorrow.

While Husayn's defeat ended prospects for a direct challenge to
the Umayyad caliphate, it also made it easier for Shiism to gain
ground as a form of moral resistance to the Umayyads and their
demands.[12] Military defeat paved the way for a deeper appeal to
Muslim consciousness. Shiism thus evolved not as a political sedition against Umayyad authority but as a moral and religious resistance to what that authority based itself upon and represented. The
moral example of Husayn has throughout the ages resonated with
many Sunnis, too.[13] For instance, the famous Indian Sufi saint Moin
al-Din Chishti, a towering figure in the history of South Asian Islam,
who now lies buried in the shrine of Ajmer in Rajasthan, wrote a
poem in which he famously said that Husayn was a king (shah) and

a protector of religion who "gave his head but not his hand to Yazid." Chishti's pithy homage to Husayn became so influential that to this day, those in South Asia who claim descent from Husayn are referred to with the honorific *shah*.

Husayn became not only Shiism's flag-bearer, symbolizing its claim to leadership of the Islamic world, but also a byword for chivalry and courage in the just cause of standing up to tyranny. Shiism is defined by its passion for Husayn, whose martyr's death is the dramatic experience that lies at the beating heart of Shia devotion. Husayn's death has left the Shia with a model of authority that differs from the one that the Sunnis commenced building at the start of the Umayyad period. For the Shia, Karbala is an emblem of suffering and solace but also connotes the refusal of true Muslim authority to be caged by pragmatic considerations and its willingness to challenge illegitimate authority—not only that of the caliphs but that of any ruler who does not measure up.[14] Shias have often invoked the Husayn story to define their conflicts in modern times: against the Shah's forces in Iran in 1979, against Israeli troops in southern Lebanon in the 1980s, and against Saddam Hussein's death squads in Iraq during the anti-Ba'thist intifada (uprising) that followed the first Gulf war in March 1991.

Shia identity manifests itself in many everyday modes besides the black pennant topped with an ornate carved hand. Devout Shia women generally wear black, as do the male religious leaders, who by tradition choose this color for their flowing robes. Shias hold their hands at their sides when praying—as opposed to Sunnis who clasp them—and are often recognizable by names derived from the proper names or titles of saints. Shias who trace their lineage to the imams carry the title *sayyid* (*seyyed* in Persian and *syed* in Urdu), which is treated by Shias as a mark of nobility. Clerics who are *sayyids* wear a black turban. Ayatollah Khomeini was a *sayyid,* as is Ayatollah Ali al-Sistani, the senior clerical leader among Iraqi Shias today.

But perhaps the most vivid distinction—and one that grates on Sunni sensibilities—is the love of visual imagery evident in Shia popular devotionalism. Sunnism tends to frown on the visual arts as possible inducements to, if not outright expressions of, idol worship. The piety of the Shia, by contrast, is steeped in visual representation. Although the Shia ulama do not condone the use of visual representations of the imams and even of the Prophet Muhammad, Shias hold them dear. Portraits of Ali and Husayn as well as depictions of the Karbala fight and other scenes from their lives adorn Shia homes and shops and are displayed in marches and festivals along with the ever-present colors of Shiism: black to express sorrow for Ali's fate, red to commemorate Husayn's martyrdom, and green to honor the Prophet's bloodline. Popular Shia artworks play much the same role that iconic images play in certain branches of Christianity. Puritanical Sunnis who condemn as un-Islamic any attempt to depict the Prophet visually or any veneration of images often cite the Shia taste for images as proof that Shiism is a form of deviance or even outright heresy.

Setting the Shia apart from the Sunni most emphatically, however, is the great feast of mourning, remembrance, and atonement that is Ashoura. From its earliest days, Shiism has been defined by the witness that it bears to the moral principles of Islam—a witness whose greatest public expression takes place in and through the rituals that remind the community of the special status of the imams. No ritual observance is more important in this regard than that associated with Husayn's death—the shaping event par excellence of Shiism. While there are indeed Shia approaches to Islamic theology and Islamic law, they developed alongside rituals.

In the days of the British Raj in India, Ashoura was an important date on the calendar of colonial officials, who inevitably had to contend with Shia customs and procession routes that raised Sunni hackles and, at times, Hindu objections. Every year around the time of Ashoura, British gazettes and newspapers would sound alarm bells regarding potential breaches in imperial security. Rudyard Kipling, who lived in Lahore in the 1880s, watched many Ashouras *(Holidays)* firsthand in the old city and wrote about them in his gazettes.[15] These observations formed the basis of his 1888 short story on the intensity of communal violence, "On the City Wall," which was set during one Ashoura. He captured the spirit of the feast and the political passions that it could unleash in the following words:

> All the processions—there were two-and-twenty of them—were now well within the City walls. The drums were beating afresh, the crowd were howling 'Ya Hasan! Ya Hussain!' and beating their breasts, the brass bands were playing their loudest, and at every corner where space allowed, Mohammedan preachers were telling the lamentable story of the death of the Martyrs. It was impossible to move except with the crowd, for the streets were not more than twenty feet wide . . . As the first *tazia*, a gorgeous erection, ten feet high, was borne aloft on the shoulders of a score of stout men into the semi-darkness of the Gully of the Horsemen, a brickbat crashed through its talc and tinsel sides . . . Then, without any warning, broke the storm . . . The *tazias* rocked like ships at sea, the long pole-torches dipped and rose round them . . . the fight became general. Half a mile away where the *tazias* were yet untouched the drums and the shrieks of 'Ya Hasan! Ya Hussain!' continued, but not for long.[16]

Every year British administrators would brace themselves for fights and riots and negotiate Shia procession itineraries and rules of conduct for each community. Today British administrators do much the same thing in Northern Ireland, when the late spring and summer "marching season" sees groups such as the Protestant Orange Lodge approach with demands to process through Catholic neighborhoods.

Ashoura's powerful focus on sorrow (*azadari*) and pageantry has a parallel in Catholic Lenten rituals, such as the Holy Week and Good Friday "Way of the Cross" processions and Passion plays that preface Easter Sunday observances in many places. Even the more extreme practices of some Shias, such as shedding one's own blood through a small cut on the scalp, resemble rituals such as those of the Penitentes, a lay Catholic brotherhood originally formed on the Iberian Peninsula. In rural southern Colorado and northern New Mexico, Penitentes hold special Holy Week reenactments of Christ's sufferings. They wear crowns of thorns and carry heavy crosses, and are even tied to the crosses and raised from the ground. Shias congregate in *husayniyas* (abodes of Husayn)—known as *imambaras* (courts of the imam) in South Asia—where they pray, chant, and lament Husayn's death. This too has a parallel in the Penitentes' *moradas* (places of worship), where they mark the sufferings of Christ.

Ashoura is a time of commemoration and penance for the vices and errors of humanity. The first Ashoura observance appears to have taken place in 684 C.E., four years after Husayn's death, when a group of penitents gathered at Karbala with blackened faces and torn garments. Every year since, the Shia have shown that they continue to share in the day's sorrow. Scholars have drawn attention to the resemblances between the rituals of Ashoura and pre-Islamic Iranian and Mesopotamian rites celebrating cosmic renewal, as well as rituals surrounding the death of Dionysus in Greek mythology and Osiris in Egyptian mythology.[17] The Shia's narrative of sorrow and faith was similarly enacted in the perennial language of ancient civilizations.

Over the years and the miles, the Shia faithful have adapted Ashoura to variations in local culture. As a result, an observance at Lucknow, in northern India, looks quite different in some ways from one in Nabatiye, in southern Lebanon. In Iraq, hundreds of thousands walk long distances to Karbala, sometimes in scorching summer heat, much as Catholic pilgrims still march between the cathedrals of Notre Dame de Paris and Chartres in France. Ashoura in northern India reflects contact with Hindu symbols and festivals. Many of its practices, while recognizable to local Hindus, would seem strange in the eyes of Shias from the Middle East.

Elephants led the processions of the royal Ashouras in Lucknow in the nineteenth century, and the crowd carried large replicas of the grand Shia places of worship in Lucknow and Iraq on their shoulders for many hours. To this day, carrying these replicas is at the center of Ashoura ceremonies in Lucknow, a practice that brings to mind the festival of Corpus Christi in Cuzco in Peru in June, during which the local people carry large sixteenth-century images of saints, especially San Cristobal and the Virgin of Bethlehem, for several days in the rarified air of the high Andes. Just as the Corpus Christi is based on ancient Inca rituals, so Ashoura in Ladakh bears the mark of Buddhism, and in Awadh and Hyderabad reflects the influence of Hinduism.[18]

In Awadh in the nineteenth century, Hindus routinely participated in Ashoura. They adopted Husayn as the god of death, "his bloodstained horse and severed head lifted aloft on Umayyad staves presenting no less terrible an aspect than Kali Durga with her necklace of skulls."[19] Hindu influence shaped Ashoura rituals—for instance, extending the festival to ten days, the same as the festival of the goddess Durga. In Hyderabad, in southern India, it is customary for Hindu fakirs, with red streaks painted on their faces, and equipped with drums and whips, to walk in front of the main Ashoura procession. They flagellate themselves as they ask onlookers for alms in Imam Husayn's name. Incense sticks burn in urns, in the tradition of Hindu religious gatherings in congregations for prayers or the reading of dirges. Hindus come to these meetings dressed in the saffron color of their religion, which provides a sharp contrast to the black worn by Shias. Before leaving, the Hindu visitors stoop over the urns and rub the ash of the incense on their eyelids, paying homage to Imam Husayn and receiving his blessing in the ways of their religion.[20]

Other South Asian displays of devotion to Ali and the imams also bear the mark of Hinduism. Shias popularly engage in "miracle reading" (mu'jizat khani), a spiritual vow to read (and hence bring to life) a particular story from the lives of imams with the expectation that a desired favor will be granted. This practice may have its origins in the devotional Hindu tradition of bhakti. There ritual readings of particular stories, known as vrats, are associated with fasting and prayers (pujas).[21]

Ashoura has traditionally been about collective atonement, not about inflicting pain on the individual. Over time, Shia communities such as those of the Turkic Azeris of northwestern Iran or the Arabs in Lebanon and Iraq have gone beyond atoning for Husayn's death to joining him symbolically in his last stand at Karbala. To taste his martyrdom in some small way, some engage not only in the abovementioned scalp-cutting but also in self-flagellation. Shia religious authorities do not condone such painful practices—most have in fact forbidden them—though they have become staples of many Ashoura processions.

Ashoura is also a time of drama, when in Iran and the Arab world passion plays (ta'ziyah) act out scenes from the battle of

Karbala, providing a dramatic visual backdrop to the commemorations.[22] The highly decorated *alams* carried at the head of each procession add to the spectacle. In larger towns and cities, various neighborhoods or guilds may each have their own processions, with unique chants and particular ways of performing the familiar rituals of the day. In South Asia every neighborhood has its own *alam*, and some families are entrusted with the custodianship of them, which becomes a badge of honor.

For Shias, the passion of Husayn carries a larger symbolic significance that is somewhat reminiscent of the meaning that Christ's passion has for Christians. In both cases, believers sadly commemorate the brutal slaying of an innocent and courageous spiritual figure, whose self-conscious sacrifice rises above the common run of events. This sacrifice reveals itself to the eyes of faith as an eternal decision that forms the conscience of and gives spiritual life to a sacred community that transcends space and time. For Sunnis, Karbala is history, albeit a dark chapter. For Shias, it is the beginning, the motif around which faith has been shaped. Karbala defines Shiism's ideals: dedication to the imams as an article of faith and commitment to pursuing justice in the face of tyranny.

Over the centuries, Shia identity and spirituality have grown up in the shadow of the Karbala narrative. Shia theologians argue that Husayn's martyrdom was the triumph of moral principles over brute force.[23] It was the supreme act of sacrifice by Husayn to seek martyrdom when he knew that pushing on to Kufa would lead to a confrontation that he could not militarily win. Yet Husayn was after a grander victory, a moral and spiritual one. The caliph's triumph was hollow, for it only served to rouse Muslim consciences to the sovereign claims of the truth represented by the Shia leaders, the descendants of Ali.

For Shias, Husayn's martyrdom is both a particular historical event, a historic turning point, and a metahistorical manifestation of the truth. Even before there was Islam or Husayn, Shia theologians say, the spiritual essence of Husayn's great deed existed as a timeless expression of divine grace. The Shia would in later years claim that Karbala and its significance had been known to all the prophets, as well as to Ali, who preceded Husayn.[24] Karbala is thus not merely one more massacre in the bloodstained annals of human wickedness, but a divine intervention meant to provide Muslims with a true spiritual signpost. Husayn willingly accepted oppression from the hand of a tyrant and embraced martyrdom as a divine favor, thereby transforming his suffering into a higher meaning and purpose.[25] It is for this reason that commemorating Karbala defines the Shias.

It is also for this reason that Shias place such a strong emphasis on their imams and the rituals associated with their deaths and are not content to limit themselves to the kind of law-governed and dutiful religious observance that forms the backbone of Sunni religiosity. Shias believe that to take part in Ashoura is to be absolved of sin, and that spirituality is to be found in the urgent drama of Husayn's martyrdom rather than in strict observance of pious duties or laws. As a popular Shia saying puts it, "A single tear shed for Husayn washes away a hundred sins." A tear shed on Ashoura is all the more rewarding. Whatever sins the Shias commit, they seek redemption in the grace and forgiveness of God and the blessing that flows from a renewal of their spiritual ties with Husayn and his progeny during Ashoura or at the resting places of their saints.

The rituals associated with Ashoura repeat themselves throughout the Shia calendar. First there is Arbaeen (or Chehelum in South Asia), which occurs forty days after Husayn's death; then the commemoration of Ali's death, which falls during Ramadan and on days of popular worship throughout the year when the faithful recite special prayers and sing devotional dirges known as *rowzehkahni* (*marsiya* in South Asia) that commemorate the sacrifice of Karbala. On Thursday nights and the twenty-nine nights of the fasting month of Ramadan, Shias recite the prayers attributed to their imams. One of the favored is the Prayer of the Day of Arafah, a long supplication by Imam Husayn during a pilgrimage to Mecca, which captures the essence of Shia piety:

Praise belongs to God
whose decree none may avert, and whose gift none may prevent . . .
O God, cause me to fear Thee as I were seeing Thee,
give me felicity through piety toward Thee
make me not wretched by disobedience toward Thee,
choose the best for me by Thy decree
and bless me by Thy determination
that I may love not the hastening of what Thou has delayed,
nor the delaying of what Thou hast hastened . . . [26]

In the end, however, what separates Shiism from Sunnism is not so much the divergences in practice as the spirit in which Islam is interpreted. First, whereas Sunnism took shape around belief in the writ of the majority and the legitimating power of communal consensus, Shias do not put much stock in majority opinion in matters of religion. Truth is vested not in the community of believers but in the virtuous leadership of the Prophet and his descendents. Whereas Sunnis have always placed greatest emphasis on the Islamic message, Shias have also underscored the importance of the vehicle for that message. Some have explained this difference by saying that Sunnis revere the Prophet because he relayed the Quran to Muslims, whereas Shias revere the Quran because the Prophet relayed it. Although most Shias stop short of holding such a view, there is no doubt that more extreme Shias have subscribed to it, and that Shiism places great emphasis on the prophetic function in tandem with the Islamic message.

Second, Shias believe that faith has an outer (*zahir*) manifestation and an inner (*batin*) meaning. Religion consists of layers of truth leading to absolute Truth. The inner meaning of religion, its esoteric dimension, can be accessed only through interpretation (*ta'wil*), and that is the domain of the imams and those who are privy to esoteric knowledge. Shias believe that the Quran contains truths that come from the other world. Only the Prophet and the imams, who like Muhammad are blessed with special knowledge concerning the things of God, can interpret those truths. Whereas the explicit meaning of the Quran can be understood through commentaries (*tafsir*), its implicit and inner meaning can be understood only by interpretation. This emphasis on interpretation and inner truth has shaped Shia piety and made philosophy and theology central to their faith. The Shia have throughout the centuries justified their religious doctrines in terms of their esoteric reading of Islamic sources.

After Karbala, the Shia continued to challenge the caliphate, but they could never dislodge the Sunni dominance over the politics of the Islamic world. To the Sunni majority, they increasingly looked like an errant interpretation of Islam, mistakenly bestowing larger-than-life importance on the progeny of Ali and alien to the tribal sensibilities of Arabs and more reflective of Iranian and, some would argue, Yemeni attachments to heroes, saints, and charismatic individuals.

Sunni caliphs worried about the Shia less as a theological deviation than as a political threat. The notion of the Prophet's blood kin asserting their right to rule and standing up against monarchs always had the potential to capture the popular imagination. The great caliph Mansour (d. 762) had to suspend the construction of Baghdad twice in order to put down Shia revolts. The fear that the Shia imams instilled in the caliphs resulted, not surprisingly, in persecution.

The Umayyad caliphs, and more so their successors, the Abbasids (750–1258), who ruled from Baghdad, imprisoned and killed Shia imams and encouraged Sunni ulama to define Sunni orthodoxy and contain the appeal of Shiism. By the tenth century Sunni jurists of the Hanbali school, known for their intolerance of Shiism, held sway over Baghdad, and fear of Shia revolts supported their penchant for purifying Islam. The last decades of that century witnessed anti-Shia violence in Baghdad and its environs—mosques and Ashouras were attacked, and Shias were even killed or burned alive. When in 971 C.E. Roman forces attacked the Abbasid domain, the first response of the caliph's forces and the angry and terrified Sunnis was to blame the Shia. Shia houses in al-Karkh (in today's Iraq)—which had become a refuge for Shias who escaped persecution in Baghdad—were torched as the attackers chanted, "You [Shias] are the cause of all evil." In a pattern of behavior that would be repeated throughout the centuries down to the present, the Shia bore the brunt of popular frustrations with the failures of Sunni rulers. Treated as the enemy within, they were the first to come under suspicion when there was an external threat to the ruling Sunni establishment. By the middle of the eleventh century, persecuting the Shia of al-Karkh had become a custom; every Saturday, Sunni mobs would show up at Shia mosques and shrines before looting the town, saying, "You blasphemers! Convert to Islam!"[27]

By the eleventh century these attitudes had also been canonized by Hanbali jurists, who condemned Shias as *rafidis,* or rejecters of the Truth. They said that Shias should not lead prayers or marry Sunnis, and that any meat that Shias slaughtered was not *halal* (permissible) for Sunni consumption. In short, the Shia were not to be treated as Muslims. After the Mongol sack of Baghdad and the destruction of the Abbasid caliphate in 1258, attacks on Shiism grew even sharper. Hanbali characterization has in recent history found a reflection in the extremist Sunnis' demonization of Shiism, which regards the faith as a heresy and a bigger threat to "true" Islam than Christianity and Judaism.

To survive, the Shia grew insular, often hiding their true faith through dissimulation (*taqqiya*), a practice that has a parallel in Judaism. The *dönme* community of Turkey descends from Iberian Jews who settled in the Ottoman empire and hid their identity behind Islamic practice. The sixth Shia imam made *taqqiya* obligatory for Shias to make sure the faith would survive. I remember a conversation a decade ago with a particularly anti-Shia Pashtun fundamentalist leader, who told me that his ancestry was actually Shia. His forebears had hidden their identity and pretended to be Sunni in public so long and so thoroughly that they had actually *become* Sunni.

The early sufferings of the Shia shaped their approach to religion. They revered their imams as specially blessed by God and immaculate from sin. The murders of these men only deepened the Shia rejection of Sunni authority and extended the emotional ties to the imams in the form of attachment to the shrines that grew up above their tombs. The Shia revere not only the holy group represented by the symbol of the carved hand but also the "Fourteen Immaculate from Sin" (*chahardah ma'sum*), which means Muhammad, his daughter Fatima, and the twelve imams. They invoke these sanctified figures in prayer and commemorate the days of their births and deaths. Shias visit the burial grounds of their imams, and of important kin of the imams, such as Husayn's brother Abbas in Karbala and their sister, Zaynab, in Damascus. Titles such as *karbalaie* or *mashadi*, meaning those who have visited the shrines of Karbala in Iraq or Mashad in eastern Iran, carry only slightly less weight than that of *hajji,* one who has made the hajj, or pilgrimage to Mecca. It is a blessing to be buried near the imams' great shrines. Shias believe that one who is buried in the shadow of a shrine will have a quicker passage to afterlife. No shrine is more blessed in this regard than the golden-domed Mosque of Ali in Najaf. Over the centuries the faithful have brought their loved ones' mortal remains from near and far to rest in Najaf. The enormous cemetery surrounding Ali's shrine, the Wadi al-Salaam (Valley of Peace), spreads for miles, thickly dotted with headstones and mausoleums.

Shias believe that their shrines are locations of spiritual grace (*baraka*), where God is present in a special way and most likely to answer cries for help. They seek blessings from these shrines and pray to saints to heal them and grant them their wishes. They believe that the shrines will imbue them with divine blessings and cleanse their souls. The shrines of the imams dot the landscape of Iraq, for that is where the Abbasid caliphs murdered so many of them. Along with Ali's tomb in Najaf, the major Shia shrines are those of Husayn in Karbala, of Musa al-Kazem (the seventh imam, d. 799) and Muhammad al-Taqi (the ninth imam, d. 835) in Baghdad, of Ali al-Naqi (the tenth imam, d. 868) and Hasan al-Askari (the eleventh imam, d. 872) in Samarra, of Ali al-Reza (the eighth imam, d. 818) in Mashad, and of Zaynab in Damascus. As pressed by Umayyad and Abbasid persecution, many members of the imams' families escaped to far-flung corners of Iran and as far as India to seek refuge, and so many more shrines emerged to serve as the pole of piety for local Shia communities.

In the nineteenth century, the Shia nawabs, or princes, of Awadh in northern India sought to reduce the burden of travel to Iraq by bringing the soil of the holy cities of Iraq (popularly known as the *atabat*) to Lucknow. That soil was enshrined in that city's opulent *imambaras*, especially the Shah-e Najaf (King of Najaf) Imambara, which holds soil from Najaf. Thus did northern India too become host to places of pilgrimage.

As soon as Saddam Hussein's regime was crushed in the spring of 2003, tens of thousands of Iranians, many poor and elderly women with nothing more than a black cloth covering their heads and small bundles of food in their hands, walked across the Iran-Iraq border, traversed minefields, and made their way through the desolate landscape of southern Iraq to visit the shrine of Imam Husayn in Karbala, which Saddam had for years barred to Iranian pilgrims. The shrine of Imam Reza at Mashad—which, like the Grotto of the Blessed Virgin at Lourdes, France, is famed as a place of sacred healing—draws an estimated 12 million visitors per year, which makes it the most popular pilgrimage site in the Muslim world except Mecca.

Shrine visits create transnational networks of people, charitable giving, and commerce. They provide Shias with a sense of community that goes beyond the merely local. A small brick at the shrine of Zaynab in Damascus bears the name of Sayyid Maratib Ali Hindi (the Indian). The brick was placed there in memory of the financial contribution that this Indian Shia merchant made to the restoration of the shrine. Today, as Maratib Ali's Indian and Pakistani coreligionists commingle with the throng of Iranian pilgrims to perform the same rituals at the shrine, they strengthen the transnational bonds of Shiism. Similarly, the beautiful tiles, mirrors, chandeliers, and carpets that grace the shrines of Najaf and Karbala have been gifts of Iranian kings, the Pahlavis included, who, along with Iranian and other merchants and pilgrims, have spent willingly on the burial places of their saints. The vast kitchens of these shrines feed the poor and rely on support from pilgrims who come to seek the saint's blessing and in turn seek to bring joy to his soul by giving food to the needy.

The sufferings of the imams lie at the heart of the Shia doctrine of martyrdom (*shahadat*). Just as early Christian saints accepted "the crown of martyrdom," steadfast in their faith and believing that their blood would be the seed of the church, so do Shias revere martyrdom. The imams died as witnesses to the faith, as did many of their followers. Husayn is popularly known as the Lord of the Martyrs (Sayyid al-Shuhada). Shias believe that martyrdom is the highest testament to faith, following the example of the imams, a deed that will gain the martyr entry into paradise just as it will strengthen Shiism. Sunnis historically frowned on this belief, but now the most extremist Sunnis seem to have embraced an especially grim version of it in the form of suicide bombing.

The Shias' historical experience is akin to those of Jews and Christians in that it is a millennium-long tale of martyrdom, persecution, and suffering. Sunnis, by contrast, are imbued with a sense that immediate worldly success should be theirs. Sunni Islam made huge strides as a force in the world very quickly. Within a generation after Prophet Muhammad, Arab tribal armies had exploded from their native peninsula to defeat three superpowers of the time, overrunning the Persian and Egyptian empires and pushing the Byzantines out of the Near East into Anatolia. Muslim armies continued to conquer, moving across North Africa, crossing the Straits of Gibraltar, (named after the Arab commander Tariq) to control the Iberian peninsula, and pushing north into Western Europe until the Franks stopped them at the Battle of Tours-Poitiers in 732 C.E. By the time the Abbasids rose to power, Islam stretched from the boundaries of India and Central Asia in the east to the Atlas Mountains and beyond in the west.

Given their history, the Shia would never associate their faith's validity with worldly success. The Sunnis, by contrast, became accustomed to celebrating their dominion in the world through the muscular temporal institution of the caliphate. As a result, Shias seem to find it less threatening than the Sunnis do to come to terms with the relative decline of Muslim power in modern times, since for the Shia such a decline does not suggest a crisis of belief.

If Sunnism is about law and the "thou shalts" and "thou shalt nots" of Islam, Shiism is about rituals, passion, and drama. Shias follow Islamic law with equal vigilance, but their piety is not defined by the law. Before there was Shia law there was Shia piety, which defines believers above and beyond the law. The current excessive legal-mindedness of Iran's ayatollahs is in some ways a "Sunnification" of Shiism—a reflection of the influence exerted in recent decades by Sunni fundamentalism, with its puritanism and intense political activism.

Of course, neither Shia nor Sunni beliefs and views of each other are monolithic. Symbolic of this is a small but important shrine on the beach in the wealthy neighborhood of Clifton in Karachi, popular with both Shias and Sunnis. The saint buried at the shrine is Abdol-Ghazi Sahab. Popular lore holds that he was a relative of the sixth Shia imam, Jafar al-Sadiq. Abdol-Ghazi fled from Abbasid Baghdad and sought protection in Sind from the local Hindu prince. For Karachi's Shias, he is a scion of the line of imams and a symbol of Shia life in Sind. For Sunni pilgrims who go to his shrine, he is simply a great saint. The shrine has for centuries brought Shias and Sunnis together around common beliefs and practices associated with popular Islam. It has fostered tolerance and comity.

Abdol-Ghazi's shrine is not unique in this regard. Others from the lines of the imams escaped from Umayyad and Abbasid rule to seek shelter in Hindu kingdoms, and their burial places are sacred to both Shias and Sunnis. In a corner of the courtyard of the shrine of Bibi Pakdaman in Lahore, where it is believed five women from the Prophet's family, including a daughter of Ali, are buried, a plaque marks the place where the great Sunni Indian Sufi saint, Sayyid Ali Hujwiri (d. 1071), once spent forty days in meditation. Such shrines symbolize a coming together of Shiism and Sunnism at a spiritual level and in the realm of popular piety.[28]

Sufism emerged among Sunnis as a powerful esoteric expression of the Islamic faith, resembling many aspects of Shia piety, as a balance to Sunni legalism and rational theology.[29] It is also prevalent among Shias, but it was among Sunnis that its concern with the inner meaning of the Islamic message found greatest expression.

Sufism and Shiism share much in ethos and temperament. Like the Shia, Sufis believe that there are outer and inner meanings to the Quran and the prophetic traditions and revere those whom they believe can grasp the more inward meaning. Much like the Shia imams, Sufi saints enjoy a special status that comes from their esoteric knowledge and their proximity to God. The spiritual essence of the saints, much like that of the imams, is a source of grace that continues to bless their followers even after the saints die. Sufi shrines, like those of the Shia, are places to which believers feel a deep sense of spiritual and emotional attachment. Among the Chishti order in South Asia or the Alawiya order in North Africa, visits to shrines are at the heart of piety. Even as Afghanistan labored under the lash of the Taliban's violent puritanism, many Afghans continued to visit shrines and practice the popular Muslim devotions associated with them.

Both the Shia imam and the Sufi saint are esteemed as special intermediaries between man and God, capable of interceding in order to secure divine healing, blessing, favor, and forgiveness, even for devotees whose daily religious habits may not have been the most diligent. In other words, Sufis accept the attitudes that define Shia piety—the very attitudes that some Sunnis have rejected as un-Islamic.

Last, Sufis share Shias' veneration of Ali and their love of the

Prophet's family. For most Sufis, Ali is a preeminent source of spiritual knowledge. He was the very first Sufi disciple and the source of the esoteric wisdom that Sufism is based on, and hence all Sufi orders save for the Naqshbandi, who trace their lineage to Abu Bakr, see Ali as the fountainhead of spiritual wisdom. (Many Naqshbandi Sufi leaders too have venerated Ali and accepted his special spiritual status.) Many of the qualities that are attributed to Ali, such as chivalry, bravery, generosity, justice, and grandeur of soul, are values that Sufis cherish as the true essence of Islamic piety. This tendency is strongest in Shia Sufism, the most important expression of which is the Nematollahi order prominent in Iran, whose doctrines weave Sufi spirituality into Shia piety.[30]

The influence of Sufism on Muslim life and thought has generated tolerance for Shiism in many Sunni societies. Where Sufism defines Islamic piety, Shias have found greater acceptance. In South Asia, for instance, the Brelwi school of Islam, which integrates Sufi teachings into Sunni theology and law, has always been more tolerant of the Shia. Both Sufism and Shiism have found much to fear from the kind of puritanical righteousness that Wahhabism (the puritanical interpretation of Islam that prevails in Saudi Arabia) and Salafism (a modern and at times violent manifestation of Wahhabism) promote.[31] Many of the forces that draw on hardline Sunni rejection of Shiism also aim harsh opposition at Sufism. In Iraq and Pakistan, the extremist forces that attack the Shia now also attack Sufis.[32] In many parts of the Muslim world today, the battle between Sufism on the one hand and Wahhabi or Salafist puritanism on the other vastly overshadows any struggle between Islamic traditionalism and modernism. Attitudes toward the two tend to ebb and flow along with puritanical tendencies inside Sunnism—the tugs between conceding to Sufism and folk Islam and asserting the claims of rigorous orthodoxy.

The two have come to make common cause in confronting their common adversary. Syria provides a modern example of cooperation between Shiism and Sufism. Facing a challenge from the fundamentalist party, Muslim Brotherhood, and its advocacy of puritanical Sunni fundamentalism, Syria's government, dominated by Alawis (an offshoot of Shiism whose beliefs deviate from Islamic orthodoxy and include elements of Christianity and pre-Islamic religions), has since the 1980s relied on the Naqshbandi Sufi order for legitimacy. Sheikh Ahmad Kaftarou, who died in 2004, was both the grand mufti of Syria and a prominent leader of the Naqshbandi Sufi order in the country. His successor as grand mufti, Sheikh Ahmad Badruddin Hassoun, is also a Naqshbandi Sufi. Kaftarou's order has provided backing against a Sunni fundamentalist challenge to a secular Alawi regime that recently has persuaded Lebanese and Iranian Shia religious authorities to declare the Alawis bonafide Shia Muslims. In Afghanistan, Chechnya, and the Balkans, wars of liberation were often begun by local Naqshbandi groups but were then hijacked by better-funded Saudi-backed groups of puritanical Sunnis. The Naqshbandi resistance to the puritanical Islam of Wahhabis and Salafis was especially evident during the Afghan war, as Naqshbandi forces fought for control of the country, first against various Saudi- and Pakistani-backed mujahideen groups such as Gulbidin Hekmatyar's Hizb-e Islami (Islamic Party) and later against the Taliban.

Chapter 2

THE MAKING OF SHIA POLITICS

Just south of Tehran, not far from where Ayatollah Khomeini is buried, there is a small Shia holy place that is open to women only. This is the shrine of Bibi Shahrbanou. It is known for the munificence of the blessings that it offers to its female pilgrims, and for being the reputed burial place of Princess Shahrbanou, who was the daughter of the last Sassanid king of Persia, Yazdgerd III, and the wife of Imam Husayn. The shrine sits on top of a hill overlooking the poorer neighborhoods of south Tehran. It is a trek up the hill to where hundreds of women mill around the princess's tomb, crying, praying, and looking for solace, healing, and favors. For Iranians, the marriage between Imam Husayn and the daughter of the last Sassanid king—who was also, of course, the mother of the fourth Shia imam—symbolizes the marriage between Iran and Shiism.

Iranians claim that their fidelity to Shiism goes back to the very beginning. Among the Prophet's companions, Salman the Persian supported Ali's candidacy to become the first caliph. It was an Iranian prisoner of war who killed Caliph Umar, who is particularly disliked by Iranians because during his caliphate Arab armies conquered Iran. Iranians also resented him for his Arab chauvinism and discrimination against Iranian converts: he forbade marriages between Arabs and Persians, for instance. He also stood accused of abusing Ali and his wife, Fatima, the Prophet's daughter.

If in Iranian eyes Umar and later the Umayyads were guilty of violating Islam's teachings on the equality of all humans before God, the Shia imams were favored for their particularly warm feelings toward Iranians. Iranians believe that Husayn was on his way to Iran to seek refuge from persecution by the caliph when his caravan was intercepted by the Umayyad army. The eighth Shia imam, Ali al-Reza, who is buried in the shrine of Mashad and whose sister, Massouma, is buried in the shrine of Qom, is believed to have said that since the Prophet's death Iranians had been accorded a special status among Muslims. If Umar had privileged the Arabs, the eighth imam had clearly had a soft spot for people from Iran, who loved him for his blessing as much as they loathed Umar for his cruelty.

Whatever the colorful lore about the early days, the ascertainable historical reality is that Shiism did not come to predominate in Iran until the sixteenth century, when the Safavids took over the country. The Safavids take their name from their ancestor Sheikh Safi al-Din Ardabili (d. 1334), who traced his ancestry to the seventh Shia imam, Musa al-Kazem (buried in the Kazemiya shrine in Baghdad) and who was an influential Sufi master of the Safawiya order. By the fifteenth century, Sheikh Safi's descendants had emerged as political rulers in northwestern Iran, the border area between Iran and Azerbaijan. Their domain and influence grew as they battled Mongol rulers. In 1501, Ismail I defeated the Mongols once and for all and established the Safavid dynasty.

Ismail was a warrior and a poet with extremist Shia beliefs. His creed combined the Sufi spiritual doctrines of the Safawiya order with esoteric Shia teachings. His warriors, the Qizilbash, literally worshipped him as a demigod. The Safavids were not content to rule over a domain that would remain Sunni. They had a genuine zeal for Shiism and wanted to bring Iran into the ambit of that faith. They also were intense rivals of the Sunni Ottoman Turks to the west and the Sunni Mughal Empire and Turkoman tribes to the east. In particular, the Ottomans and the Safavids competed for domination in the heartland of the Muslim world.[1] That competition took sectarian overtones as the Safavids became a Shia empire and the Ottoman emperors—who ruled over Arab lands and officially laid claim to the caliphate and made Istanbul its seat in 1517—became the spokesmen of Sunnism.

It is not that there was much of a real caliphate for Shias and Sunnis to fight over by the sixteenth century. What the Ottomans inherited was not a functioning institution but the purely symbolic leadership of the Sunni world. The more concrete focus of struggle was the competing assertions of dynastic and imperial Shia or Sunni power over the larger region. The Safavids were the champions of Shia aspirations to regional hegemony. The Safavid model was not rule by the imams but power to the shahs. The Safavid dynasty was a new kind of vehicle for Shia ambitions.

The Ottomans and the Safavids fought many wars. For a brief time the Safavids controlled Iraq (in effect, the eastern flank of the Arab world). But soon enough the line between the two rival empires came to follow very much the same path as today's border between Iran on the east and Iraq and Turkey to its west. While the Safavids used their power to make Shiism the religion of Iran, as much by coercion as by persuasion, the Ottomans put the Shia to the sword in Anatolia. Only the Alawi offshoot of Shiism survives in what is today southern Turkey. In this climate of antagonism, Shiism gave Iran its distinct identity, so that Iranians are distinguished from most Arabs and Turks not only by language and culture but also by religious belief and practice. The boundary between Shiism and Sunnism thus came to coincide with the boundary between empires, with what is today southern Iraq extending as a kind of Shia salient into Sunnism's flank.

Under the Safavids, Shia religious learning and artistic expression flourished. They built their capital in Isfahan, in central Iran, and the magnificent architecture of that city is a Safavid legacy. The Safavids brought Shia ulama from Lebanon's Jabal Amel mountains, the Qatif region of the Arabian peninsula, and Bahrain—the backwaters of the Muslim world—to build new centers of Shia learning.[2] To deepen Shiism's roots in Iran, they also actively propagated the faith among the populace, relying on itinerant dervishes who went from town to town and village to village to tell people the great Shia stories.[3] These dervishes relied less on theology and law than on myth and passion. For this reason, Iranian Shiism is deeply and emotionally attached to narrative. The wandering dervishes also did a lot to encourage Sunni-bashing, which of course served Safavid political interests.

The ulama, theologians, and philosophers who were patronized by the Safavids produced large numbers of treatises and books and built the foundations of Shia scholarship. Seminaries, libraries, and mosques not only entrenched Shiism in Iran but also gave it new intellectual vibrancy. The Shia tradition of esoteric interpretation laid the foundations for a distinctly Shia school of Islamic philosophy that would rival the Peripatetic school associated with the great Avicenna (Ibn Sina, d. 1037) and the tradition of Greek philosophy.

At the same time, the scholarly ulama and legal experts (*faqihs* or *mujtahids*) became functional replacements for the authority of the imams. These scholars and experts in religious law were the fore-runners of today's ayatollahs (literally, signs of God). They shoul-dered the task of ministering to the community's spiritual needs as well as its social and political interests. Thus, since Safavid times the Shia religious establishment has been closely tied to Iran. (This changed somewhat under the Ottomans, when Shia ulama in what is now Iraq became active in Iranian politics and religious life. And yet in turn, influential Iraqi Shia clerics have come from Iran. The last two leading Shia ayatollahs of Iraq, Abol-Qasim al-Khoi, and Ali al-Sistani, were of Iranian origin. The Arabic prefix *al-* was added to their names after they settled in Najaf. Sistani, who communicates principally by writing and through sermons delivered by his lieu-tenants, speaks Arabic with a noticeable Persian accent.)

Not only did the ulama take over some of the functions that the *imams* had performed until the tenth century, but, more important, they were viewed as guardians of the faith, as successors to the Twelfth Imam in managing the affairs of the community and express-ing his will. Shias believe that the line of the imams continued through the tenth century, when the Twelfth Imam, Muhammad al-Mahdi (the Guided One) was withdrawn by God into a miraculous state of occultation (hiddenness) in 939 C.E. The Twelfth Imam, as he is usually known, is believed to have been only five years old when he succeeded his father in 872 C.E. The Shia believe that God hid the Twelfth Imam from physical access in order to preserve his life. The return of this Mahdi or Hidden Imam will herald the end of time and the advent of perfect divine justice—a messianic view very similar to those among Jews and Christians. During his occultation, the Twelfth Imam is the unseen Lord of the Age (*imam al-zaman*), the permanent imam until the Day of Judgment.[4] With his "second coming" there will be a reign of justice until the return of Jesus, at which time the world will end. The events surrounding the return of the Twelfth

Imam closely parallel Judeo-Christian prophecies about the end of time and the Battle of Armageddon. Historians have suggested that Shia messianism bears traces of Zoroastrian and Judeo-Christian influence, though Shias believe that their messianic doctrine was mandated by God and any similarity it may have to that of other religions is proof of its validity, reflecting the divine plan for humanity.

Among Muslims as a whole, only the Shia embrace such messianism. Sunnis do not believe in the second coming of a particular individual whose advent will culminate in the end of the world. For Sunnis, the Mahdi is merely a descendant of the Prophet named Muhammad who will revive the faith, as was the case with the most famous of such revivalists, the nineteenth-century Mahdi of the Sudan, whose tribal warriors defeated a British army and killed General Charles "Chinese" Gordon at Khartoum in 1885.

Although like Christians and Jews the Shia early on postponed the coming of the Twelfth Imam to the end of time, removing it from their everyday lives, still they live in waiting for his return. As has been the case in Christianity and Judaism, at times of crisis this expectation has found greater immediacy as the faithful look urgently for "signs of the times" and the impending "rapture." For the Shia, jihad (holy war) has meaning most clearly in the context of their millenarian expectations: doing the bidding the Twelfth Imam and hastening his advent.

As successors to the Twelfth Imam, the Shia ulama enjoy a privileged spiritual status that their Sunni counterparts have never had. Sunni ulama are religious functionaries, learned in religious matters but no different from other believers. The Shia, by contrast, revere their ulama not only for their knowledge but for the link to the Twelfth Imam that they represent.

The insular nature of the Shia community and its persecution at the hands of Sunnis have strengthened the authority of the ulama, but Shias have differed over what kind of role the ulama are to play in the religious life of the community. Most rely on the ulama not only to interpret religion but to make new rulings to respond to new challenges and push the boundaries of Shia law in new directions. These are known as Usuli (fundamentalist) Shias. They are distinguished from a minority of Shias that emerged in eighteenth-century Iraq and today are found for the most part in Bahrain, known as Akhbaris (traditionalists). Usulis look to the ulama to use reasoning to devise legal opinions, protect the community's interests, and if necessary assert its political prerogatives. Akhbaris accept only the Quran, the prophetic sayings, and the recorded opinions of the imams as sources of law and reject the notion that reasoning can lead to the creation of new laws. For Akhbaris, therefore, the ulama hold far less power both in religion and in politics. The two schools competed for the soul of Shiism from the seventeenth to the nineteenth centuries.[5] In time the Usulis overshadowed the Akhbaris. The Iranian revolution, with its political empowerment of the ulama, further promoted the Usuli position, which is now popular among previously Akhbari communities such as that of Bahrain.

Shia ulama are first and foremost lawyers—they interpret and expand on religious law, first codified in the eighth century. The sixth Shia imam, Jafar al-Sadiq (d. 765), developed a Shia jurisprudence (known as Jafari law) separate from the Sunni legal learning that was being codified at about the same time, differing on matters regarding inheritance, religious taxes, commerce, and personal status. Most famously, Shias practice temporary marriage (*mut'a*), which, as the term suggests, is a religiously sanctioned marriage with contractual obligations but for a finite period of time.[6]

Shia ulama also attend to the spiritual as well as the social and political needs of the community. As guardians of the faith, they exercise enormous authority over their flock. The ties between Shias and their ayatollahs are akin to those of East European Jewish communities and their rabbis or traditional Catholic communities and their priests. In fact, ayatollahs are very much like Catholic cardinals, though Shiism has no pope. (It is hardly surprising that when Saddam fell, the Shia clerics who had endured his brutality alongside their followers emerged as the new Iraq's main power brokers.)

Shia clergy are educated at seminaries, the most important of which are clustered around Najaf in Iraq and Qom in Iran. Seminarians attend many years of tutorials and lectures at the feet of senior ulama. They have to complete particular sets of lectures and excel in law, jurisprudence, and theology as well as philosophy, logic, rhetoric, and, at times, literature. When a student has completed this regimen to his superiors' satisfaction, he receives permission (*ijaza*) to become a bonafide member of the ulama, someone who can practice *ijtihad* (independent reasoning to give a new ruling)—a *mujtahid*—collect religious taxes, and serve as the guardian of a flock. Clerical students and seminary dropouts form the lower ranks of the clergy, carrying out a variety of religious functions from performing marriages to leading prayers and public liturgies.

The rank of a Shia cleric is determined by the stature of his instructors, especially the one who has most closely overseen his intellectual development. In a fashion somewhat like that of the peer-reviewed world of academia, Shia clergy also judge one another on the quality of their scholarship and publications. The community too plays an important role in determining the rank of the clergy and bestowing such lofty titles as ayatollah and *hojjat al-Islam* (proof of Islam).

The most senior clergy are sources of emulation (*marja'al-taqlid*) for the Shia. Every Shia follows a *marja'* of his choosing, although it is usually a cleric of lower rank—the representative or follower of the *marja'*—that most Shias turn to when addressing their religious concerns. Believers ask for opinions and rulings from their ulama, and follow the religion as specified by them. The most senior ulama claim the largest congregations directly, as well as through underlings who help in serving the believers' needs.

Also helping to determine a cleric's status are the religious taxes and donations that believers give him for charitable purposes and to help educate seminary students. The bigger a senior cleric's purse, the wider a patronage network he can build in the clerical ranks below him. Because the Shia hierarchy depends not only on knowledge but on money, its desire to maintain strong ties to the bazaars has always been among its major priorities. The most senior clerics, such as Iraq's Ayatollah Sistani, take in funds from across the Shia world and give out opinions that are studied and followed from India to Lebanon. They have representatives (*wakils*) in various Shia communities, who receive and disperse funds on their behalf and propagate their rulings in competition with those of other senior ulama. At the top of this hierarchy sit the most senior ulama, the *marja'*s, who have traditionally resided in Najaf or Qom. Today the most senior of these grand ayatollahs, with the broadest following, are the Iranian Sistani, the Afghan Muhammad Ishaq al-Fayyad, the Pakistani Bashir al-Najafi al-Pakistani, and the Iraqi Muhammad Said al-Hakim, who are collectively known as the *marja'iya* (sources of emulation) in Najaf; Muhammad Taqi Mudarressi in Karbala; Muhammad Husayn Fadlallah in Lebanon; Mirza Javad Tabrizi, Taqi Behjat, and Hossein Ali Montazeri in Qom; and, for a minority of ideologically oriented Shias, Ali Khamenei in Tehran.

With the exception of Grand Ayatollah Muhammad Husayn Boroujerdi (d. 1965), there has never been a sole source of emulation—a universally accepted supreme ayatollah. Although Khomeini tried to become that and to establish a Shia "papacy," his fiat never extended beyond Iran. Shias everywhere accepted him as a political leader, but many continued to look for religious guidance to Grand Ayatollah Abol-Qasem al-Khoi, Ayatollah Sistani's mentor and fellow Najaf resident. The Shia in fact pride themselves on the pluralism of their religious authority and institutions. It is not permissible to adopt a dead *marja'* as the source to follow; hence, Shia law continues to evolve. It is also discouraged for one *marja'* to follow another, ensuring diversity of opinion. After Khomeini died, the Islamic Republic failed to produce a leader of Khomeini's or Sistani's standing, and so the religious leadership of Shiism reverted to quietist ayatollahs in the seminaries of Qom and Najaf.

It was also during the Safavid era that the foundation of a new Shia political doctrine was laid. The rise of an avowedly Shia monarchy ruling over a Shia domain was a new development. After the line of imams ended in 939 c.e., with the occultation of the Twelfth Imam, the Shia mood turned consolidationist. Shia theologians reasoned that the imam's withdrawal must mean that in the interim before his return, political authority could never escape imperfection. Until the end of occultation, there could be no true Islamic rule, and anyone who claimed to be setting up such a regime would by definition be a pretender. Their goal from then on was to keep faith until the imam's return. Passive resistance replaced active rebellion. Shias would not recognize the legitimacy of Sunni rule, but they would not directly challenge it either. The final reckoning with Sunnism would come only at the end of time. In this regard, Shia thought resembles that of Orthodox Jews, who argue that restoring the fortunes of the Jews is the job of the Messiah and who at first condemned Zionism for taking on the messianic task of returning Jews to Palestine.

Just as the dislocating experience of the Babylonian captivity spurred the Israelites to gather together the writings that became the Hebrew Bible, so the imam's occultation convinced the Shia that it was time to set about systematically codifying and organizing their body of religious knowledge. The imams had provided a living gateway to the Prophet. When it swung shut in the tenth century, the time had come to take stock and put things in order. During the three centuries between the occultation and the late 1250s, when the Mongols overran much of the Middle East, Shia theology and religious sciences took shape. The intellectual leaders of this project included Ibn Babuya (d. 991), Sheikh al-Mufid (d. 1022), and Khwaja Nasir al-Din Tusi (d. 1274). This era also saw the compilation of the Nahj al-Balagha (Path of Eloquence), a compendium of Ali's sermons and letters that Shias consider the most important source of Islamic teachings after the Quran and the sayings of Prophet Muhammad. Since Shias regard Ali's brief caliphate as the *beau idéal* of perfect Islamic rule, the compendium is also considered a fount of political wisdom, while its eloquence and impact on Arabic political prose has been compared with the words of Confucius in Chinese or Cicero in Latin.

Among Ali's letters collected in the Nahj al-Balagha is his instruction to his governor in Egypt, Malik al-Ashtar, a foundational document in Shia political theory. In that letter Ali wrote:

> Know, O Malik, that I am sending you to a land where governments, just and unjust, have existed before you. People will look upon your affairs in the same way that you were wont to look upon the affairs of the rulers before you . . . So let the dearest of your treasuries be the treasury of righteous action.

Control your desire and restrain your soul from that which is not lawful to you . . . Infuse your heart with mercy, love and kindness for your subjects. Be not in the face of them a voracious animal, counting them as easy prey, for they are of two kinds: either they are your brothers in religion or your equals in creation. Error catches them unaware, deficiencies overcome them, and evil deeds are committed by them intentionally and by mistake. So grant them your pardon and your forgiveness to the same extent that you hope God will grant you His pardon and His forgiveness. For you are above them, and he who appointed you is above you, and God is above him who appointed you . . . Never say "I am invested with authority, I give orders, and I am obeyed," for surely that is corruption in the heart and enfeeblement in religion.[7]

There was much in Ali's conception that supports an accountable government, if not a representative one in the full-blown modern sense. By the time of the Safavids, Shias had become used to living as a minority under Sunni rule. They neither legitimated the authority of those rulers nor expected recognition from them. In fact, after the Twelfth Imam went into occultation, the Shias were notionally just waiting for the end time, with no hope of truly legitimate government until then, so what were they to make of the Safavids? These kings were not Sunni caliphs, but not the Twelfth Imam either. The Safavids had created a safe haven for Shiism in Iran, propagated the faith in their domain, established Shia law as the law of the land, and patronized Shia scholarship. The Shia ulama, many of whom became a part of the Safavid aristocracy as landowners and courtiers, crafted a new theory of government. According to this theory, Shia ulama would not recognize the Safavid monarchy as truly legitimate but would bless it as the most desirable form of government during the period of waiting. Shia shahs would protect and propagate the faith, ensuring that it would prosper in anticipation of the coming of the Twelfth Imam. For as long as the shahs did so, they would receive religious support. The "Safavid contract" survived for nearly five hundred years, until the Iranian revolution of 1979, when the ayatollahs and the monarchy parted ways and Khomeini imposed his theocratic doctrine of *velayat-e faqih* (guardianship of the Islamic jurist) on Iran.[8]

As Shiism spread over time and space it became culturally diverse. This enriched Shia life and thought and added new dimensions to the faith's historical development that went beyond its roots in the Arab heartland of Islam. The practice of the faith itself adapted to new cultures as its message spread eastward from the Arab lands to Iran and India. Succession crises through the ages led to offshoots that broke away from the main body of Shiism—also known as Twelvers, for recognizing twelve imams. Following the death of the fourth imam in the eighth century, a minority followed one claimant to the imamate who rose in rebellion against the Umayyads. They are known as Zaydis (named after Zayd ibn Ali), or Fivers, for following only five imams. Today most Zaydis live in Yemen and are closer to Sunnism in their practice of Islam.

A graver schism occurred after the death of the sixth imam, the law codifier Jafar al-Sadiq, in 765 C.E. Jafar's eldest son, Ismail, had died before his father. A group of Shias claimed that Ismail had inherited his father's religious charisma while both men were still alive. Others disputed this and located the succession in a living younger son. Those who affirmed the charisma of Ismail came to be known as Ismailis or Seveners, for breaking off from the main body of Shiism after the seventh imam.

Ismailis remained a small denomination, but one that accentu-

ated the cult of the imams and emphasized their function of reveal-
ing the inner meaning of Islam. They had an esoteric bent and
became immersed in philosophy and mystical practices, eventually
breaking with some of the fundamental teachings of Shiism and
even Islam. In the tenth century, Ismailis rose to power in Egypt and
founded the Fatimid dynasty (909–1171). The Fatimids left an
imprint not only on Cairo's Islamic architecture but also on Islam in
Egypt, where the level of special devotion to the Prophet's family is
more intense than anywhere else in the Sunni world.[9] The Ismailis
also produced the cult of the Assassins in the twelfth century, when
Ismaili warriors terrorized Iran's then Sunni leadership.

The descendants of Ismail and the Fatimids continue to serve as
living imams of that community. The current imam is Prince Karim
Aga Khan, who looks after his community's welfare from his seat in
Paris. Ismailis pay tithe to the Aga Khan, who in turn oversees his
flock, guiding them in religious matters as well as ensuring their
material prosperity. The Aga Khan has built universities, schools,
and hospitals in Ismaili communities and used his influence with
kings and presidents, generals and businessmen to further the interests of Ismailis wherever they live.

There are Arab Ismaili communities—for instance, in the remote
Najran province of Saudi Arabia—but in recent centuries Ismailis
have largely been an Indo-Iranian community. Most Ismailis have traditionally lived in a circular pattern of settlement that runs from
India into western China, Tajikistan, Afghanistan, northeastern Iran,
and back down into Pakistan. The fall of the Soviet Union and certain openings in China have allowed the Ismailis to form renewed
ties across this vast arc and the many international borders that it
traverses. Under the British Raj, India's Ismaili merchants did well
and often migrated along imperial trade routes. Many settled in
British East Africa and formed the merchant classes of Kenya,

Tanzania, and Uganda. Africanization campaigns in that region in the 1970s—the worst one was part of the reign of terror that gripped Uganda under the dictator Idi Amin—sent many Afro-Indian Ismailis into exile. Some went to the United States or Britain, but most migrated to Canada. Over the centuries Ismailis have spun off smaller communities, including the Bohras of India, and have deeply influenced other small offshoots of Shiism, such as the Druze of the Levant, the Yezidis of Iraq, and the Alawi of Syria and Alevis of Turkey.

Shiism exists not only in time but in space and within various cultures that it has both helped to shape and been shaped by. Like Islam, Shiism appeared first among the Arabs but soon found a foothold in Iran, whose farther reaches provided Shias with refuge from their Baghdad- or Damascus-based persecutors. In the tenth and eleventh centuries, Shiism was strong in North Africa and southern Syria, while Iran was the seat of Sunni theology and religious sciences. Then older Shia dynasties in Egypt and the Arab lands began to decline, while newer Shia dynasties were emerging in Iran and India. The net result was that Shiism's geographical center of gravity shifted eastward. Iran's own ethnic and linguistic tensions with the Arab-led Islamic empire and the country's cultural and religious ethos made Shiism an attractive creed.

Today, Shiism has a diverse ethnic base. The largest groups are Arabs, Persian-speaking Iranians, and the Turkic-speaking Azeris, who live in northwestern Iran and the former Soviet republic of Azerbaijan on the west coast of the Caspian Sea. The Azeris have played a little-appreciated but important role. Azeri tribes came down into the Middle East from the steppes of Central Asia as part of the Turkic wave that swept into the Muslim heartland beginning roughly around the year 1000. These horse-riding conquerors even-

tually embraced Islam even as they began politically displacing the
Arab caliphs and spreading out to form empires and monarchies
across swaths of present-day Turkey, Iran, and South Asia. Azeri
tribes pushed south into Iran at about the same time that their fellow tribesmen were driving west into Anatolia and south from
Kabul into India. It was convert Azeris who took Shiism into what
was then a largely Sunni Iran. While decades of Soviet rule seem to
have robbed Shiism in Azerbaijan of much of its vibrancy, Iranian
Azeris continue to be a strong pillar of the faith in the region. Some
of the most prominent Shia ulama since the nineteenth century,
such as Ayatollah Abol-Qasem al-Khoi, have been Azeris.

South Asia is home to a number of Shia communities, from the
Qizilbash, Farsiwan, and Hazara of Afghanistan to Sindhi, Punjabi,
Bengali, and Gujarati Shias, to name a few, in Bangladesh, India, and
Pakistan. While the Arab cities of Najaf and Karbala continue to
play an important role in Shia religious life, Iran, India, and Pakistan
today account for the majority of Shias, and provide no small share
of Shia intellectual leadership as well.

Waves of migration over the centuries, and especially during the
course of the twentieth century, have also taken smaller Shia communities to Africa, Europe, and North America. Along the east
coast of Africa, in trading towns such as Mombassa and Zanzibar,
Shia communities have deep roots. Shias went to Africa as traders
from southern Iran, Bahrain, and the Arabian peninsula as part of
the robust commerce that crisscrossed the Indian Ocean in the eighteenth and nineteenth centuries. In the early decades of the twentieth century others migrated from India with the British, following
in the footsteps of their Ismaili brethren to settle in Kampala,
Nairobi, Dar es Salaam, and Durban. Like the Ismailis, East African
Shias, were pushed to leave Africa for exile in the United States or
Canada. Farther to the west, Shia communities are largely com-

posed of recent migrants from Lebanon, who escaped the ravages of war and poverty to seek their fortunes in places like Kinshasa and Freetown. More Shias—some displaced African exiles, others with origins in the Arab world, Iran, or Pakistan—have settled in the West. Cities such as Toronto, Detroit, Washington, D.C., and London now have sizable Shia communities in their midst.

The spread of Shiism has inevitably been tied to the way the faith has fared in the halls of power. Although Shias never seriously challenged the Sunni domination of the early Islamic empire, there were periods when Shia dynasties ruled, often over Sunnis. The Persian Buyids ruled Baghdad in the middle of the tenth century, and Ismaili Fatimids ruled over Egypt. Elsewhere, smaller Shia principalities prevailed. The Shia Bahmani Kingdom (1347–1526) ruled over the Deccan in southern India, and the Nawabs of Awadh (1732-1856) ruled over Lucknow in northern India. In these instances, Shia rulers patronized Shia ulama and intellectuals and provided havens from Sunni persecution, but they did not produce a Shia domain.

Since that feat was achieved by the Safavid kings of Iran, the faith has become closely enmeshed with Iranian identity, and the two have influenced each other. After the Safavids, Iran became even more homogeneously Shia as European colonial powers began stripping away Iranian-run but Sunni-populated territories in the Caucasus, Central Asia, and Afghanistan in the nineteenth century. The renowned French scholar of Shiism, Henry Corbin, even characterized Shiism as *Islam iraniene*, or Iranian Islam.[10] While the existence of Persian or Iranian influences at the roots of Shiism remains much debated, there is no doubt that the development of the faith since the sixteenth century has had a large Iranian component to it, and that a far greater proportion of Iranians identify with Shiism than do Arabs, who have mostly remained Sunni. Aside from the Azeris, no people has embraced Shiism as fully as the Iranians have.

In 1722 the Safavid empire fell to Sunni armies from Afghanistan, who were then followed in power by the great Iranian king Nader Shah. Nader restored Iranian power as an eminence between the Ottomans to his west and the Mughals to his east. Yet he was a Sunni. Although neither the Afghans nor Nader were able to make Sunnism the religion of Iran, their triumph ended the Shia political challenge to Sunni regional domination. Yet the identification of Iran and Shiism endured, with highly provocative consequences for the Middle East in the twentieth century.

Chapter 3

THE FADING PROMISE OF NATIONALISM

The voice on the tape was grainy, but all Iraqis could tell who it was. Saddam Hussein was sending them a message. Recorded at his hiding place shortly before he was arrested and addressed to "the Iraqi people and the Arab nation" on the occasion of his birthday, April 28, 2003, the tape was vintage Saddam. The fallen dictator blamed traitors for the way his troops had failed so quickly, letting U.S. forces storm into Baghdad in just a few weeks of high-speed maneuver warfare. He exhorted Iraqis to resist the occupation and to remain true to their Arab honor and sense of nationalism. They would be triumphant if they remained defiant, he said.

Saddam had always had a flair for drama and a keen sense of history. To make sure that his countrymen felt the meaning of what had happened as well as to poison the well for the United States, he compared Baghdad's fall to the Americans in 2003 to its fall to the

Mongols in 1258. That earlier conquest had spelled the end of the caliphate and is remembered by Sunni Arabs as a calamity, when the rivers of the cultured Abbasid capital are said to have run black with ink from books and red with the blood of the Mongols' massacred victims. Iraqis, Saddam hoped, would come to see resisting the coalition's occupation as an Islamic duty. He then made an ominous comparison in which he likened the Shias' lack of resistance to the Americans to the alleged offense of Ibn al-Alqami, the last caliph's Shia vizier, who supposedly helped the Mongols to sack Baghdad. "Just as [the Mongol chieftain] Holagu entered Baghdad," he ranted, "so did the criminal Bush enter Baghdad, with the help of the Alqami."[1] His implication was clear: just as the Shia had betrayed Islam in 1258, he was saying, so they were betraying it again in 2003.

Since Saddam raised the ghost of Ibn al-Alqami, references to him have become ubiquitous in communiqués of insurgents and Sunni extremists. As the bloody travails of war and occupation have unfolded in Iraq, the Shia have once more been held responsible for failures of the Arab world. Long persecuted and suppressed by the Sunni-dominated Iraqi state, now they are being blamed for the debacle that Sunnis face in the new Iraq—and by extension in the whole Middle East.

The ready way in which a "secular" Ba'thist figure such as Saddam can ring a change on a seven-century-old Sunni grudge to appeal to sectarian prejudices is a sign that the concepts and categories that are often cited in order to explain the Middle East to Western audiences—modernity, democracy, fundamentalism, and secular nationalism, to name a few—can no longer satisfactorily account for what is going on. It is rather the old feud between Shias and Sunnis that forges attitudes, defines prejudices, draws political boundary lines, and even decides whether and to what extent those other trends have relevance.

The rise of modern states changed the makeup of Shia society by loosening the ties that had once bound so many Shias tightly to their communities and leaders. Middle- and upper-class Shias tended to be educated in secular schools either in the West or at home in institutions built by European missionaries, such as Kinnaird College or Foreman Christian College of Lahore, Baghdad College, the American College of Tehran, and the American University of Beirut, and later those run by their countries' modern educational systems. Some became secular in lifestyle as well, or embraced Sunnism for the sake of easier upward mobility, the way a Southern Baptist might become an Episcopalian in some quarters of American society. Others became enamored of Sunni fundamentalism, which was gaining adherents and both political and religious stature. In Pakistan in the 1970s, as in Azerbaijan in the 1990s, for instance, Shiism was seen as politically passive and overly concerned with matters of ritual. Sunni activism, by contrast, had a heroic image: it was fiercely puritanical, dynamic, and politically engaged. Many young and upwardly mobile Shias felt the pull of this image and either became Sunnis or else began to practice Shiism as if they were Sunnis.

Modernization also led to a secularist trend that was particularly visible among middle- and upper-class Shias in Lebanon, Iraq, Iran, and Pakistan. This secular elite has played an important role in leftist politics across the broader Middle East, which some attribute to Shiism's intuitive identification with the poor and dispossessed and others to a Shia desire to focus politics on matters of ideology that distract attention from painful questions of religious identity. In Iraq to this day, the leading members of the local Communist Party have always been Shia. In Pakistan, likewise, the vast majority of Shias typically vote for the secular, left-of-center Pakistan People's Party, the political vehicle of the Bhutto family—a political habit that only increases Pakistan's right-of-center Sunnis' suspicion of their Shia neighbors.

Modernization has also changed ties between Shia elites and their communities. Early in the process of state formation in Pakistan, Iraq, Bahrain, and Lebanon, landlords and tribal leaders represented the Shia community. These notables (za'im in Arabic or zamindar in Urdu) cut deals with the Sunni ruling classes, and it was through these elite-level bargains that rank-and-file Shias found their mostly humble places in the new states. The notables would benefit from their ties to power and in turn were expected to represent and control their community. That is still the case in Bahrain and Saudi Arabia, where Sunni rulers limit Shia political participation to a game of notables. In many other places, however, social change gradually loosened the grip of landlords and tribal leaders. Few rural landowners, for instance, exert much influence in the big cities, where both middle-class and poor Shias can now be found in large numbers. "City air is free air," as the saying goes, and Shias who are no longer tightly bound by the venerable strictures of village life and its slower agrarian rhythms urgently want and expect to have a direct voice in politics.

This process changed Shia politics in Lebanon in the 1970s. Lebanon's sectarian politics divided spoils among communities, with Shia landlords such as the al-Khalil, al-Asad, and al-Zayn families nominally standing in for all Shias but in fact protecting their own interests. Growing tensions of various kinds in southern Lebanon spurred a mass Shia exodus to the southern slums of Beirut, while many Shias with more resources left for brighter prospects in Africa, Latin America, and the United States. Social change and migration loosened the notables' hold. Imam Musa al-Sadr, the religious head of the community, brought together the fragmented Shia communities of the Beqaa Valley in the West and southern Lebanon and organized them into a new political movement, Harakat al-Mahrumin (Movement of the Deprived), which in the 1970s became the new voice of the Shia in Lebanese politics. When Lebanon's civil war began in 1975, the Harakat gave way to a political organization and militia, Amal (Hope), which dominated Shia politics until Hezbollah (the Party of God) emerged in the 1980s, with Syrian and Iranian backing.[2] Amal became the party of many Lebanese Shia merchants in Freetown, Accra, Kinshasa, and greater Detroit, and the affluence of these diaspora communities became an important financial factor in Shia politics.

Interestingly, it was not secular Shias who benefited most from the change in Shia society and politics but the ulama. In Lebanon, Imam Musa, and later such turbaned chieftains as Muhammad Husayn Fadlallah and Hezbollah's Hasan Nasrallah, grew in prominence. To the south and east in Iraq, a similar process unfolded. Land reform in the late 1950s freed Shia peasants from the notables' political control. The cities of Baghdad and Basra, and others, swelled much as Beirut had, as strife, persecution, continuing high birthrates, and rural underemployment drove millions of Shias off farms and out of villages. These people streamed into vast and poverty-stricken conurbations such as the Zafaraniya neighborhood of South Baghdad or Sadr City, the enormous Shia neighborhood that skirts the eastern and northern edges of Iraq's capital. The poor of Baghdad or of Basra in the far south had little connection anymore with the rigid authority of their ancestral farms and marshes. In the slums, desperately needed social services came via the efforts of such clerical leaders as the ayatollahs Muhammad Sadeq al-Sadr (executed by Saddam Hussein in 1999, and the father of Muqtada al-Sadr), Abol-Qasem al-Khoi, and Ali al-Sistani. As a result, when Saddam's regime fell before U.S. tanks, it was not the mathematician-turned-politician Ahmad Chalabi or the doctor-turned-politician Iyad Allawi who emerged to lead the Shias, but Sadr, Sistani, and the clerics of the Supreme Council for the Islamic Revolution in Iraq (SCIRI).[3]

In Iran too, after decades of modernization, it was the ayatollahs rather than secular leaders who inherited the mantle of the shahs. This has to do with the traditionally strong ties that the ulama have had with their flock. But change in the ranks of the ulama is also important. Many like Musa al-Sadr, Khomeini, and Baqer al-Sadr and the Hakims adopted a new approach to politics. They became involved in social mobilization and used many of the ideological and political tools of the left even as they were competing with it for support among the youth.

That competition was important in pushing Shia intellectuals and religious leaders seriously to engage the Western ideologies that dominated the public sphere. In the 1960s, the Iranian ayatollah Morteza Motahhari, who would become a leader in the revolution, called attention to the popularity of the left among the country's young people. In Iraq, Muhammad Baqer al-Sadr wrote on philosophy and economics in a new style that adopted language and concepts from Western thought. The aim was to present Shiism to the young as the equal of Western thought. Sadr's two-volume study of economics, *Iqtisaduna* (*Our Economics*), presented a Shia view of social justice in terms and language that were familiar to readers of Karl Marx. Sadr was competing with Marxism even as he was reflecting its influence.

The Shia also embraced nationalism enthusiastically. In the aftermath of World War I, new national identities were forged—sometimes out of thin air—to define the struggle against colonialism and the character of the nation-states that were to follow. For the Shia, especially where they were a minority, secular nationalism was an inclusive identity. It defined them above and beyond the polemical debates of old and as equals to Sunnis in the eyes of the nation. Shias had failed to dominate the Islamic world theologically or politically and had faced the pains and perils of marginality. The modern state showed them a path forward that was free of the baggage of their religious identity. In Iran nationalism did not have these connotations, because Shias were a majority; but where Shias were a minority or ruled by Sunnis, nationalism appealed to them in the same way that inclusive ideologies attract minorities, who are drawn by the promise of a level playing field. Shias therefore embraced Arab nationalism, Pakistani nationalism, and Iraqi or Lebanese nationalism, in each case imagining a community where Shia-Sunni divisions would not matter. The modern world, at least in its nationalist guise, held the promise of ending centuries of painful prejudice and persecution.

The promise, however, proved to be illusory, as the modern states grew increasingly authoritarian and showed a penchant for using Sunni sectarian prejudices to shore up their own authority. They entrenched the very divisions that the Shia hoped they would bridge.[4] These nations solidified Sunni rule and Shia marginality and, worse yet, gave impetus to sectarianism. The founding ideas of these nations, despite a certain surface rhetoric of inclusiveness, never truly encompassed the Shia. Nor did they make provisions to include the socioeconomically disadvantaged classes, who often were predominantly Shia (as in Iraq and Lebanon). Marginality continued to dog the Shia as they faced institutionalized discrimination, persecution, and vicious prejudice in their everyday lives.

The fading promise of nationalism was most evident in the Arab world, but even in India Shias' enthusiasm for Muslim nationalism during the years leading up to partition, independence, and the birth of Pakistan in 1947 was to lead to disappointment. The Pakistan movement won early support from the Ismaili leader, the Aga Khan, and was generously bankrolled by Shia financiers such as M. A. Ispahani and Raja Mahmoudabad of Lucknow, a Shia prince and the biggest landowner in north India. Unlike Arab nationalism, the nationalism that drove the creation of Pakistan was pan-Islamic rather than specifically Sunni. The idea of Pakistan as a separate homeland for the Muslims of British India was at the outset openly inclusive of both Shias and Sunnis, and the initial composition of the bureaucracy and the military in the new state reflected this stance.

Pakistan's founder, Muhammad Ali Jinnah, was an Ismaili by birth and a Twelver Shia by confession, though not a religiously observant man. He had studied at the Inns of Court in London and was better versed in English law than in Shia jurisprudence, was never seen at an Ashoura procession, and favored a wardrobe that often smacked as much of Savile Row as of South Asia.[5] Yet insofar as he was Muslim and a spokesman for Muslim nationalism, it was as a Shia. His coreligionists played an important role in his movement, and over the years many of Pakistan's leaders were Shias, including one the country's first governor-generals, three of its first prime ministers, two of its military leaders (Generals Iskandar Mirza and Yahya Khan), and many other of its leading public officials, landowners, industrialists, artists, and intellectuals. Two later prime ministers, the ill-fated Zulfiqar Ali Bhutto and his Radcliffe-educated, currently exiled daughter, Benazir Bhutto, were also Shia. Feeling the wind shift in the 1990s, Benazir styled herself a Sunni, but her Iranian mother, her husband from a big Shia landowning family, and her father's name, the name of Ali's twin-bladed sword, make her Shia roots quite visible. In a way, Benazir's self-reinvention as a Sunni tells the tale of how secular nationalism's once solid-seeming promise has given way like a rotten plank beneath the feet of contemporary Pakistan's beleaguered Shia minority.

Benazir's father came from a family of large Shia landowners who could afford to send him for schooling to the University of California at Berkeley and to Oxford.[6] He cut a dashing figure. Ambitious, intelligent, and secular, he was a brilliant speaker, with the ability, it is said, to make a crowd of a million people dance and then cry. His oratory manipulated public emotion as the best of Shia preachers could, and his call for social justice resonated with Shia values. His party's flag conveniently displayed the colors of Shiism: black, red, and green. Although he never openly flaunted his Shia background, he commanded the loyalty of Pakistan's Shia multitudes, around a fifth of the population. What he lacked in the area of regular religious observance he made up for with his zeal for Sufi saints and shrines, especially that of Lal Shahbaz Qalandar, the widely popular Sufi saint of Shia extraction whose tomb is a major shrine in southern Pakistan.

Zulfiqar Ali Bhutto's years in power (1971–77) marked the pinnacle of Shia power in Pakistan and the high point of the promise of an inclusive Muslim nationalism. But the country that Jinnah built and Bhutto ruled had over time become increasingly Sunni in its self-perception. The Sunni identity that was sweeping Pakistan was not of the irenic Sufi kind, moreover, but of a strident and intolerant brand. Bhutto's Shia-supported mix of secularism and populism—sullied by corruption and his ruthless authoritarianism—fell to a military coup led by pious Sunni generals under the influence of hard-eyed Sunni fundamentalists. In April 1979, the state hanged Bhutto on questionable murder charges. A Sunni general, Muhammad Zia ul-Haq, strongly backed by Sunni fundamentalist parties, personally ordered that the death sentence be carried out, even after Pakistan's highest court recommended commutation to life imprisonment.

The coup of 1977 ended the Pakistani experiment with inclusive Muslim nationalism. Shia politicians, generals, and business leaders remained on the scene, but a steadily "Islamizing" (read "Sunnifying") Pakistan came to look more and more like the Arab world, with Sunnis on top and Shias gradually pushed out. Pakistan in many regards captures the essence of the political challenge that the Shia have faced. The promise of the modern state has eluded them as secular nationalism has been colonized from within by Sunni hegemony.

In the Arab world, the Shia learned the harsh lesson that secular regimes and ideologies may come and go but Sunni biases endure. The governments that followed Ottoman rule or European colonialism began as pan-national but were filiations of the same power structure that long had supported Sunni supremacy. The same Sunni elites—landowners, tribal elders, top soldiers, and senior bureaucrats—often ran the day-to-day show both before and after independence.

In the Sunni-dominated Iraqi state that British administrators created in conjunction with the princely clan of the Hashemites from the Arabian peninsula, there was a cosmetic sprinkling of Shia statesmen and notables in the parliament but not much more in the way of Shia influence.[7] Despite their preponderance in numbers, Shias have never ruled or even had anything like a fair share of power in modern Iraq. Whether under the Ottomans before 1921 or the British Mandate authorities and their handpicked Hashemite king-clients after that year, the Sunnis formed the police, military, and administrative class that effectively ruled the Land Between the Rivers.[8] Shias made a convulsive bid for power in the summer of 1920, when they joined Sunni tribes to rise against the British, but the rebellion failed; the Shias got the blame and received the brunt of the British reprisal. In the wake of the revolt, the British clung even more tightly to the local Sunni—Arab and Turkish—*gendarme* class that surrounded the throne of King Faysal I (Lawrence of Arabia's friend and a Bedouin prince who was a son of the hereditary Sherif of Mecca). The Sunnis compensated for their minority status in Iraq by merging the country's identity with that of the larger Sunni Arab world. In this scheme Shias were not seen as partners in nation, but instead, accused of representing Iranian interests and hence disloyalty to the Arab cause, were marginalized. Iraq did not have a Shia prime minister before 1947, some twenty-eight years after the country's formation. The beaten Shia found themselves pushed to the edges of national life. Many of their religious leaders fled from Najaf and Karbala to Iran. Exhausted and defeated, the Shia conceded to Sunni rule in a depressing aftermath to hotheaded revolt, which haunted the imagination of Ayatollah Sistani eight decades later. He cautioned the Shia against reprising the blunders of 1920 as he encouraged moderation during and after the U.S.-led military destruction of Saddam's regime. Otherwise, he feared, the United States and Britain would hand the keys to the country to Sunnis and lock the Shia out of power once again just as the British had done before.

Arab nationalism, which defined national and regional identity for most of the post-independence period, is at its heart a Sunni phenomenon—although many of the thinkers who gave shape to the idea, and especially its most virulent expression, Ba'thism, were Christian. It inherits the mantle of the Umayyad and Abbasid empires and the Ayubid and Mamluk monarchies—the historical expressions of Muslim and Arab power. Arab nationalism's promise of triumph and glory evoked memories of medieval Islamic power and drew on that legacy to rally the masses to its cause. The flag-bearer states of Arab nationalism—Egypt, Syria, and Iraq—had all been seats of Sunni power. Leaders of the latter two countries in particular claimed leadership of the Arab world from capitals whose prestige was tied to their past status as seats of the Umayyad and Abbasid empires. Nominally secular-patriotic in outlook and socialist by creed, Arab nationalism was the secularization of Sunni political identity in the Arab world.

Although Syria's politically dominant Alawi minority, the home base of the ruling Asad family, does not identify with Shiism, it has its roots in the faith. It was not until the late 1970s that Alawis admitted this. Facing rising Sunni consciousness among Syria's population at large, the Asad regime turned to Imam Musa al-Sadr and Ayatollah Khomeini for fatwas that declared Alawis to be Shias and hence Muslim. Arab nationalism in Syria even under the Asad regime has always appealed to Sunni political consciousness. The growing Sunni activism in Syria since the late 1970s—fitfully if at times very brutally suppressed by the Asad regime—has only confirmed that at heart Syria is a very Sunni country.

Arab nationalism therefore holds an inherent bias against the Shia. Shias whose mother tongue is Arabic are not by that fact equal members of the Arab nation. The pull of sectarianism is too strong, and they are among the distrusted quasi-outsiders, the "Arabs of the second class." It did not matter how enthusiastically they joined the Ba'th Party by the banks of the Tigris and Euphrates, sang the praises of Nasser by the banks of the Nile, or fought for the Palestinian cause by the banks of the Jordan. Shia blood, sweat, and tears for the Arab cause might be welcomed and expected, but equal rights would not be meted out even as the wages for such sacrifice.

Owing to institutionalized discrimination, Shias have never been well represented in the bureaucracy or military officer corps of an Arab state. In Saudi Arabia, most of the oil industry workers are Shia (the kingdom's petroleum reserves are mostly beneath a pre-

dominantly Shia east coast province), and in Iraq Saddam's large
conscript army was mainly Shia. Their numbers have made them
important to presidents and generals on occasion, but Shias have
never risen beyond the glass ceiling that separates them from the
Sunni elite. A few, such as Saddam's last and highly colorful information minister, Muhammad Saeed al-Sahhaf, rose to prominence.
But they were tokens in a world where Shia feet never trod the real
halls of power. Saddam Hussein liked to make much of the second
part of his name before his Shia subjects—especially during the
Iran-Iraq war of the 1980s—but he nevertheless characterized Shias
as Iranian lackeys, and he periodically purged the Ba'th Party of its
Shia members in order to make sure that the levers of state power
and the banner of Arab nationalism remained firmly in Sunni
hands. Shia privates filled the ragtag conscript ranks of Saddam's
poorly equipped and ill-trained regular army, but the elite
Republican Guards and Special Republican Guards were Sunnis
almost to a man. Iraqi Shias revealed what they thought of the Ba'th
Party when they insisted on including a clause in the August 2005
draft constitution that would ban all "racist" institutions, meaning
among other things the Ba'th Party, and that barred former Ba'thists
from holding office.

The rise of Islamic fundamentalism in South Asia and the Arab
world from the 1970s on lent new intensity to age-old anti-Shia bias.
The Muslim Brotherhood in the Arab world and the Jamaat-e Islami
in Pakistan both talk of Islamic unity, but what they mean is unmis-
takably a unity consistent with and actuated by rigid Sunni orthodoxy. Islamic fundamentalism was born first among Sunnis as a
response to the decline of Muslim power. It was closely tied to a
Sunni conception of history featuring belief in a Sunni right to rule,

and to a Sunni anxiety to uncover the reasons for Islam's (Sunnism's) relative decline in worldly power under modern conditions. Fundamentalism emerged in the early decades of the twentieth century in the works of Mawlana Abul-Ala Mawdudi (d. 1979) in India and later Pakistan, and Hasan al-Banna (d. 1949) in Egypt. These thinkers equated Sunni theology and law with true Islam, and they wished to impose Sunni values on society. Their ideal was the restoration of Sunni power, a power that Sunnis saw as proof of God's special favor toward them and theirs.

These thinkers had ample precedent in Sunni intellectual history, which over a millennium developed along different trajectories and produced many schools of thought. Still, regardless of what path Sunnism followed, its attitudes toward Shiism remained the same. Puritanical, reformist, and modernist tendencies each imparted a different spirit to Sunni theology and law but reiterated the refutation of Shiism. No one has been as important in giving religious legitimacy to popular prejudices, carving arguments, charges, and innuendoes against Shiism in stone, than the prominent Sunni jurist Ibn Taymiya (d. 1328). He saw the Shia as the enemy within, guilty of polluting Islam and facilitating the fall of its cherished institution of the caliphate during the Mongol invasion. He dismissed Shiism as heresy and sanctioned violence against its followers. More important, he put forth a formal Sunni refutation of Shiism that set the tone for much of the sectarian conflict even to this day. He is enormously popular with those who insist on puritanical and fundamentalist interpretations of Islam, such as the Wahhabis and the Salafis. To scratch their current theological and political claims is to find Ibn Taymiya lurking just beneath the surface. His anti-Shia polemics have had a long reach. Indeed, it might not be going too far to say that the surge of extremist Sunnism that troubles the Muslim world and hence the globe today is unimaginable without this one long-dead jurist.[9]

In a tome entitled *Minhaj al-Sunna al-Nabawiya* (*Path of Prophetic Traditions*), Ibn Taymiya refuted Shia beliefs and practices. He rejected the Shia view of the imams, arguing that there is no mention of them in the Quran or the traditions associated with the Prophet. In his view, the imams could not glean any more meaning from the Quran and the prophetic traditions than any other Muslim could. Outlining what has since become a staple argument of Wahhabis and Salafis, Ibn Taymiya emphasized that religious sources had no esoteric meaning; they had to be read and understood literally.[10]

Ibn Taymiya had even less tolerance for Shias' expectation of the return of the Twelfth Imam. What good, he asked dismissively, is a leader who is absent from the world and who thus cannot guide his people? Faith in some hidden imam, he continued, was irrational and simply underscored the Shias' folly. Likewise Ibn Taymiya rejected the special status that Shias accord to Ali as the chosen one of God.[11] How could God choose a leader who failed three times in his bid to become caliph and whose caliphate, when he finally attained it, ended in the debacle of civil war, his own assassination, and the triumph of the Umayyads? Islamic history in its glory and power is a testament to God's favor to Sunnis. Unmoved by the apocalyptic battle between good and evil that drives Shia theology, Ibn Taymiya saw worldly success as the most obvious measure of God's favor. The same logic drives Sunni insurgents in Iraq today and explains their determination to deny Shias worldly power and successful consolidation of their hold over that country.

Extending this logic, Ibn Taymiya chided Shias for misunderstanding the Sunni view of authority. Sunnis accepted their rulers not because they were the best of Muslims or because better leaders could not exist but because they performed the functions of leadership well—they provided order and governed effectively. In this pragmatic view, the proof of a leader's worth was his ability to grab power. Good leadership began with ascent to power. That Shia imams, beginning with Ali, were not able to win power made them ipso facto unworthy of having it. If imams lack special powers or a special right to rule, then the only legitimacy they can possibly enjoy must come from their ability to assert their power (*showkat*). This for Ibn Taymiya was the clinching reason to reject the Shia imamate, for by the same logic the Umayyads and the Abbasids were worthier rulers than the imams. This was why Sunni ulama had supported the caliphs in Damascus and Baghdad. Sunni theologians and political theorists have always measured the worth of authority in terms of power—a fact that has not been lost on modern-day Arab dictators.

Rejection of Shiism was not limited to the kind of puritanism that Ibn Taymiya promoted. The Shia found Sunni religious reformers to be equally unbending in their refutation of Shiism. Reform movements that emerged in the Sunni world from the seventeenth century onward, most notably that of Muhammad Abdul Wahhab (d. 1792), revisited Ibn Taymiya's condemnation of Shiism, this time as part of their prescriptions for reforming and reviving Islam and reversing its gradual decline in power as a world civilization.

Wahhabism emerged in the Arabian peninsula as a "back to the roots of Islam" reform movement in the nineteenth century.[12] Its base of power was in the oases that dotted the barren landscape of the desert of Nejd, the interior plateau region that is also the seat of the House of Saud, the princely ruling clan of today's Saudi Arabia. Abdul Wahhab was a purist. His creed reflected the simple ways of the desert tribesmen of Nejd, natives of what was then a fringe region of the Islamic world. He sought to cleanse Islam of all the cultural practices that it had borrowed and incorporated over the centuries. They had corrupted and weakened Islam, he said, and must be purged. Following the example of Ibn Taymiya, he rejected anything other than a literal reading of the Quran and the prophetic traditions.

Wahhabism rejected the notion of any mediating authority between man and God as untrue to the original essence of Islam. Even the Prophet was seen as a mere messenger of God, the equal of all other mortals and undeserving of any special veneration. In 1804, Abdul Wahhab's sentinels burst out of the desert into the holy city of Medina and made a show of their zeal by destroying the Prophet's tombstone in order to stop their fellow Muslims from "worshipping" it.

Wahhabis condemned the veneration of saints and their shrines as polytheism and viewed Muslims who engaged in this action as heretics. Before setting their eyes on the Prophet's mosque, in 1802, Wahhabi armies had invaded Karbala and desecrated the shrine of Imam Husayn—an event that has left an indelible mark on Shia historical memory. The Wahhabi conquest of the Arabian peninsula involved violence against the Shia. In 1913 the fanatical Ikhwan (Brotherhood) army of the Wahhabi commander (and later first king of Saudi Arabia) Abdul-Aziz Ibn Saud invaded the Shia region of al-Hasa and tried to impose Wahhabism on the population. In 1925 Ibn Saud's forces destroyed the cemetery of Jannat al-Baghi (Tree Garden of Heaven) in Medina, where the Prophet's daughter and the second, fourth, fifth, and sixth Shia imams were buried. To this day, during hajj Shia pilgrims sneak off to the site of Jannat al-Baghi to pray—that is, if they can escape the canes of Saudi Arabia's morality police, the feared *mutawaeen*.

After their conquest of al-Hasa, the Ikhwan called for a jihad against the Shia, asking Ibn Saud either to convert them or to sanction killing them. Ibn Saud wavered, but the Ikhwan often took matters into their own hands, and in 1926 in a burst of fury they put large numbers of Shias to the sword.[13] The bloodletting forced Ibn Saud, whose attention was now focused on state-building, to rein in the Ikhwan. He would not allow a pogrom, but the Shia had already experienced the worst of Wahhabism. As the Saudi state took form in the 1930s, the Shia were systematically marginalized and stripped of their public role. They were tolerated but not accepted by the Wahhabi state; they were the undesirable and heathen minority.

The bad blood between Wahhabis and Shias still colors their attitudes toward one another. Since the 1970s, as Wahhabism has become increasingly influential across the Muslim world and become the theological driving force behind Salafist movements, the tenor of Shia-Sunni conflict has become more strident. In many ways the greater violence of Shia-Sunni conflict in recent years flows from the spread of Wahhabi influence.

The Taliban in Afghanistan and jihadi fighters in Kashmir both have their origins in the anticolonialist strains of Sunnism that developed in India under the British, and in response to a brief period of Shia ascendancy there. In the eighteenth century, Shiism gained in influence as the Mughal empire weakened. The turn in Shia fortunes was evident in Emperor Bahadur Shah's decision to import Shia practices into his court at Delhi in the early 1700s. The trend was even more evident in the smaller kingdoms that were beginning to emerge in what had been Mughal imperial lands. The princely state of Awadh (rising in the 1720s), and later also that of Bengal, were the domains of Shia rulers known as nawabs.[14] In south India, the largest princely state, that of Hyderabad, was ruled by a Sunni nizam (as Hyderabad's ruling prince was called) but was by and large a Shia domain. Persian nobles, courtiers, scribes, and poets dominated the opulent political and cultural scene at the court of Hyderabad.

(William Dalrymple vividly reconstructs the life and times of late-eighteenth-century Hyderabad in his 2002 book *White Mughals*, which revolves around the romance between the British Resident and a Persian princess.) Shia influence was also pervasive at the courts in Mysore and Madras. Shia rulers patronized Shia ulama and encouraged them to debate their Sunni counterparts. These nawabs funded Shia seminaries and helped disseminate Shia culture. With royal money and patronage behind them, Shia practices such as Ashoura became grand public occasions. As the eighteenth century turned into the nineteenth, Awadh emerged as north India's preeminent seat of Shia culture, art, and religious study. And the Indian city of Lucknow is arguably second only to Isfahan in Iran as a showcase of Shia art and architecture.

To India's Sunni Muslims, the Shia ascendancy appeared to be a consequence of Britain's growing commercial and political influence. The Sunnis also saw the Shia domination as a manifestation of Islam's local decline—a divine plague attendant upon the improper practice of the faith. Sunni religious leaders began to stress the need for Islamic revival, which to them meant first of all the refutation of Shiism. The eminent Indian Islamic scholar and Naqshbandi Sufi leader, Shah Waliullah of Delhi (d. 1763), who himself venerated Ali, insisted that the Shia were wrong to deny the legitimacy of the first three caliphs. He encouraged them to consider that Abu Bakr and Umar deserved respect for fostering peace and unity among Muslims while expanding the amount of territory under Muslim rule.[15]

Sayyid Ahmad of Rae Bareli (d. 1831), who is best known for his jihad against the British, pursued a more radical reformist agenda, according to which the revival of Islamic power in India required the outright refutation of Shiism as part of a reform campaign designed to restore Muslim belief and practice to their originally intended condition. Influenced by Wahhabism, he identified false

Sufism, Shiism, and errant popular customs as the sources of religious corruption and hence declining Muslim power.[16]

India's Sunnis tended, like Sunnis elsewhere, to draw extremely direct lines between divine favor and worldly success. Seeing their own stock go down as British interlopers and Shia deviants took the lead, they sought to explain why power (God's blessing on his own) had left them and how they could get it back. In their eyes, Shia influence appeared as both a cause and a gauge of Muslim decline. For those Sunnis who felt most urgently concerned about what had gone wrong and what could be done to fix it, the Shia thus became a preoccupation. In a pattern that would also appear in the Arab world, colonialism angered the Sunnis, who then directed no small share of their ire at that already-suspect minority in their midst, the Shia.

Sayyid Ahmad's position on Shiism became a staple of reformist movements among India's Sunni ulama in the nineteenth century. The so-called Deobandi movement (named after a town in north India), which emerged late in the century to protect Islamic identity by defining and then propagating orthodox Islamic practice in British India, as well as the Ahl-i Hadith movement, which sought to purify the faith much as Wahhabism did, both rejected Shia theology and popular practices.[17] Both traditions were a response to British colonialism, seeking answers to India's turn-of-the-century tumult via new (but overtly restorationist) interpretations of Islam. The Deobandi movement sought to school Indian ulama in its views, while the Ahl-i Hadith focused on purifying religious practices to create a "true" Muslim community capable of defending Islam from the shocks of colonial subjugation.

The Deobandi area of influence still stretches from Bangladesh west to southern Afghanistan, which is, not coincidentally, the homeland and redoubt of the Taliban. The Deobandis became associated with Sunni extremism during the Afghan war in the 1980s, and some in their midst—in conjunction with Saudi and American money and Pakistani military intelligence agents—gave rise to the Taliban. Many other of South Asia's Sunni extremists, responsible for violence in Kashmir or against Shias and other minorities in Pakistan, hail from the Deobandi tradition, while Ahl-i Hadith inspires the jihadi fighters of the Lashkar-e Tayiba (Army of the Pure) organization, which has fought in Kashmir.

The fin-de-siècle attempt to reform Islam found renewed urgency not only in South Asia but in Arab contexts such as that of Egypt as well. A form of response to colonialism gave rise to the Islamic modernist school of thought most immediately associated with Jamal al-Din al-Afghani (d. 1897), Muhammad Abduh (d. 1905), and Rashid Rida (d. 1935). The modernists wished to restore Islam's position and prospects by reconciling it with modern thinking. Like the restorationists, who preceded them by a few decades, the modernists saw the path to Islam's reempowerment as running through a return to authentic Muslim practices and a model of state and society shaped by the early experience of the faith.[18]

The only difference was that the modernists found the example of the West to be deeply impressive and sought to identify in their own religion and history those values that accounted for the West's rise to global preeminence. The modernists in their own way shared the fundamentalists' belief that Islam's decline was payback for the embrace of "deviant" practices. They criticized popular religion, the layering of syncretistic cultural accretions over the purity of original Islamic doctrines, and the rise of a congeries of empires and monarchies in place of the original and at least notionally unified caliphate. In fact, they regarded the period of the first four caliphs as an age of true "Islamic democracy" that authentically embodied the value on which the West tended most to pride itself. Modernists rejected Sufism and Shiism, with their mystical doctrines, their emotional rituals, and their air of folk piety. They urged their fellow Muslims to look to the period of the first four caliphs as the sole authentically normative period in Islamic history; what had followed did not even deserve the name, for it was more a sad tale of Muslims caught in the toils of the "un-Islamic" than the narrative of true Islam working itself out faithfully across time. The deep irony that shadows the modernists and their legacy is that it was they who in many ways inadvertently taught the fundamentalists to be preoccupied with early Islamic history and to trumpet its authoritative character, although not the methods by which it is pursued today.[19]

The modernists also cherished a vision of unity among all Muslims. Al-Afghani was the great champion of pan-Islamism.[20] This unificationism dovetailed neatly with the modernists' idealized conception of the early Islamic period as a time free of ethnic rivalries, national divisions, sectarian disagreements, theological disputes, and contending legal interpretations. This appetite for idealizing an allegedly untroubled past had an ominous flip side, for it could easily mean denying and detesting the pluralism characteristic of "actually existing" Islam as found on the ground a millennium and a half or so after the time of the Prophet. In truth, Islamic modernism has really meant mostly Sunni modernism. Al-Afghani himself was Iranian by birth and most likely a Shia. He took the name Al-Afghani ("the Afghan") to mask his national origin, for he knew that a champion of Islamic unity and modernist reform would have to have Sunni credentials even to get a hearing.

A wily politician, al-Afghani traveled far and wide in the Muslim world. He was in India at the time of the Great Mutiny in 1857 and was a frequent visitor to Tehran and Istanbul, in each of which he was privy to court intrigues. There is even a story that he helped the

Ottoman sultan arrange the assassination of Iran's king Nasir al-Din Shah. Al-Afghani eventually settled for a time in Cairo, where he lectured on Islamic issues and became a major influence on the budding Islamic modernist trend. His ideas were forged in the struggle against imperialism. He was less interested in theology than he was in organizing a Muslim response to Western pressure. Although he belonged to both the Shia Iranian and Sunni Ottoman worlds and frequented both, he was not interested in laying the basis for a theological reconciliation between Shias and Sunnis, but rather wanted to persuade all Muslims to start presenting a politically united front to the West.

The modernist challenge to Shiism became more direct with Al-Afghani's and Abduh's students. Rashid Rida, who coined the term *Salafi* (virtuous ancestors), was concerned with emulating the Islam of the first four caliphs. Although his enterprise had its roots in modernism, his emphasis on early Islamic history spelled a puritanical approach that had much in common with that embraced by the reformists of the eighteenth century. Rida inspired some of the twentieth-century fundamentalists who followed in modernism's footsteps. His polemics were openly anti-Shia, and found reflection first in the Muslim Brotherhood and later in Salafist ideologies.

The Shia reaction to the modernist challenge was mixed. Shia ulama responded to Islamic (meaning functionally Sunni) modernism in the same way they had answered Sunni criticism since the attacks of Ibn Taymiya centuries earlier, using a mix of theological and historical arguments. The Arab world was where the modernist argument found greatest currency among Sunnis and hence posed the most direct challenge to Shias, so it is not surprising that the strongest responses, reaffirming Shia beliefs and rejecting modernism as yet another face of anti-Shia polemics, came from Shia scholars there, such as the Iraqi cleric Muhammad Husayn Kashif al-

Ghita and the leader of Lebanese Shias, Abdul-Husayn Sharafuddin Musawi.

The response to modernism from the Shia world's educated (but nonclerical) classes was both more receptive and more apologetic. Some, such as the Indians Chiragh Ali and Amir Ali, even became supporters and passionate advocates of Islamic modernism. Chiragh Ali dedicated his treatise on reform under Muslim rule to the Ottoman Sultan Abdul-Hamid II, who was, of course, also the nominal caliph. Others sought to replicate Sunni modernism in their own faith. This trend became particularly prominent in Iran, where the top-down "command modernization" policies of the Pahlavi monarchy (1921–79) challenged traditional Shia beliefs and authorities and threatened Shias' place in society. Intellectuals such as Reza-Qoli Shariat Sangelaji and Mehdi Bazargan sought to reform Shiism and thereby reconcile its theology and law with modernity. Shia modernism continues to resonate in the works of the Iranian dissident intellectual Abdol-Karim Soroush, who criticizes core Shia beliefs in light of the needs of modernization.

In many regards, Shia modernism resembled its Sunni counterpart. Shia modernists joined Sunnis in attacking popular Shia practices in the name of a more puritanical reading of the faith. With regard to Islamic history, Shia modernists continued to defend the Shia view of Ali and the imams, but sought to reduce the importance of imams and devotional piety in favor of religious observances that could be shared with Sunnis. Their approach to theology revealed the imprint of Sunni puritanism and its literal and narrow reading of Islamic texts. Their critics came to see this approach as "Sunnification" of Shiism and rejected reform for both its modernism and its crypto-Sunnism. Shia modernism did not become a notable force, though it has left some marks on Shia thought and practice.

The political interpretations of Shiism that became prominent in the 1960s and 1970s revealed modernist tendencies but did not proclaim themselves as modernism. Their advocates preferred instead to dwell on matters such as establishing the individual's place in society, confronting the power of the state, and securing liberation from foreign control. Still, in responding to the challenges before them, they ended up reforming aspects of Shia thought. Ali Shariati of Iran, Imam Musa al-Sadr of Lebanon, and Muhammad Baqer al-Sadr of Iraq related Shia doctrines to struggles for social justice and political freedom in the 1970s against the Pahlavi regime in Iran, the Christian- and Sunni- dominated political establishment in Lebanon, and Ba'thist rule in Iraq. They borrowed from modern ideologies, most notably Marxism in Shariati's case, to connect faith to modern concerns. Although they did not claim to be modernists, the result of their labor was a kind of Shia modernism that has proven to be of direct relevance to politics in the Shia world.

Debates between Sunnis and Shias may have had their own internal dynamics, but events on the ground also imposed a certain logic on them. The end of World War I brought important changes to the Muslim world. The Ottoman empire collapsed, and within its core region of Asia Minor arose the modern, secular-nationalist Republic of Turkey under its military founder and first president, Mustafa Kemal Atatürk. Kemalism's anti-Islamic program would in one form or another become the model for emerging Muslim states across an area far wider than Anatolia. Nationalism and secularism replaced Islam as the credo of state leaders, and muftis (Sunni religious leaders) and ayatollahs alike found themselves relegated to the margins of society, or at least politics. In 1924 the Turkish Republic abolished the caliphate, ending the last vestige of Muslim unity and the most prominent single symbolic link to the Muslim past. Finding much of itself overrun by colonialist infidels and now bereft of a notional center of gravity, the Muslim world became gripped by a new sense of foreboding.

In the turmoil of political and religious movements that followed, Shias and Sunnis found pressing reasons to join forces. Intra-Muslim polemics began to appear trivial in the harsh light cast by colonialism and secularism. Shia leaders in India supported the Khilafat (Caliphate) Movement, which swept the subcontinent to protest Turkey's putative betrayal of Islam via its abolition of the Ottoman-cum-Sunni caliphate. Iraqi Shia ulama who had supported the Sunni rebellion against the Ottomans during the war accompanied Shia ulama from Iran to the Caliphate Conference in Jerusalem in 1931. The conference was convened to determine what should be done about the caliphate. That Shia religious authorities should come to the caliphate's defense, cooperating with Sunni efforts to restore this cherished flagship institution of Sunni authority, was a momentous development, a rare coming together of the two millennium-old rivals, rising above the legacy of their conflicts and debates and bloody history together to stand united as Muslims in the face of what they saw as a grave threat to Islam. The Shia, for their part, took the view that while the Sunni caliphate was not a legitimate form of Islamic rule, its demise was a sign that far more worrisome threats than the end of a venerable but nominal Islamic institution were in the offing.

In the 1920s, centers of Shia religious learning in Iraq and Iran came under assault. As the decade began, Shias in Iraq were reeling from the dire consequences of their collapsed revolt against the British, while in Iran the Pahlavis aped Atatürk and pushed secularism by decree as a prelude to modern development. Shia authorities and other traditionalists saw secularism and colonialism as twin threats facing the Muslim world. To counter them would require making common cause with Sunnis. Thus, helping Sunnis somehow to preserve the caliphate was in the interest of Shias. The two sects disagreed on matters of religion, but not on the importance of religion itself or on the nature of the threat confronting it.

The spirit of cooperation led to a period of harmony and reconciliation. In 1959, the most influential center of Sunni learning, al-Azhar University in Cairo, authorized the teaching of courses on Shia jurisprudence as part of its curriculum. In a fatwa, al-Azhar's rector, Sheikh Mahmoud Shaltut, recognized Shia law as the fifth school of Islamic law. While Shaltut was a man of tolerance and Cairo has always had a special place in its heart for the Shia saints (al-Azhar was founded by the Ismaili Fatimids), the Sunni rector was also responding to the same impulse that had sent Shia ulama to the Caliphate Conference two decades earlier.[21] The challenge of secularism, now manifested in Egypt by President Gamal Abd al-Nasser's Pan-Arab nationalism, necessitated sectarian harmony. This spirit prevailed in the Muslim world for as long as secularism seemed to pose the most urgent threat. The rise of Shia and Sunni fundamentalisms in the late 1970s and the weakening of secular states—manifested in the fall of the Pahlavi monarchy in Iran and the slow death of Arab nationalism after the debacle of 1967's Six-Day War with Israel—at a time of growing regional instability changed the context once again. The specter of secularism no longer seemed fearsome enough to compel harmony, and with Islam dominating the Muslim world's politics, the long shadow of Ibn Taymiya and the sectarian polemics embedded in Sunni intellectual history once again stretched over the Muslim scene.

The growing importance of fundamentalism over the years has "Sunnified" the political climate in the Arab world and Pakistan. As national states have faltered in their missions, their vision of secular Arab or Pakistani nationalism has been not a new conception of society and politics but simply a "Sunnification" of that conception. Fundamentalism aims to fulfill the same promise as the nationalist state, but it claims that Islamic ideology will prevail where Arab nationalism or Pakistani nationalism failed. For the Shia, the "Sunnification" of the political sphere has meant adding a renewed spirit of religious dispute and oppression to the list of discriminations they already had to confront.

In the Arab world, the treatment of Shias as outsiders—as "lesser Arabs"—has always found justification in the accusation that they are Iranian, and that their demand for rights is nothing more than a modern-day reenactment of the Iranian-led *sho'oubi* revolt against Arab rule in the early centuries of Islam. In the heady days of the 1960s, when Arab nationalism was at its height and proclaimed a chauvinistic dislike of Turks and Iranians, ethnic identity was a measure of loyalty to the Arab cause. If religious belief made the Shias' fealty to the Sunni identity of the Arab state suspect, the charge of Iranian ethnicity was meant to place them on the other side of the pale from the "real" Arab nation. The rivalry between Nasser and the Shah in the 1950s and 1960s, and more so that between Iraq's long line of radical Arab nationalist rulers and Iran in the 1960s and 1970s, as well as Iran's friendly ties with Israel at the time, cast Iranians as Arabs' enemies. There were Shia communities of Iranian origin (*ajami*, literally meaning Iranian), whose founders had migrated to Iraq in the sixteenth century and to the Levant in the eighteenth century. It is said that when modern Iraq was formed, 75 percent of the population of Karbala was Iranian. Over time, however, most *ajamis* had become Arabs, adopting the Arabic language and Arab identity. Still, Arab Shias' religious affinities with most Iranians were used unfairly to cast them as lackeys of Iran.

That there were ideological and ethnic dimensions to the divide that separated the Arab world from Iran is not to be doubted, but the rivalry's historical mainstay was always the Shia-Sunni split. In the emirates of the Persian Gulf, Iran's growing regional power under the Shah and later Khomeini was always a source of concern. The prominence of Iranian merchants and traders in local economies heightened the fears. The main market in Doha, Qatar, is called the Irani Bazaar. The trading class in Dubai and Kuwait has always had a large Iranian component. I once shared a ride with a senior government official of the United Arab Emirates (UAE). As soon as we were alone in the car, he began speaking to me in fluent Persian. Noting my surprise, he discussed his belief that a healthy majority of the official citizens of Dubai, the UAE's expatriate-heavy economic boomtown, are of Iranian origin. Ethnic Iranians, he added, are disproportionately well represented in UAE government and business ranks. Fear of Iran meant fear of the Shia, and this led the emirates to tie their fortunes to Arab identity in the hope of withstanding Iranian aggrandizement. It was this nervous insistence on Arabism that explained my acquaintance's hesitancy to speak Persian unless in conditions of absolute privacy.

Many Arab regimes warn of the hidden "Shia agenda" and have depicted the Shia as the Iranian fifth column. In Iraq, Saudi Arabia, and Bahrain, such claims have been or are used to help justify dictatorship. Interestingly, these hoary rhetorical chestnuts of Arab nationalism have in recent years become a staple of Wahhabi and Salafi sermons and al-Qaeda communiqués. This no doubt speaks of Sunni anxiety in the face of the recent power gains by the Shias of Iraq, which is now in the extraordinary position of being the first Arab-world country to adopt a political system that gives a majority (and in this case, a Shia majority) its full scope in government via free elections.

While Shiism's association with Iran is long and even predates the Safavids' adoption of Shiism as their official version of Islam a half a millennium ago, and while the Gulf emirates as well as Najaf and Karbala have substantial numbers of ethnic Persian residents, the fact is that most Arab Shias are ethnically Arab and have roots in Iraq as deep as those of their Sunni counterparts. Nevertheless, Sunni extremist propaganda would make them out to be sinister interlopers.[22]

Fearful of a Shia challenge to Ba'thist rule in the wake of the revolution next door in Iran, Saddam Hussein in 1980 put to death the Shia leader Muhammad Baqer al-Sadr (Muqtada al-Sadr's granduncle), along with his sister. The execution was accompanied with the expulsion of tens of thousands of Iranians and Arabs of Iranian origin in 1979 and again in 1980. Nine years earlier the Ba'thist regime had expelled another 75,000, including ayatollahs, from Najaf and Karbala—"purifying" Iraqi Shias and severing their ties to Iran. Some of these people went to Lebanon, Jordan, Syria, or Persian Gulf emirates, where they are known as *ajamis*, but most were simply dumped at the Iranian border.[23]

Discrimination eventually sapped the Shia of their enthusiasm for the Arab nationalist ideal. They began to turn their backs on an ideology that had never delivered on its promise of inclusion. The Shia of Lebanon were the first to break away from the unhappy family of Arab nationalism. Throughout the 1960s and especially the early 1970s, in the days leading up to Lebanon's second civil war, the situation for the Shia worsened as radicalism and violence grew exponentially.

In 1959, Ayatollah Muhsin al-Hakim, the most senior Shia cleric in Najaf, sent the young Iranian cleric Musa al-Sadr as his representative to Lebanon. Musa al-Sadr arrived shortly after the civil war of 1958 and found himself in a land that was becoming the favorite battleground for Arab nationalist movements of all types. Nasserists, Ba'thists, Marxists, and all hues of radical nationalism were represented in Lebanon. At that time the Shia were not taken seriously in the confessional equation in the country. Lacking a clear political identity of their own, they followed the Sunnis' lead, fervently supporting Arab causes. They joined the Lebanese Communist Party or the leftist Lebanese National Movement of the Druze leader Kemal Jumblatt, along with various Palestinian fedayeen ("sacrificers") factions. The Shia fought the Christian Lebanese Forces, which were arraying against Palestinians and leftist factions as the spiral toward civil war continued. Always eager to prove their fidelity to Arab nationalism, they took their cue from Ayatollah Hakim in Najaf to back the Palestinian cause fully. Shia youth joined radical Arab anti-Israeli groups, and many trained with Palestinian fedayeen militiamen in order to join the fight along the border with Israel.

After the Black September struggle of 1970, when Jordan's Hashemite king, Hussein, and his mostly Bedouin army crushed the state-within-a-state of the Palestine Liberation Organization (PLO) and drove out its cadres, many of the Palestinian fighters fled to Lebanon. Left out of the negotiations following the 1973 Arab-Israeli war, the Palestinians (most of whom are Sunnis) decided to make their presence violently felt. Southern Lebanon, the traditional home region of the country's Shias, became willy-nilly a Palestinian armed camp. Palestinians took over the Shias' farms and villages, cut off their roads, and forcibly recruited their young men into their militias. The Shia were now forced to fight for the Palestinian cause, and even to sacrifice their own and their children's lives and property for it. The entire Shia community found itself forcibly entangled in the Palestinian struggle against Israel, as Palestinian attacks launched from Lebanese soil brought Israeli reprisals and incursions. With their villages destroyed and their land turned into a battle zone, Shias began to stream out of southern Lebanon to seek their fortunes in faraway Africa or North America, or, if they did not have the resources to take them that far, in the sprawling slums of south Beirut—the eleven-square-mile so-called belt of misery that by the 1990s was home to almost a million people. Musa al-Sadr's repeated pleas for help for the Shia and consideration for their plight fell on deaf ears in Beirut as well as across the region. This lack of wider Arab-world interest in Shia suffering was sadly typical. For all their pains, the Shia received no recognition or appreciation. Many began to question the wisdom of wholeheartedly supporting the Palestinian cause. Arab nationalism had brought them only suffering. It was Musa al-Sadr who showed them a path forward.

Iranian, young, and without patrons in Lebanon's ruthless politics, Musa al-Sadr was an improbable leader for the Lebanese Shia, but in the end he proved to be the deliverer that they needed and had been yearning for. He was a new kind of leader, an activist cleric engaged in the life of his community. He was tall and handsome, with piercing green eyes. He was worldly wise, had a law degree from Tehran University, and spoke several languages. He was as conversant in Shia theology as he was in Western thought. Much like the activist Catholic priests in Latin America who would pioneer liberation theology, Musa al-Sadr worked tirelessly to improve the lot of his community—to give them a voice, to protect them from the ravages of war and intercommunal strife, and to give them identity and power in Lebanese politics.

Sadr combined social activism with Shia identity to produce a distinctly Shia approach to political discussions, one that was true to the nationalist demands of the Arabs but also asserted Shia interests. He was largely successful in giving Lebanese Shias a new political identity distinct from Sunni-led Arab nationalism. Following his lead, the Lebanese Shias abandoned their blind loyalty to the Arab cause. Instead they demanded recognition and rights as Lebanese Shias, and by organizing politically and rallying behind their own militias they were able to wrest control of their destiny. The mark that Musa al-Sadr left on them was so deep that it became popular in parts of Lebanon to mimic his Persian accent. Sadr and his Amal militia—which also ran social services and acted as a political organization—became signal beacons for the Shia awakening and the standard-bearers of a Shia challenge to both the gauzy fiction of pan-Arab unity and the cement-hard reality of Sunni hegemony. Sadr even inspired Shias elsewhere in the region. In the 1970s, Amal camps trained Iraqi, Iranian, Saudi, and other Arab Shia activists. In fact, Iran's Islamic Revolutionary Guard Corps was first organized by veterans of Amal training camps.

Sadr's path of empowering the Shia looked like treason in Sunni eyes. That he was of Iranian origin only confirmed the worst suspicions about him and his movement. A Persian was leading the unsteady Shia to betray Arabism. The Shia awakening that Sadr had sparked was a threat to the Palestinians and to the Sunni establishment in Lebanon and by extension elsewhere in the larger Arab world. Before Sadr left on a trip to Libya in 1978, Rifaat al-Asad, Hafiz al-Asad's feared younger brother and the head of Syrian security, summoned the Iranian ambassador to a meeting in Damascus.[24] Musa al-Sadr had an Iranian passport, and Asad did not want to damage newly improved ties with Tehran. So he told the Iranian envoy that Libya's ruler, Muammar Gadahfi, was going to kill Sadr. Sadr disappeared in Libya, to become forever a "vanished imam" to his followers.

But Shia anger was not Sadr's creation, nor did it die with him. A new mindset had emerged among Lebanese Shias, and they were eager to express it. Even at the academic level, the first open attack on the orthodoxy of Arab nationalism came from a Lebanese Shia,

Fouad Ajami. In his *Arab Predicament* and later his passionate biography of Musa al-Sadr, *The Vanished Imam*, Ajami strongly criticized the underlying assumptions and promise of Arab nationalism.[25] His detractors attributed Ajami's "blasphemy" and "treason against the Arab cause" to many things, but near the heart of the matter were the volumes that his disillusioned account spoke about the badly soured Shia attitude toward the promise of Arab unity.

The depth of Shia anger at Palestinians and Arab nationalism became evident in 1982, when the Shia greeted the invading Israeli army as liberators, with flowers and open arms. "Palestinians had been expanding in disturbing ways" and it was time for "the Lebanese scene to free itself from the burden of the Palestinian problem," argued Muhammad Husayn Fadlallah, who would gain renown as the spiritual leader of Hezbollah.[26] When the Israeli Defense Forces (IDF) expelled the PLO from Lebanon, the Shia found ample room to flex their muscles. They became the dominant Muslim force. Amal showed its newly gained power in a series of attacks on Palestinian refugee camps around Beirut, such as Sabra and Shatila—camps that had gained international notoriety after Israel was accused of sanctioning a bloody massacre of civilians there by Christian militias—and Bourj al-Barajneh. In these "camp wars," which lasted three years, Amal wreaked revenge upon Palestinians. Shatila and Bourj al-Barajneh were at one point put under siege for some six months. Cut off from water and food, the residents faced starvation. Shia politicians such as the current Amal leader, Nabih Berri, continued to support anti-Palestinian legislation. The Shia were only absolved of the "sin" of supporting Israel and attacking Palestinians after Hezbollah emerged on the scene to take on the IDF and force it to retreat from Lebanon, overshadowing Amal as the face of Shia politics in Lebanon.

Hezbollah was from the outset closely tied to Iran. Its fighters were trained by Iran's Revolutionary Guards under the watchful eyes of Iranian clerics, most notably Fazlollah Mahallati, who was sent from Tehran to organize the group. Hezbollah quickly developed into a lethal and highly organized military force, far more radical in its views than Amal—committed to pan-Islamic revolution rather than merely the empowerment of Shias within Lebanon. It was led from early on by militant clerics, most notably the charismatic Fadlallah, who became the organization's most articulate spokesman. Unlike Amal, which is still active in Lebanese politics and commands the loyalty of many Lebanese Shias, Hezbollah has shunned an openly sectarian posture and has instead defused Shia-Palestinian tensions by focusing attention on the fight against Israel.

Hezbollah has dealt with the Palestinian issue by subsuming Palestinian politics under its own drive for power. Today its television station, al-Manar (Lighthouse), is the second most popular in the region (after al-Jazeera), in part thanks to its strong following among Palestinians across the Middle East. In 1994 Lebanon began a process of naturalizing its Palestinian refugees. To avoid disturbing the country's delicate confessional balance, Palestinians, regardless of their actual faith, will be naturalized in equal portions as Shias, Sunnis, Druze, and Christians. The first to be naturalized were around 30,000 people in southern Lebanon, who are now officially Shia—in other words, the Shia can claim that many more in terms of their numbers in Lebanon. These new Shias will not be likely to turn out for Ashoura processions but will vote—predominantly for Hezbollah. Hezbollah's war on Israel since 1982 has made the organization a hero to the Palestinian cause. It is Israel, the common enemy, that will define Palestinian Shias' relation to Hezbollah.

As Shias elsewhere also began to opt out of Arab and other nationalisms and to think of gaining power through the assertion of what might be called the politics of Shia identity, many have looked to the Lebanese model. There have been other paths as well, however. Starting in the 1930s, some turned to communism. Egalitarian ideologies of the left had always held a certain attraction for Shias. If Arab nationalism's failure lay in its inability or unwillingness to transcend Sunni identity, then communism's more radical approach, some hoped, offered the prospect of at last generating enough ideological thrust to escape the deadening gravitational field of Sunni dominance. If Arab nationalism became the creed of the Sunni in the Arab world, communism became identified with the Shia—although many Sunnis joined the ranks of communist parties as well—and the attitudes towards the *shoyou'i* (the word for communism in Arabic) came to reflect those toward the Shia.[27]

This trend toward the left ran strongest in Iraq. The backbone of Iraq's Communist Party was always its cadre of Shia intellectuals (including the famous poet Muzaffar al-Nawwab), bureaucrats, professionals, and military men such as Hasan Sari', who was a leader in the coup against Colonel Abdul-Salam Arif in July 1963. So closely was the Communist Party associated with the Shia that the town of Shatra in southern Iraq was nicknamed "Little Moscow." The party, which was suppressed by Saddam, reorganized after the Iraq war. Its leader today, Hamid Majid Musa, is a Shia and was counted as such in the head count of Shias in the governing body that the United States set up after Saddam's fall. Communism has also found some middle-class Shia support in other Arab-world countries as well as Pakistan. It has never come close to being a majority penchant in the Shia world as a whole, however. Most Shias are not keen to replace one secular ideology with another. Moreover, neither atheistic materialism nor schemes of radical social change hold much charm for the majority of Shias, who remain at heart devout and fairly conservative.

More importantly and more ominously, the Shia began to look to the other enemy of Arab nationalism, Islamic fundamentalism, as a model. While Arab-world Islamic fundamentalism in fact had an anti-Shia edge, it could and did influence the Shia at the same time. In the wake of the 1967 Arab-Israeli war, Islamic fundamentalism proved capable of challenging and defeating Arab nationalism intellectually. In this, fundamentalism succeeded where communism had failed in Egypt, Syria, and Iraq. In 1967 a group of young Iraqi Shia activists formed the Hizb al-Da'wa al-Islamiya (the Islamic Call Party). Da'wa was a revolutionary organization dedicated to creating an Islamic state in Iraq. It was made in the mold of Arab fundamentalist organizations and drew ideological inspiration from Muhammad Baqer al-Sadr and Ayatollah Khomeini's writings.[28] Da'wa gained strength in the 1970s as it developed an organizational structure and recruited from among the ulama and Shia youth. Its growing prominence worried Saddam, who suppressed it and pushed it underground in 1980. Ibrahim al-Jafaari, Iraq's first elected prime minister, is a member of Da'wa.

In exile in Kuwait in the 1970s to escape the persecution of Shias in Saudi Arabia, the Saudi Shia leader, Sheikh Hasan al-Saffar, was powerfully influenced by Sunni fundamentalist works of the Muslim Brotherhood and Jamaat-e Islami, which called for an organized resistance to the secular state, Islamic revolution, and creation of an Islamic state.[29] In Iran too the turn to fundamentalism came to dominate Shia politics, culminating in the Iranian revolution and the rise of its brand of Islamic fundamentalism.

Chapter 4

KHOMEINI'S MOMENT

ehdi Haeri Yazdi was a philosopher and a jurist—a grand ayatollah in his own right. His father was one of the most important Shia clerics of the twentieth century. Back in the 1920s he had established the Iranian city of Qom as a center of learning to rival Najaf. He had also been Ayatollah Seyyed Ruhollah Khomeini's teacher and mentor. The younger Haeri's niece was married to Khomeini's son, and Haeri himself had studied mystical philosophy with Khomeini. During the 1950s, Khomeini had taught Mehdi Haeri and a few other seminarians *al-Asfar al-Arba'a* (*The Four Journeys*), a mystical text written by Mulla Sadra during the Safavid period.

Khomeini had in his early career been a noted philosopher (with a specialty in the study of Aristotelian logic) and had dabbled in mysticism, probably while influenced by his reading of the Andalusian Sufi mystic, Ibn Arabi.[1] He even wrote mystical poetry, though none of it was published before his death in 1989. Most important for his reputation among Shia clerics, he had shown great mastery in analyzing Sadra's *Four Journeys*, a particularly complex spiritual text that has always been popular in Iran's centers of religious study. In this work, Sadra charts the search for Truth as a four-part journey, during the course of which man is led to God, learns to open himself up to spiritual wisdom, and then returns to the world as one who has become united with God, reflecting his divine attributes and qualities.

Haeri told me that one night during the dark years of the Iran-Iraq war, as the 1980s were being consumed in blood, with countless thousands of young Iranian men perishing at the front, he went in distress to visit his old teacher. He found Khomeini alone, sitting on a rug in his garden before a small pool. Like many Iranians at the time, Haeri was deeply troubled by the war's horrors, which included missile attacks on civilian neighborhoods in the cities of both belligerent states. He opened up his heavy heart to Khomeini and asked his mentor if he could not find a way to stop the awful slaughter.

"It is not right for Muslims to kill Muslims," Haeri began. "Hundreds of thousands are dying in a war that has no end and no good purpose." Khomeini made no sound until Haeri stopped talking. Then, without turning his head and in even but reproachful tones, he asked, "Do you also criticize God when he sends an earthquake?"

Shocked at Khomeini's implicit comparison of himself to the Almighty, Haeri got up and left without a word. He would never speak with Khomeini again. Years later, he recalled his realization that evening that Khomeini had come to see himself as embarked on the last leg of Sadra's journey—as one who had become so closely identified with God and his divine attributes that he, while human, could function as a virtually divine lawgiver.

While to outsiders Khomeini might have seemed the epitome of traditionalism in his flowing robes and black *seyyed's* turban, he was a drastically new kind of Shia leader, with a movement behind him that represented a major break in Shia history. Dour and unbending, he had strong convictions and soaring confidence in his own spiritual stature. He was intelligent and commanded great respect from his students. Most important, he had a clear sense of destiny—his own, Shiism's, and Iran's. His politics and religious views reflected not so much Shia history and theology (indeed, he was something of a theological innovator and maverick) as the authority that he claimed by virtue of his understanding of mystical doctrines. His was a new Shiism, interpreted by someone who claimed direct knowledge of the Truth.

Khomeini used the emotional power of Shia lore and imagery not only to help him seize control of Iran but to lay claim to Shiism's very soul.[2] In the process he also made Islamic fundamentalism a political force that would change Muslim politics from Morocco to Malaysia.

Khomeini had not always been a revolutionary. His worldview evolved in reaction to the changes that the modernizing trends of the twentieth century (Khomeini was born in 1900) brought to Iran. In the sixteenth century, the Iranian Shia ulama had made a deal in which they agreed to affirm the monarchy's legitimacy as long as the throne defended Shia identity and the Shia realm. The first cracks in the partnership between the shahs and the ayatollahs came in the nineteenth century. At that time Iran was finding itself falling prey to European commercial and political pressures, though not actually colonized. The Qajar monarchy (1795–1925) had restored Shia government but proved weak and increasingly did the bidding of Britain and Russia. The tentacles of colonialist influence threatened the Shia realm by subjugating the country economically and taking away its political independence. With the shahs unwilling or unable to defend the nation, ayatollahs stepped into the breach to defend national rights and interests.

In 1892 the monarch Nasir al-Din Shah used his formally absolute power to give exclusive control of the tobacco trade to a British company. Popular opposition mounted. Iranian merchants complained to their religious leaders, and a powerful member of the ulama, Mirza Hasan Shirazi, issued a fatwa from his home in Samarra (then part of the Ottoman empire, now within Iraq) banning tobacco use. In effect, he was challenging the shah to stand up for the nation's rights. The shah could grant a tobacco monopoly, but an ayatollah could decide whether that grant would mean anything. The women in the shah's harem quit smoking, and his servants refused to prepare his water pipe. The ordeal ended only when the shah bowed to the ayatollah and cancelled the concession. The Shia ulama had become Iran's first line of defense and loudest spokesmen against colonialism.

Almost a decade later they went further, joining the constitutional movement of 1905–6, which liberal intellectuals and social activists had started in hopes of placing limits on the monarchy. Worried that the shahs' power might again become a tool of colonialism, the ulama leaned toward vesting more authority than ever in the people. Ayatollah Muhammad Husayn Na'ini led most of the ulama in defending the rule of law and democracy as compatible with religious teachings, provided secular laws did not impugn Islamic law or infringe on Shia interests. The ulama did not promote their own vision of the Islamic state, which would vest sovereignty in God, and instead accepted a constitution that declared the people sovereign, within certain limits. This outlook was essentially the same as the one articulated by Ayatollah Sistani during debates over a new constitution for Iraq in the summer of 2005.

The importance of protecting the Shia realm thus pushed the clerical stewards of Shiism in a new and more democratic direction. In Iran early in the twentieth century, defending the Shia realm meant constitutionalism. In Iraq after World War I, when the British took direct control of the country after having conquered the Turks, the response was outright revolt.

In Iran, the twentieth century saw the old partnership of kings and clerics strained to the breaking point. In 1925 the Shia ulama—Haeri's father prominent among them—persuaded an army officer named Reza Khan, who had staged a coup, to declare himself shah. They feared the rise of a Kemalist ruler, and believed that whatever the faults of a Shia monarchy, it would be preferable to an aggressively secular republic of the sort that Mustafa Kemal Atatürk was building next door in Turkey.[3] But the clerics got more than they bargained for, since the Pahlavi monarchy that Reza Khan founded turned out to have less to do with preserving Shiism than with acting as a modernizing republic parading in royal trappings. The Pahlavis never conceived of Iran as a Shia realm and refused to see defending Shiism as their duty. On the contrary, they perceived Shiism as a stumbling block to their modernizing agenda.

Before the first Pahlavi shah took the throne, he had taken part in Ashoura, beating his chest while calling out to Imam Husayn. The shah included the name of the eighth imam, Reza, which he also carried, in every one of his sons' names. Nevertheless, he saw a Turkish-style secular state as vital to Iran's modernization. Reza Shah secularized the legal system and the courts, banned the veiling of women, deemphasized Iran's Shia identity, and marginalized the ulama—when need be, brutally. The ulama resisted—at times violently—but the combination of a powerful government and a modernizing society caused clerical influence to fade.

One area where the ulama could still make their weight felt was the struggle against imperialism. Clerics supported both the nationalization of Iran's oil industry in 1951 and the popular movement that it created. The nationalization led to a confrontation between Iran and the West, which ended in 1953 with a CIA-backed military coup that ousted the nationalist premier, Muhammad Mossadeq, and restored power to the young shah, Muhammad Reza Pahlavi, who was Reza Shah's son. While many in the Shia ulama supported Mossadeq's goals, at the end of the day the most senior clerics backed the restoration of the monarchy because they badly feared chaos and a communist takeover. They set aside their sympathy for the nationalist cause and reacted to the same fears that led the U.S. to support the coup. They had made, thought the top clerics, yet another hard choice in order to defend the realm of the true (Shia) faith.

Whatever they meant at the time, however, the events of the early 1950s did not signal the birth of a lasting rapprochement between the throne and the Shia clergy. On the contrary, the 1960s and 1970s saw the state of relations between the two hit a new low. Rapid socioeconomic development, political repression, the growing influence of Western culture, the close ties between Tehran and Washington, and a growing gap between rich and poor all fed worsening social tensions. The ulama read these signs of the times as cause for worry, but also as an opportunity to undercut the religiously wayward Pahlavi monarchy. Some among the ulama also believed that unless Shiism took a leading role in the social and political struggles of the day, it would lose more ground and find itself shoved to the sidelines by leftists. To prevent this, the ulama would have to wax political as never before.

By the 1970s, alienated and angry ulama had become a potent

bloc within the growing opposition to the Shah. Behind the scenes, the Shia religious establishment wrestled with the question of what institution, if not monarchy, would defend the faith and the Shia realm. Khomeini, then an exile in Najaf, framed the most influential response. In a 1971 lecture series that became a book titled *Islamic Government (Hukoumat-e Islami)*, he put forward a new model for Shia government.[4]

Khomeini argued that God had sent Islam for it to be implemented. No one knew religion better than the ulama, who were trained in its intricacies and who carried the Twelfth Imam's mandate to safeguard its interests. God had commanded an Islamic government, and the ulama had to rule if that command was to be executed. Shia ulama had always been the guardians; Khomeini argued that that function could now be properly performed only if they ruled. With this theory of "guardianship of the jurist" (*velayat-e faqih*), Shiism would look to its ulama as a class—and among them the most respected cleric—rather than its shahs to rule and protect its interests and identity.

Not all Shia ulama were persuaded by Khomeini's argument. Some found his line of reasoning and the sources on which it relied weak.[5] Others saw it as a violation of Shia historical tradition and even theology. No one among Khomeini's peers was more vocal in his criticism than the grand ayatollah Abol-Qasem al-Khoi, Ayatollah Sistani's mentor. Khoi and Khomeini did not like each other. During Khomeini's Najaf years (1964–78), the two had kept their distance and often exchanged barbs through their students. In fact, Khomeini's lectures on Islamic government were a response to a provocation from one of Khoi's students. Khoi saw *velayat-e faqih* as an innovation with no support in Shia theology or law. He showed his disdain by sending the Shah an agate ring along with a special prayer at the height of the Iranian revolution in late 1978.[6]

After Khomeini assumed power in Iran, Khoi went further and denounced his theory as a deviation from Shiism. Khoi had supporters among the Iranian ulama, but fear of retribution kept them quiet when Khomeini took power and made himself a kind of turbaned shah under the title "supreme leader of the Islamic Revolution." One such dissident, the grand ayatollah Muhammad Kazem Shariatmadari, was defrocked by Khomeini, an affront that no shah had ever contemplated.

Khomeini knew philosophy, and his ideal of Islamic government under the ulama relied heavily on the Platonic notion (probably meant ironically by the original Platonic Socrates of *The Republic*) of a specially educated "guardian" class led by a "philosopher-king" wise enough to know transcendent truth and able with that knowledge to produce and maintain a perfect government that would safeguard all national and spiritual interests. This was Shiism reduced to a strange (and, as it would turn out, violent) parody of Plato.

While the Islamic Republic of Iran has converted the Shia ulama into a ruling class—a political as well as a religious "guardian" elite—it was less Plato than Marx who set the tempo of the Iranian revolution. The tectonic shifts in Iranian Shia politics that took place under the Shah coincided with a period of strong leftist activism in the country. Young clerics read Marxist works and found themselves impressed by communist ideas and activism. Some shared jail cells with left-wing activists and learned about revolution from these prisonmates. The organizational abilities and ideology-driven forcefulness of leftists made a mark on still other clerics.

Mahmoud Taleqani was a chain-smoking cleric with a gaunt face and a serious demeanor.[7] He was a veteran of years of struggle against the Pahlavi regime. He had been to jail several times during different decades, as a young preacher, as a mid-ranking cleric, and as a senior religious leader just before the revolution. During his time in jail he met many leftists, ranging from Stalinists in the 1950s to the younger breed of Maoists who dominated campuses in the 1970s. Some were thinkers and intellectuals. Others were guerrilla fighters. Lionized in the eyes of interlocutors by the scars he bore from his prison days, Taleqani liked to tell jailhouse anecdotes and was particularly fond of talking about his interactions with leftists.

During his early stints behind bars, Taleqani kept his distance from leftists. He read his Quran and shunned atheists. But gradually he began joining in leftist debates, defending his faith from Marxist materialism and charges that religion was unthinkingly conservative. Realizing that the Quran would have to match the *Communist Manifesto* if religion were to remain relevant in modern Iran, he became determined to show that Islam was just as progressive and revolutionary as Marxism. Taleqani would never openly admit that he had borrowed anything from leftists, but it was clear that he had a soft spot for them. He understood them, and he shared their worldview. He wrote a famous book, *Islam and Ownership* (*Islam va Malekiyat*), which as the title suggests dealt with a favorite theme of Marxism, arguing in support of collective ownership as if it were an article of faith in Islam.

Taleqani represents an influential clerical tendency to blend Shia with Marxist ideals in order to compete with leftist movements for youthful supporters as well as to put religion to political use more generally. No thinker was more instrumental in this regard than Ali Shariati, a lay intellectual who died just before the revolution, in 1977.[8] Shariati was raised in a religious family, but like many in his generation he received a secular education. He went on to study sociology in Paris, where he frequented leftist circles and befriended

Algerian nationalists. (It was President Houari Boumédienne of Algeria who in 1975 used the occasion of a peace summit between Iran and Iraq in Algiers to plead with the Shah to release his old friend Shariati from jail.) Shariati was keenly aware of Shia theology and history, but his worldview was shaped by the Marxism and Third Worldism that he encountered in Paris. He was sold on Marxist ideas and believed in class war, revolution, and the Marxist utopia. He wrote of Islam in clear Marxian terms: "Fourteen hundred years ago a few slaves, date sellers, camel herders and workers followed the religion of Muhammad. Today it is workers, farmers, merchants, bureaucrats and students who must revive it. Movements always arise among people because aristocratic ruling classes promote conservatism and prevent social change to protect their position . . . Many religious scholars (ulama) also take on the color of aristocrats for fame and glory or because the aristocrats hire them to preserve their interests."[9] For Shariati, the challenge was how to translate Marxist ideas into cultural symbols that the Shia masses could relate to—how to make Marx go down easier by giving him a Shia coating, so to speak.

Shariati saw Shiism as a creed of revolution. Its history told the tale of a grand quest for justice. Its saints were revolutionary heroes. He saw Imam Husayn as a seventh-century Che Guevara and Karbala as a revolutionary drama. Shia history was none other than the famous dialectic of class war, culminating in a revolution. It had all begun in Karbala and would end with an Iranian revolution. In Shariati's thinking, Karbala was no longer an eternal manifestation of the truth but a revolutionary act by a revolutionary hero, which could be duplicated in the late twentieth century. As Shariati often said, "Every day is Ashoura, every place is Karbala." Shariati criticized the Shia ulama for having turned a revolutionary creed into a quietist faith. In his opinion, Shiism had lost its way during the

Safavid period, to become a creed of scholarship and piety rather than social justice and revolution.

Shariati called his brand of Shiism "red Shiism," which he distinguished from "black" or Safavid Shiism. Red Shiism greatly resembled the roughly contemporaneous Catholic movement known as liberation theology, which began with the writings of the Peruvian priest Gustavo Gutierrez and those of the Brazilian Franciscan friar Leonardo Boff. Much like leftist Catholic thinkers and priests in Latin America, Shariati was inspired by Marxism and driven by his reading of what Catholics call "the signs of the times." In the process, he convinced many Iranians that their faith demanded social action, even to the point of embracing martyrdom in the cause of social justice, as the Shia saints had done.

Many among the ulama criticized Shariati for his Marxist leanings. Some saw him as a closet Sunni because of his attacks on the ulama, whom he said were at best unnecessary (for the revolutionary content of the faith was open to all) and at worst perverters of Shiism into a counterrevolutionary doctrine. Still others claimed that it should be up to the Twelfth Imam to heal the world's ills. Shariati's answer to this quietist objection was highly reminiscent of the open and urgent apocalypticism that had proved such a potent force in the history of early modern Christianity in Europe, where it influenced everyone from Christopher Columbus to Martin Luther, John Milton, Isaac Newton, and Oliver Cromwell: Shariati said that Shias should not merely await the imam in a passive state but instead should feel themselves called upon actively to work for the hastening of his return.

The critics scarcely dented Shariati's standing with Iran's young people, or impeded his success in popularizing a revolutionary reading of Shiism. "Islamic Marxism," as the Shah called it, became the credo of the revolutionary youth.[10] In fact, by the late 1970s many junior ulama fell under Shariati's influence, and they too defined Karbala as merely a model for social revolution.[11] Iran's current supreme leader, Ayatollah Ali Khamenei, was close to Shariati and shared many of his ideas. Others concluded that the only way to curb Shariati's influence was to appropriate some of his ideas as their own. As a result, Shariati's Marxist reading of Shiism came to define Khomeini's movement. Khomeini's arguments against the monarchy and in favor of clerical rule were thus married to Shariati's Shia Marxism to forge a revolutionary movement.

If Shariati looked to Karbala to legitimize revolt, Khomeini also relied on Shia messianism to confirm his own leadership of that revolt. Unlike Sunnism, Shiism strongly cultivates millenarian expectations, which give the religion its framework for understanding history and current politics as well as the mysteries of salvation and the end time. The Iranian revolution drew on the power of that framework, but it was not unique in that regard. In Lebanon, the disappearance of the popular Shia leader Imam Musa al-Sadr in 1978 evoked tales of miraculous occultation. After the fall of Saddam in Iraq the firebrand cleric Muqtada al-Sadr named his militia the Mahdi Army (Jaish al-Mahdi), clearly implying that his cause was that of the Twelfth Imam, and that those who fought him were the enemies of the promised Mahdi—who went into occultation over a millennium ago.

Throughout the revolution, Khomeini's followers used messianic symbols and language to give him an aura of power. He assumed the title imam. To the Sunnis the title literally means "leader," as in those who lead prayers at a local mosque. For the Shia, by contrast, it is a much more evocative term, conjuring up images of Ali and his eleven descendants. Only Musa al-Sadr had used that title, but

Lebanon had a strong Sunni presence and the routine use of the title in that country had reduced its symbolic value. In Iran, references to "Imam Khomeini" not only raised him above other ayatollahs but equated him with the saints. This became all the more the case as Khomeini's followers manipulated popular piety to enhance his religious standing. In the heat of the revolution, his cadres spread rumors that they had seen Khomeini's face in the moon, which was said to prove that God had blessed his cause.

Khomeini referred to the Shah's regime using terminology that had been reserved in religious texts for describing the enemies of the Twelfth Imam, such as *taghut* (false god) and *mofsidin fi'l-arz* (corrupters of the earth). Many government officials were executed by the revolutionary regime on charges of fighting against the Twelfth Imam—implying that the revolution was the promised return of the Twelfth Imam. After Khomeini assumed power, his titles became loftier still. He was referred to as Na'eb-e Imam (Deputy to the [Twelfth] Imam). On one occasion a parliamentary deputy asked him if he was the "promised Mahdi." Khomeini did not answer. Fearing that Khomeini had not heard, the MP repeated the question. Khomeini still did not answer, astutely neither claiming nor denying that he was the Twelfth Imam.

All this was designed to compel support for the revolutionary movement by suggesting that the choice before Iranians was between absolute good and absolute evil. Those who failed to fight on behalf of the Twelfth Imam were condemned to damnation. This notion was also used to garner support for the battle against Iraq and to motivate the troops at the front. In September 1980, Saddam Hussein sent Iraqi troops east across the border to occupy part of the oil-rich Iranian province of Khuzistan. It was early in the revolution. Emotions were running high, but the country was vulnerable. Many of the Iranian military's most seasoned officers had been purged or had fled into exile. The seizure and holding of the hostages from the U.S. embassy, which lasted from November 1979 to January 1981, had left Iran internationally isolated. In other words, conventional means of repelling the Iraqi invasion were hard to come by.

The revolutionary government therefore resorted to mobilizing hundreds of thousands of volunteers to defend the Islamic Republic. These untrained, ill-equipped innocents gathered at the front, where each received a plastic key representing the key to the gates of paradise. Many nights during the war, Iranian soldiers would wake up to see a white-shrouded figure on a white horse blessing them. These apparitions of the Twelfth Imam were professional actors sent to boost morale. The common soldiers, often peasant boys raised in an atmosphere of simple piety, would then carry the tale to their relatives and friends in the villages and small towns they called home, if they lived to make it home.

Convinced of the religious significance of their sacrifice, the volunteers launched human-wave attacks by the tens of thousands. Empty-handed, they confounded the Iraqi army's conventional tactics by using their bodies to set off mines and even to swarm Iraqi tanks or overrun Iraqi gun positions. Young Iranian men died by the hundreds of thousands, but in the end they forced Saddam's army off their soil. Pure willingness to die had matched the military superiority of the Iraqi army. The volunteers fought not for nation but for faith—or perhaps it would be better to say that they made no distinction between the two. They were sentinels of the Twelfth Imam, and to them the war was a spiritual as well as a physical fight.

The regime said that those who died in combat were guaranteed a place in heaven. Many lie buried in the Martyrs' Cemetery in Tehran, where a fountain with red water memorializes the blood that they shed. The more demanding the war became, the more the regime depicted it as the battle of good and evil—of the Twelfth Imam versus his enemies. The fervor bred a cult of martyrdom in the populace and made sacrifice for the faith a central feature of revolutionary Shia politics.

That cult of martyrdom proved equally important to Shia politics in Lebanon, where Hezbollah used it to launch its campaign of suicide bombing against the Israeli army in the 1980s. The willingness to die for the Shia cause was a watershed in Middle East politics. It gave Iran's revolutionary Islamic regime an edge in pursuing its domestic and international goals, and it made Islamic extremism and terrorism more lethal by encouraging what were in the 1980s called "martyrdom missions." In the Middle Eastern context at least (the Hindu Tamils of Sri Lanka have also extensively used suicide bombers), willingness to die for the cause has until fairly recently been seen as a predominantly Shia phenomenon, tied to the myths of Karbala and the Twelfth Imam.

Many in the religious establishment found these appeals to messianism disconcerting. Just as ultraorthodox Jews may oppose Zionism for presuming to do the messiah's special work, ultraconservative Shias were unhappy with Khomeini's messianic aura. Members of a powerful messianic society dedicated to the Twelfth Imam and named after him as the Hojjatieh were opposed to the Pahlavi monarchy and supported the goals of the revolution, but were uncomfortable with Khomeini's insinuation that he was or represented the Twelfth Imam. The Hojjatieh were disbanded after the revolution, but many members joined the revolutionary regime and some, like the current Iranian president, Mahmoud Ahmadinejad, became prominent figures in it. Reflecting Hojjatieh's dedication to the Twelfth Imam but also seeking to recapture Khomeini's power over the masses, Ahmadinejad declared soon after he became president that the real ruler of Iran was the Twelfth Imam and that government policy should be guided by the goal of hastening his return.[12] He even instructed his cabinet to sign a symbolic pledge of allegiance to the Twelfth Imam.[13] Most Iranians were not eager to recognize Khomeini as the messiah, but messianism continues to have appeal in many circles.

The Shia state that resulted from the revolution was a populist theocracy. Its vision of state and governance was drawn from Khomeini's *velayat-e faqih*, but its relations with society revealed the imprint of leftist ideologies. The Islamic Republic of Iran relied for its ability to govern on the religious enthusiasm and economic frustrations of the poor. It was built on the religious values that Khomeini defined, but it functioned as a domineering Third World state, with a centralized authoritarian government, a large public sector, and left-populist economic policies. It fused Plato's rarified notion of government by an elite with a certain street-smart, play-to-the-galleries authoritarianism.

Beyond the nonnegotiables of rule by the ulama and the enactment of Islamic law, Khomeini had never given much thought to what an Islamic state should look like. He once famously answered a question about his economic policies by declaring that "economics is for donkeys." Later he observed in his dour way that "we did not make a revolution to slash the price of watermelon." Khomeini, in short, was a classic big-picture man. To him, the details of governance mattered little, if at all. Still, his lieutenants had a country to run. Many borrowed ideas from the copious works of Sunni fundamentalist thinkers in Pakistan and the Arab world to give shape to the Islamic Republic. The state that Khomeini built would be an intolerant theocracy in which Islamic law was narrowly interpreted and implemented to limit individual and minority rights and erase all Western influences on society and culture.

Shiism since its inception had been defined by the spirit of

Karbala and the passionate rituals whose performance kept the intensity of that searing experience alive and burning bright. While Shias take the notion of Islamic law seriously, their faith is not primarily a law-bound or law-ruled phenomenon. Khomeini's Islamic Republic, however, was all about law, and had little interest in the values associated with Karbala and even less in the rituals associated with Husayn's martyrdom. There were no grand observances of Ashoura presided over by Khomeini, no parallels to the royal Ashoura processions of Iranian shahs and Awadh's nawabs. In truth, Khomeini and his coterie discouraged popular Shia piety, and even more, Shia traditions. During his years as Iran's leader, Khomeini not only eschewed Ashoura observances but also never bothered to visit the vastly popular shrine of the eighth imam in Mashad. In his own mind, he was above all that.

Iranian leaders visiting Pakistan would often shock their Pakistani Shia hosts with their disdain for Shia traditions. Faezah Rafsanjani, the daughter of former president Ali Akbar Rafsanjani and herself a leading member of parliament in the 1990s, once offended a senior Pakistani parliamentarian who invited her to visit a Shia shrine by cavalierly declaring that shrine visits were un-Islamic. Her attitude clearly betrayed the influence of modern Sunni puritanism. Shia fundamentalism appealed to Shia identity but did not draw on Shia spirituality. Its legal-mindedness and strict observance were and are, in fact, very "un-Shia."

Forcible cultural change in Iran had something eerily modern about it. The same mindset that managed the Chinese Cultural Revolution of the 1960s was also at work during the Iranian version a decade and a half later, when universities were purged of leftists and society of whatever was said to smack of the West and its ways. Religious edicts and the erasures of Western cultural influence were enforced for the most part brutally, through violence and intimidation.

Khomeini and his coterie managed the masses by wrapping their regime in Shia symbolism and evoking the great Shia stories. They adroitly manipulated popular beliefs to cultivate loyalty to and veneration for Khomeini and to compel the population to sacrifice for the revolution. Nowhere was this trend more evident than during the grind of the Iran-Iraq war.

Khomeini and his followers pushed their mythmaking to the point of claiming that the Iranian revolution was an event of equal significance to Shia history and piety to Karbala—a "new Karbala" of sorts. The revolution was to shape Iranian Shia identity and piety, just as Karbala had in the seventh century.[14] Friday prayer sermons began to assert this claim, and more recently, in a speech in Qom in May 2005, on the eve of his election to the presidency, Mahmoud Ahmadinejad reminded his audience that the Iranian revolution was of the same "essence" as Imam Husayn's movement.

When Khomeini died, his successors modeled his mausoleum after the shrine of the Imam Reza in Mashad and actively encouraged visitors to perform rituals usually reserved for visits to an imam's final resting place. The Islamic Republic of Iran as a worldly government may have been changing over the course of the past two decades, but the intent of Iran's rulers has been to enshroud the Iranian revolution and Khomeini in myth—to give them an eternal quality and surround them with an aura of religious awe.

For a while the Iranian revolution looked as if it would create a Shia "papacy." The Shia religious establishment had always resembled the Catholic hierarchy. The only difference was that Shiism did not have a pope to enforce doctrine and define the hierarchy, and it was the congregation rather than the hierarchy that decided how prominent an ayatollah was. Khomeini's assumption of the title imam and his claim to be the supreme religious authority in Shiism clearly pointed to his aim to be recognized as the supreme Shia leader.

Khomeini's ambitions also extended beyond Shiism. He wanted to be accepted as the leader of the Muslim world, period. At its core, his drive for power was yet another Shia challenge for leadership of the Islamic world. He defined his revolution not as a Shia one but an Islamic one, and saw the Islamic Republic of Iran as the base for a global Islamic movement, in much the same way that Lenin and Trotsky had seen Russia as the springboard country of what was meant to be a global communist revolution. Khomeini rose rapidly as a Shia leader because he appealed to Shia myths and popular beliefs, but he found it difficult to transform himself into an Islamic leader acceptable to the Sunni world.

Outside Shia contexts, Khomeini sought to downplay his Shia image. He posed as a champion of Islamic revival, and presented the Iranian revolution as the Islamic revolution that the Sunni thinkers of the Muslim Brotherhood and Jamaat-e Islami had been claiming was necessary if Islam's fortunes were to be restored. Iran, the bastion of Shiism, was also the vanguard of the global Islamic revolution. This was a hard sell, and most Sunnis were not buying. Although many Islamic activists in the Sunni world admired Khomeini and sought to emulate his example, still they were reluctant to accept his leadership. Khomeini sought to address this problem by focusing on secular issues that united all Muslims rather than on religious questions that were likely to divide them. He became the tireless foe of imperialism, and more anti-Israeli than the Arabs. He sought to focus Islamic activism on these issues—the battle against outsiders—rather than on Islamic concerns. His anti-Americanism had roots in Iranian history but was in many regards a byproduct of his ambition to be recognized as the leader of all Muslims, to find a cause that would unite Shias and Sunnis under his cloak.

Idealism is contagious, and Khomeini and his followers captured the imagination of many. However, although Iran inspired Islamic activism and forever changed the politics of the Muslim world, the final impact of the revolution would be far from what Khomeini had hoped for. He failed to achieve Muslim unity and the leadership position that went with it, but he managed to escalate anti-Americanism and inculcate fear and distrust toward Islam in the West as his glowering visage became the virtual face of Islam in Western popular culture.

The Shia world welcomed the Iranian revolution with great pride. After all, Shias had achieved the lofty goals of Islamic revolution and Islamic statehood that Sunni activists in the Muslim Brotherhood and the Jamaat-e Islami had talked about for so long. The Iranian revolution had changed the stature of the Shia. They had moved up in the world, thanks to Khomeini. Shortly before he died, one of the most important ideologues of Islamic fundamentalism, the Pakistani leader Mawlana Mawdudi, said that he wished he had accomplished what Khomeini had, and that he would have liked to have been able to visit Iran to see the revolution for himself. That sort of endorsement and envy gave the Shia pride.

The revolution also awakened the Shia. They became bolder in their demands for rights and representation, secure in the belief that Khomeini would support them and that they had a model for political activism which would succeed in challenging authority. Khomeini once sent a message to the Pakistani military ruler Zia ul-Haq, telling him that if he mistreated the Shia, "he [Khomeini] would do to him what he had done to the Shah."[15] Hence, when

Pakistan's Shias went by the tens of thousands to Islamabad in 1979 to demand exemption from Islamic taxes based on Sunni law, the government had no choice but to concede.

During the decade following the Iranian revolution, Shia politics in Afghanistan, Pakistan, Saudi Arabia, Kuwait, Bahrain, Iraq, and Lebanon began to stir. Shias started to abandon Arab nationalism or leftist ideologies to join the ranks of avowedly Shia political movements—many of which received financial and political support from Tehran—in order to push for specifically Shia agendas. (For example, Adel Abdul-Mahdi, a vice president in Iraq's first postwar elected government and a leader in the Supreme Council for the Islamic Revolution in Iraq, was once a member of Iraq's Communist Party.) These groups included not only the Amal movement of Musa al-Sadr in Lebanon, but al-Da'wa (the Islamic Call) in Iraq, Hizb-e Wahdat (Party of Unity) in Afghanistan, Tahrik-e Jafaria (Shia Movement) in Pakistan, al-Wifaq (the Accord) in Bahrain, and the Saudi Hezbollah and Islamic Reform Movement (al-Haraka al-Islahiya al-Islamiya) in Saudi Arabia.

Shia demonstrations, riots, and violent clashes with ruling regimes occurred in various parts of the Middle East. There was a failed coup attempt in Bahrain in 1981, and terrorist plots in Kuwait in 1983 and 1984. The greatest fear then was for Saudi Arabia's oil fields, which lie in the Shia region of the kingdom and have traditionally relied on Shia workers for their operation. In 1979–80, the kingdom's oil-rich eastern provinces were scenes of riots and disturbances. The Saudi princes and the region's other rulers responded to such unrest with sticks, suppressing pro-Khomeini activists.

Saddam Hussein's Iraq, a Sunni-ruled state with a Shia majority, was particularly worried about shock waves that might emanate from the revolution next door. The normally decisive and ruthless Saddam had not been entirely sure how to react to Khomeini's rise, but it troubled him deeply. At one point before the end of Khomeini's Iraqi exile (he was deported and moved to Paris in 1978), Saddam even let the Shah know that the Iraqi secret police would be willing to kill the troublesome cleric. The Shah turned down the offer.[16]

In 1975 the Shah and Saddam had signed a peace treaty normalizing relations between their two countries. Made nervous by the Shah's inaction in the face of Khomeini's rising challenge, Saddam warned Iran's Queen Farah during her 1977 Iraqi pilgrimage that Khomeini's success would bode ill for both Iran and Iraq.[17] He said that hundreds of thousands would die unless the Shah got tough and smashed the revolutionaries. In later years Saddam would say ruefully that he should not have asked the Shah for permission to deal with Khomeini, and that the single biggest mistake of his career had been to let the ayatollah leave Iraq alive.[18]

When Shia activism began to stir in Iraq, Saddam reacted quickly and violently. He killed the leaders of al-Da'wa and pushed the organization underground. He purged the Ba'th Party and senior military ranks of Shias and added a "carrot" to his policy by spending more money in poor Shia neighborhoods, towns, and regions of the country. His decision to attack Iran sprang from his assumption that an Iraqi victory would crumple the brittle revolutionary government in Tehran. Saddam was clearly unfamiliar with the history of revolutions, going back to France at the end of the eighteenth century. They thrive on war and gain strength when challenged. The brutal war of 1980–88 did not undo the Iranian revolution but radicalized it and entrenched its control over Iran. After Iran's costly campaign to regain its territory, Khomeini decided to push his way to Baghdad. The war seesawed back and forth, killing nearly a million and inflicting billions of dollars in damage on the two countries. Trench fighting, chemical weapons, and some of the biggest tank battles since 1945 characterized the conflict. A number of nervous Sunni-dominated Arab countries, including Saudi Arabia, Kuwait, Jordan, and Egypt, lent Iraq financial or logistical support. Monarchies, pro-American regimes, and Sunni-minority regimes all had an interest in seeing Iran lose or at least sustain major wounds. It was a war of two nations, but also a Sunni-Shia sectarian war cast in national terms.

Khomeini's style and the challenge that he posed unnerved the region. When a delegation of Muslim heads of state went to Tehran to mediate an end to the war, Khomeini made them wait for two hours, sat on the floor and spoke untranslated Persian for ten minutes while his visitors stood, and then left.[19] The moral to be drawn was clear: the ayatollah-cum-"imam" was a force that the region's leaders would fail to contain only at their peril.

Iran had hoped that Iraq's Shias would answer Khomeini's call to rebellion. In 1982, Iranian troops reached the outskirts of Basra, the biggest city of Iraq's heavily Shia Arab southern region, and began siege operations. Despite appeals to Shia solidarity, however, the Shia population of Basra and the city's Iraqi Shia garrison remained unmoved. They may have been Shia, but they were patriotic Iraqis as well. They fought against the siege until the Iranian offensive collapsed. After several years of stalemate, Iraq at last gained the upper hand. In 1988, with Iranian land under Iraqi control, Khomeini had to accept a humiliating ceasefire—a "poisoned chalice" was what he called it. The war had not crushed the Iranian revolution, but it had contained it—and not only because Sunnis had drawn a line in the sand, but because Iraqi Shias had done so too. The revolution that the Iranian Shias had made may have held a certain appeal for their Arab cousins, but the idea of Iranian overlordship emphatically held none.

The only place to which the Iranian revolution managed to spread a measure of lasting influence was Lebanon. Amal had trained a number of Iranian revolutionaries in its military camps. Many of the first (and soon to be purged) Iranian Revolutionary Guards', commanders were Amal alumni. Still, Amal was not a favorite in Tehran. Musa al-Sadr and his followers saw Khomeini as a political upstart with unorthodox views on religion and politics. Khomeini, for his part, found Amal insufficiently radical and too lost in Lebanon's Byzantine internal politics to be a genuine revolutionary movement. Iran therefore decided to build its own force in Lebanon, that is, Hezbollah. The opportunity came in 1982, when Israel delayed its withdrawal from southern Lebanon and began asserting authority over Shia towns and villages. Fearing a Palestinian fate, Shia resistance rose. Shia clerics such as Muhammad Husayn Fadlallah and Muhammad Mahdi Shamsuddin appealed to the myth of Karbala and called for a Shia jihad against Israel. As the conflict intensified and Shia resistance took a religious turn, a faction of Amal split off to form Islamic Amal, which later became Hezbollah.

Hezbollah adopted the cult of martyrdom that had been evolving in wartime Iran and used it as a part of its battle against Israel in Lebanon. Martyrdom gave suicide bombing a gloss of Islamic religious legitimacy. Between 1982 and 1984, Hezbollah killed about six hundred Israeli soldiers, a heavy toll that did much to help force Israel out of southern Lebanon. Hezbollah's victory and its vociferous rhetorical sallies against Israel lionized the group in Arab lore from Jordan through Syria and Lebanon in years to come, and its methods became a model for Hamas's fight against Israel in the Palestinian territories.

That a Shia force had scored this rare victory over Israel only added to the aura of Shia power that still glimmered amid the afterglow of the Iranian revolution. Shias had carried out the first and only Islamic revolution and established the first Islamic state. Now Shias had done it again, besting Israel in an area where the Palestinians had tried and failed.

Hezbollah also joined Iran's anti-American campaign. In October 1983, a suicide truck bomber almost certainly sent by Hezbollah killed 241 U.S. Marine peacekeepers at their lightly defended barracks in Beirut. Fifty-eight French troops died in a similar attack on their barracks the same day. The Reagan administration withdrew U.S. forces. Martyrdom tactics had shown themselves just as gruesomely effective in Lebanon as they were proving to be in the meat grinder of the Iran-Iraq war. Hezbollah's success boosted Iran's influence in Lebanon and consolidated that gain by laying the basis for a regional alliance that included Syria and Hezbollah. The alliance was anti-American and anti-Israeli, but was also a Shia front cutting through the heart of the Arab world. It connected the two most radical parts of the Shia world, Iran and Lebanon, as something like two wings of Khomeini's project.

The effects of that revolutionary project spread like a ripple across the region. Once the reality sank in that Shia uprisings would not take place through the sheer force of example, Tehran began spreading around money and organizational help to create Shia militias and revolutionary groups that would call for Islamic revolutions. Next came encouragement for challenging ruling secular and pro-America regimes from Pakistan to Egypt through armed conflict, street protests and rebellion, and acts of terrorism. Iran named a street in Tehran after Anwar Sadat's killer, Khalid al-Istanbuli. In the case of Iraq, Tehran hoped that the revolution would be carried into the country by victorious Iranian troops. Iran saw the various communities of the Shia world as vanguards in the larger struggle for the pan-Islamic revolution. It did not see the contradiction in the hope that mobilizing the Shia to lead revolutions would lead to Sunni support as well. In majority-Shia Iran, Shia activism and Islamic activism were one and the same. That was not true elsewhere in the Middle East. What eluded Tehran was the continuing importance of sectarianism. Where Iranian revolutionaries saw pan-Islamic revolutionary stirrings, Sunnis saw mostly Shia mischief and a threat to Sunni predominance. Khomeini's call to Islamic revival could not will away the old sectarian suspicions.

Not all Shias fell under Khomeini's spell. Ayatollah Khoi, Khomeini's old rival from Najaf days, was probably more than any other person a barrier to Khomeini's influence in the Shia world. Although no one ayatollah was recognized as supreme in 1979—only later would Khomeini claim that status—Khoi enjoyed the greatest reverence among the group of five incomparably senior ayatollahs that also included Khomeini. He was a native of Iran, but his presence in Najaf gave him great sway among Arab Shia communities as well as in the South Asian Shia orbit, which had strong traditional ties to Najaf. Khoi also had access to wealthy endowments (Najaf's status as a pilgrimage site brought in large charitable donations) and a network of dedicated students who were senior clerics in their own communities. Although some of these students, such as Muhammad Husayn Fadlallah of Lebanon (who for a while served as Khoi's representative in that country) and Arif Husayni of Pakistan, eventually embraced Khomeini, the majority remained loyal to Khoi. From early on, Khoi had rejected Khomeini's theory of *velayet-e faqih* as a bogus innovation and had openly urged followers to ignore the other ayatollah.

In many parts of the Shia world, Khoi's disdain weakened Khomeini's appeal and at times divided the Shia. In a village in northern Pakistan in 1989, I asked Shias which ayatollah they followed. The answer came back: "In religious matters Ayatollah Khoi, and in political matters Ayatollah Khomeini." If the Iranian revolution was about fusing religion and politics, Shias in Pakistan were apparently intent on separating the two, and were even assigning each domain to a different ayatollah. In Lucknow, India, I found Khoi referred to with the new title used for Khomeini in Iran, Na'eb-e Imam (Deputy to the [Twelfth] Imam). It seemed that Khoi would get an automatic promotion in title every time that Khomeini did. Given that the Iranian regime was actively promoting Khomeini, the tenacity of the loyalty that Khoi inspired was surprising, and may account for the influence that his student and successor, Ayatollah Sistani, now enjoys.

Khoi came from the ethnic Azeri community in Iran. He spoke both Persian and Arabic with an accent heavily redolent of the Azeris' own Turkish-related native tongue. His persona was drastically different from Khomeini's. Khoi was religiously conservative, and to him a key part of that principled conservatism was loyalty to the traditional quietist position that Shia ulama had embraced since the Safavid period. Khoi's importance in placing limits on the reach of Khomeini's ideas and prestige is often underrated and underrecognized. He kept alive a tradition of Shia thought that accords more leeway to the idea of distinguishing between religious and political authority, and he did so until the Iranian revolution lost its allure and its appeal subsided. The degree to which Ayatollah Sistani has been able successfully to articulate a moderate Shia politics in Iraq, based in part on traditional quietism, since 2003 is in no small part traceable to the legacy of his mentor and teacher. The restrained constitutional model that may now be emerging in Iraq appears to have prospects of becoming a realistic alternative to the Islamic Republic of Iran and its overweening claims about religious authority over political decisions. If that moderate model manages to thrive, Khoi's tenacious resistance to Khomeini should get a good-sized share of the credit.

Chapter 5

THE BATTLE OF ISLAMIC FUNDAMENTALISMS

I vividly remember a 1989 research meeting with a prominent Sunni religious leader in Faisalabad, Pakistan—a city that would become a hotbed of anti-Shia extremism in the 1990s. My purpose was to conduct a scholarly interview concerning the history of Islamic politics in Pakistan. Once my host realized that I was of Iranian extraction, he began wagging his finger and accusing Khomeini of sowing discord (*fitna*) among Muslims and falsely seeking to undermine the authority of the Sunni ruling clan in Saudi Arabia, the Islamic religious heartland. My protestations of academic objectivity were of no avail. My host saw only a Persian, whom he associated with Khomeini and Shiism. This was a golden opportunity to give his "adversary" an earful, and he could not let it slip by. He ended his finger-wagging by citing a rather minatory-sounding passage from Chapter 105 of the Quran, entitled "The Elephant":

Did you not see how your lord dealt with the people of the elephant?
Did he not turn their plan astray,
Did he not send against them birds of prey, in swarms,
raining down stones of fire,
making them like blasted fields of corn?[1]

The point was to warn the Shia (through me, then an MIT gradu-ate student) of the terrible fate that awaited them unless they dropped their challenge to the House of Saud.

It was clear that Khomeini grated on Sunni sensibilities in many ways. Iran's Islamic revolution may have popularized Islamic funda-mentalism, but it clearly had fallen somewhat short, a decade on, of bringing harmony to every fractious quarter of the Muslim world. With the Shia awakening in Iran, the years of sectarian tolerance were over. What followed was a Sunni-versus-Shia contest for dom-inance, and it grew intense.

None of this is to say, however, that Sunni fundamentalists did not benefit in some ways from the Iranian revolution. For starters, watching Khomeini and his lieutenants taught Sunni militants a good deal about how to organize and manage a mass social move-ment. The revolution even moved leftists in Muslim-majority coun-tries such as Indonesia, Turkey, and Lebanon to look at Islam with renewed interest. After all, in Iran, Islam had succeeded where left-ist ideologies had failed. Islam had proven its worth as a successful ideology of resistance. But admiration for what had happened in Iran did not equal acceptance of Iranian leadership. Indeed, Islamic activists outside Iran quickly found Iranian revolutionaries to be arrogant, offputting, and drunk on their own success.

Moreover, Sunni fundamentalism in Pakistan and much of the Arab world was far from politically revolutionary. It was rooted in conservative religious impulses and the bazaars, mixing mercantile

interests with religious values. Its goal, as the French scholar of contemporary Islam Gilles Kepel puts it, was less to tear down the existing system than to give it a fresh, thick coat of "Islamic green"
paint.[2] Khomeini's fundamentalism, by contrast, was "red"—that is,
genuinely revolutionary. Its goal was to shatter the existing state and
replace it with something completely new. Khomeini's version of
fundamentalism engaged the poor and spoke of class war. Its success in Iran suggested that for fundamentalism elsewhere to succeed, it too would have to go beyond concerns about personal
morality in order to encompass social revolution. Although some
Sunni fundamentalists were open to such a shift, most were not.
Nor were their backers in bazaars and among the merchants exactly
pining for a socioeconomic revolution that would redistribute
wealth to the poor.

Moreover, just as fundamentalists in the Sunni world learned
from Khomeini's success, so too did Sunni rulers profit from the
Shah's mistakes. The stark contrast that the Shah had allowed to
appear between the Islamic values of the opposition and his own
regime's assertive secularism seemed an especially noteworthy
source of weakness to avoid. In countries such as Saudi Arabia,
Pakistan, Bangladesh, and Malaysia, the government already
enjoyed considerable Islamic legitimacy. In others, such as Indonesia
and Egypt, officials quickly moved to bolster the regime's religious
credentials. While talk of Islamic fundamentalism was everywhere
in the 1980s, the cleavage between fundamentalism as revivalism
and fundamentalism as revolution was deep and for a long while
coincided closely with the sectarian divide between the Sunnis—the
Muslim world's traditional "haves," concerned more with conservative religiosity—and the Shia—the longtime "outsiders," more
drawn to radical dreaming and scheming.

Two developments transformed reluctance to follow Iran's leadership into active opposition. First, the Shia awakening from India to Lebanon appeared to Sunnis in general (to say nothing of the Sunni fundamentalists whom Khomeini expected to become his allies) as a threat to both social stability and their position of power. The Iranians could speak of "the Islamic revolution" in their country, but to most Sunnis its Shia character was prominent. Keeping the Shia at bay meant rejecting the ideas that were emboldening them. Sunni religious leaders and intellectuals first began to criticize Khomeini mildly, then questioned the religious basis of his claims, and eventually dismissed him as yet another misguided or malicious Shia.

It was Khomeini's direct challenge to Saudi Arabia that galvanized Sunni opposition to the Iranian revolution and the Shia awakening. Khomeini saw the Saudi monarchy as an American lackey, an unpopular and corrupt dictatorship that could be easily overthrown. No doubt the ailing and weary Shah's decision not to suppress his opponents with brute force of the kind that Saddam or Hafez Asad almost certainly would have applied if they had been in the Shah's shoes had led Khomeini to overrate the power of revolutionary rhetoric. Soon after the Iranian revolution toppled the Shah's regime, a group of Wahhabi fanatics led by Juhaiman al-Utaibi took over the Grand Mosque in Mecca in what was seen as a bold challenge to the authority of the House of Saud. While many in the West thought that Khomeini was behind the takeover, rumor spread across the region that the United States had instigated the defiling of the Grand Mosque. That in turn led to the torching of the American embassy in Islamabad, leading many to believe that the Iranian revolution was rapidly spreading across the region. Seeing all this, Khomeini concluded that the Middle East, and Saudi Arabia in particular, was like a ripe apple ready to fall into his hands.

More important, Khomeini underrated the degree and intensity of Sunni religious support for the Saudi regime (as illustrated, for instance, by my finger-wagging Pakistani interlocutor's assertive solicitude for the House of Saud). Khomeini ridiculed Saudi Arabia for being named after a single family and on several occasions used the annual hajj to stage protests with the aim of fomenting trouble in the kingdom as well as spreading revolutionary messages among the faithful from around the world. On one such occasion, in July 1987, things got so out of hand that clashes between Iranian pilgrims and Saudi police left 402 people dead.

Iranian revolutionaries encouraged the Shia minority in Saudi Arabia, between 10 and 15 percent of the population, to organize and demand change. Tehran had an even loftier goal, however: to restore genuine Islamic rule to that special land with its long religious history, the Arabian peninsula. Given the symbolic significance of the two holy cities of Mecca and Medina for Muslims everywhere, Khomeini was no doubt eyeing control of the kingdom as an important stepping-stone to his goal of claiming Muslim-world leadership for himself and his movement. He argued that the guardianship of Mecca and Medina should not be the domain of any one country or government—especially if they were not genuinely Islamic. The implication for many Sunnis was clearly that Shias had designs on Mecca and Medina. As a result, Khomeini's call for genuine Islamic control of the holy cities was seen as a Shia plot.

Many Shias found Khomeini's anti-Saudi rhetoric delightful. This was the first time that a Shia leader had stood up to Wahhabism and had in fact taken the battle to them. The memory of the Wahhabis' sack of Karbala in 1802 and anger at the destruction of Shia holy sites in Medina no doubt made Khomeini's bold challenge especially gratifying. The same reading of what was afoot gave Wahhabis a chill, and in turn helped them garner support from other Sunnis. When King Fahd responded to Khomeini's challenge by assuming the title of "protector of the two holy sites" (*khadim al-haramayn al-*

sharifayn), he received the ringing endorsement of the Sunni world. A Sunni king was seen as a more suitable guardian of Mecca and Medina than a Shia ayatollah.

Wahhabism was not as isolated in the Muslim world as Khomeini had assumed, and the House of Saud in the 1980s was not as vulnerable as the Pahlavi regime had been in 1979. He saw Fahd as Westernized, soft, and corrupt. Fahd, however, had become king only in 1982, and the image of Fahd's elder brother, Faysal, was more important at the time to the religious legitimacy of the House of Saud, both within the kingdom and across the Muslim world.

Faysal, who died in 1975, was a Muslim hero. He had been a capable king who had brought stability and financial security to his country. He was a practicing Muslim, simple in his ways and close to the tribal and Islamic roots of Saudi society. He lived humbly, a world apart from the ostentatious lifestyles that his luxury-loving younger brothers and other kinsmen notoriously embraced. He championed Muslim causes and lent his support to such projects as promoting Islamic education and Islamic economics long before it became fashionable or prudent for Muslim leaders to do so. He once told Henry Kissinger that his one wish before dying was to pray at the Al-Aqsa Mosque in Jerusalem. I have heard this story repeated with fondness in many parts of the Muslim world.

Faysal attained hero status with the oil embargo of 1973. During the Arab-Israeli war that fall, he led Arab members of OPEC to cut oil exports to countries that supported Israel. There were pragmatic reasons for Saudi Arabia to adopt such a strategy, but to Muslims it seemed an expression of Muslim power—the first time that a Muslim leader had stood up to the West. Faysal's challenge also removed the stigma of pro-Americanism from the Saudi regime, at least for a while. Ironically, Faysal was assassinated in 1975 by a fanatic from the ranks of the junior princes, enraged in part by the king's role in bringing television to the country. His prestige survived him for a surprisingly long time, however, and Saudi petrodollars have underwritten many a Faysal mosque, Faysal hospital, and Faysal housing development across the Muslim world. Faisalabad, a city of some two million in Pakistan, is named for the murdered monarch. When Khomeini took on the Saudi regime, it was not merely Fahd or the jet-set princes that he had to contend with but the far more formidable memory of King Faysal.

The House of Saud had not only the legitimacy but also the means to confront Khomeini. Throughout the 1960s, Saudi Arabia had combated Arab nationalism. During the heyday of Nasserism and Ba'thism, when alliances and unity pacts promised the Arab masses socioeconomic transformation and victory over Israel, Faysal alone had stood up to Nasser and Ba'thism, branding their ideas as atheism. Faysal stopped the Arab world's dominoes from falling to Arab nationalism when he intervened to stymie a coup by pro-Nasser officers in Yemen. He supported royalist tribes, and Yemen became engulfed in civil war, forcing Nasser to send troops to support the coup. The war became Nasser's Vietnam. Egypt was forced to withdraw, and Faysal's tribesmen won the day. Later Faysal would be the first to recognize Anwar Sadat's promise and help him—both financially as well as by securing the Muslim Brotherhood's support— defeat Nasserism and change Egypt.

Faysal resisted Arab nationalism in the name of Islam. Saudi Arabia not only relied on its Wahhabi identity to ward off the lure of secular nationalist (and probably therefore republican populist) ideology at home, as well as across the Arab world. Faysal supported the Muslim Brotherhood, many of whose members took refuge in Saudi Arabia's royal-run universities and Islamic think tanks. The cross-fertilization of ideas between Wahhabism and other brands of Islamic fundamentalism began in the 1960s as part of Saudi Arabia's strategy of strengthening Islamic identity as a bulwark against secular Arab nationalism.

Thus bonds that had been forged to stop Nasser and the other Arab nationalists could be mobilized to thwart Khomeini. Far from lacking religious legitimacy, Saudi Arabia in fact had impressive ideational and organizational resources at its disposal. To counter Shia fundamentalism, the House of Saud could mobilize Sunni fundamentalism. In fact, the Saudi regime saw an opportunity in containing Shia resurgence to turn the sharp edge of the rising religious extremism inside the kingdom—which manifested itself not only in the seizure of the Grand Mosque but in the growing number of Saudi youth trekking to Afghanistan to join the jihad against the Soviets—away from the ruling regime and toward defending Sunni power.

The implications of the Saudi-Iranian—or Sunni-Shia—divide for Muslim-world politics became clear in 1982, when the Alawi regime of Hafez al-Asad in Syria crushed a Muslim Brotherhood uprising in the city of Hama, killings tens of thousands. Iran had built an alliance with Syria around the two countries' opposition to Saddam's regime in Iraq. Sunnis such as the Muslim Brothers often reviled Alawis as beyond the pale of Islam and therefore not fit to rule Muslims. This belief only gave greater intensity to their rebellion against the Asad regime. Khomeini's refusal to support the Muslim Brotherhood during the Hama uprising earned him the Brotherhood's lasting contempt and showed that despite his eagerness to pose as a pan-Islamic leader, relations between Shia and Sunni fundamentalists were breaking down along familiar sectarian lines. When it came to choosing between a nominal Shia ally such as Asad and the militantly Sunni Brotherhood, Khomeini had not hesitated to stick with the former.

As rising oil prices poured untold billions into Saudi coffers from 1974 on, the kingdom began to subsidize various Islamic causes through charities and funds such as the Islamic World League (Rabita al-Alam al-Islami). This was a facet of the Saudis' growing confidence and claim to leadership of the Islamic world. A portion of the money went to propagating Wahhabism. Once upon a time, Wahhabi tribesmen had invaded Arabian cities to spread their faith. Now that work became the task of financial institutions funded by the Saudi state and Wahhabi ulama. Thousands of aspiring preachers, Islamic scholars, and activists from Nigeria to Indonesia went to Saudi Arabia to study, and many more joined Saudi-funded think tanks and research institutions.

Muslim Brotherhood activists were joined by Jamaat-e Islami thinkers and leaders from South Asia as well as many more Islamic activists from Africa and Southeast Asia. Saudi Arabia did not just sponsor Islamic activism but facilitated its ideological growth. Many of those who studied and worked in Saudi Arabia then spread throughout the Muslim world to teach and work at Saudi-funded universities, schools, mosques, and research institutions. Today ambitious ventures such as the International Islamic Universities in Islamabad, Pakistan, and Kuala Lumpur, Malaysia, are staffed by men who were trained in the kingdom. These de facto ambassadors for the Saudi viewpoint, influenced by the harsh simplicities of Wahhabi theology and financially dependent on Saudi patronage, work not only to entrench conservative attitudes in communities from Kano, Nigeria, to Jakarta, Indonesia, but also to defend Saudi Arabia's interests and legitimacy.

Patronage of Islamic causes from 1974 onward gave Saudi Arabia great reach across the Muslim world, from opinion makers to activists in leading political, religious, and educational institutions, sometimes all the way down to the level of small mosques in provincial towns and villages. Investment in Islamic causes gave the kingdom the means both to withstand Khomeini's challenge and even to close vast swaths of the Muslim world to his influence.

After Iran and Iraq went to war in 1980, Saudi Arabia threw its weight behind Saddam, financing his war effort to the tune of tens of billions of dollars. This was an Arab-Iranian war but also a Sunni-Shia war. If in Iraq it was Saudi-supported military might that would stop Khomeini, elsewhere Saudi Arabia had other resources to limit the spread of Khomeini's message.

Saudi propaganda underscored Khomeini's Shia identity on the one hand and the divide between Shiism and Sunnism on the other. It was clear to Riyadh and other capitals in the region that the surest and perhaps the only way to contain Khomeini was to play the sectarian card. This not only made it less likely that individual Sunnis would accept Khomeini as an Islamic leader but also enabled various governments to crack down on Islamic activism more easily, and after Khomeini's threat was gone to resist political reform. Any movement that got out of hand could be characterized as Iranian-generated or -inspired and hence a form of Shia rebellion against the proper order of things.

Governments from Nigeria to Bahrain, Indonesia, and Malaysia sought to drive wedges between Sunnism and Shiism, casting the former as "true" Islam—and the incumbent government as its defender—while branding the latter as obscurantist extremism. In 1998 the Nigerian government of General Sani Abacha accused the Muslim Brotherhood leader Sheikh Ibrahim al-Zak Zaki of being a Shia just before he went on trial for antigovernment activism. In the 1990s the government of Bahrain repeatedly dismissed calls for political reform by labeling them as Shia plots. In Malaysia in the 1980s, the government routinely arrested Islamic activists on the pretext that they were Shias, thus avoiding the appearance of clamping down on Islamic activism while projecting an image as Sunnism's champion against subversive activities.

In India and Pakistan, Sunni ulama confronted the Khomeini challenge head-on, branding his vitriol against the House of Saud as a species of *fitna* (sedition) wielded against the Muslim community. The Saudi rulers, conversely, were routinely painted as Sunnism's greatest defenders and the symbols of its resistance to Shia attempts at "usurpation" in a historical context stretching all the way back to the early Shia rebellions against the Umayyad and Abbasid caliphates. The Shia-Sunni struggles for the soul of Islam that had punctuated Islamic history were thus reenacted in the late twentieth century, with the Saudi princes in the caliphs' role.

Saudi Arabia continued to pursue its strategy of containing Shiism by working closely with Wahhabi ulama to build a network of seminaries, mosques, educational institutions, preachers, activists, writers, journalists, and academics that would articulate and emphasize Sunni identity, push it in the direction of militant Wahhabism, drive all possible wedges between Sunnism and Shiism, and eliminate Iran's ideological influence. As one observer remarked concerning the geographical distribution of the Saudi-funded Sunni extremist madrasahs, or seminaries, that opened in Pakistan in the 1980s, "They form a wall blocking Iran off from Pakistan."[3] It was in this context that one of Faysal's sons, the Saudi intelligence chief Prince Turki, laid the basis for a Saudi-Pakistani strategic relationship that would underwrite the Taliban's conquest of Afghanistan and its renting out of that country as a training ground for various "holy warrior" outfits.[4] The Pakistani-trained Taliban reflected traditional Pashtun biases against Shias, including the Afghan Hazara, whose plight is depicted so vividly in Khalid

Husseini's 2003 novel, *The Kite Runner.* Taliban fanatics declared Afghan Shias to be infidels and massacred at least two thousand of them in Mazar-i Sharif and Bamiyan in 1997 and 1998, and many more in pogroms across Afghanistan up until the U.S. invasion.[5] Others were told to convert to Sunnism or face death; many fled to Iran or Pakistan.

One of Saudi Arabia's aims was to stretch that Sunni wall from Pakistan north through Afghanistan and into Central Asia. The brand of radical Islam that began spreading across Central Asia and the Caucasus in the 1990s did not come from Iran but was a Sunni radicalism born of the deliberate Saudi policy of containing Iran.

Riyadh's strategy of turning militant Sunnism into a growth stock raised few Western eyebrows right through the 1990s, when Iran and its brand of Shia extremism still seemed to be the most dangerous face of Islam and the main threats to Western interests. It was the Shia who popped first into Western minds when Westerners thought about anti-Americanism, revolution, terrorism, hostage-taking, and suicide bomb attacks. The political fervor that emanated from Tehran and the kind of violence that it perpetrated were seen as flowing naturally from the Shias' apocalyptic bent and cult of martyrdom. Even hotheaded Sunnis seemed less dangerous by comparison. They may have been hard-shell reactionaries who despised modern and Western ways, the thinking went, but they entertained no religious doctrines bloodthirsty enough to match those of the Shia, with their fixation on killing and dying for the cause. This inclined the West toward complacency when it came to Sunni extremism and its spread, first to Pakistan, then to Taliban-era Afghanistan, and then across Central Asia. Also largely unnoticed was Sunni sectarianism's role in the horrors visited upon Iraq's Shias after the first Gulf war and the failed uprising of 1991.

———

In the tall and forbidding mountains—the world's highest—where the borders of China, India, and Pakistan converge and the Silk Road once meandered its way east sits the Hunza Valley. Tucked away in the shadow of K2 and Nanga Parbat at the extreme northeastern tip of Pakistan, Hunza is a magical place, with soaring snow-covered peaks, green slopes, winding ravines, deep gorges, and small villages hugging the mountainsides. Apricot orchards cover the land, enveloping mosques and houses built in the style of the Pamir.

At the valley's heart sit two villages, Karimabad and Aliabad. The former's residents are mostly Ismailis, while the latter's are principally Shias, like most people in Hunza. Shiism and Ismailism were brought to this region from the north over the Karakoram and Hindu Kush by itinerant missionaries. Karimabad in particular was a kind of South Asian Brigadoon: its breathtaking charm even served as the source of inspiration for the fabled settlement of Shangri-la in James Hilton's 1933 novel *Lost Horizon*.[6] The village is to this day as Hilton described it, its buildings and pavilions included.

Pakistan has never made Hunza and its surrounding region into a province (preferring to leave them as the unincorporated "Northern Areas"), partly because such an entity would have a Shia majority and would be the only Shia-majority province in the country. Instead, the government in Islamabad has sought to give Sunnis (historically a bit less than a third of the local population) more influence in Hunza. The methods used have not been gentle. In 1988 marauding bands of Sunni extremists acting with Islamabad's encouragement went to Hunza and attacked businesses in Gilgit, the valley's main town, just a short drive south from Karimabad. The raiders murdered 150 townspeople. Then came the erection of an imposing Sunni mosque in the middle of the Shia and Ismaili town. The government no doubt was keen to assert Sunni presence in a region that borders on Kashmir, where Pakistan was planning to launch Sunni jihadis against the Indian half of that disputed region. Attacking Gilgit was a practice run for attacks in Srinigar, the capital and main town of the Vale of Kashmir, in the 1990s.

Since 1988 there has been very little peace in Shangri-la. Shia and Sunni militias have been arming, intersect relations are tense, and there are periodic attacks on mosques and community leaders. A region known for its serene beauty and suggestion of timeless harmony between nature and the human soul is now riven by hatred.

In the 1980s and the 1990s, South Asia in general and Pakistan in particular served as the main battleground of the Saudi-Iranian and Sunni-Shia conflict. India and Pakistan were far more vulnerable to Shia assertiveness than the Arab countries. Pakistan has the second largest population of Shias, about 30 million, after Iran. Pakistan was where Iran focused its attention first. There, as contrasted with the situation along the Iran-Iraq border, it would not be conventional war but rather ideological campaigns and sectarian-inspired civil violence that would decide the outcome.

In 1977, shortly before the revolution in Iran, Pakistan's military took power and wreaked its revenge on the Shia prime minister, Zulfiqar Ali Bhutto. Zia ul-Haq, the top general, was a conservative Sunni deeply impressed by Islamic fundamentalism. He set out to "Islamize" Pakistan, building from the top down an Islamic state that would reflect the ideology of the country's Sunni fundamentalist parties. Emboldened by Khomeini's rise to power and encouraged by Tehran to assert themselves, many among the fifth of all Pakistanis who were Shia began refusing to abide by the military-sponsored host of fresh Sunni laws and regulations. What was presented as "Islamization," these Shias pointed out, turned out in practice to be nothing other than "Sunnification."[7] In July 1980, some 25,000 Shias gathered in Islamabad to protest the Islamization laws. They virtually shut down the capital and gave the Islamization campaign a public relations black eye. Caught between Tehran and his own restive Shia citizens and worried about maintaining good ties with the United States while the anti-Soviet war in Afghanistan took off, Zia gave way and granted Shias an exemption from "Sunni" laws. While the Shias got their way in this respect, however, their complaints helped to make sectarian divisions a central issue in the country's politics.

Zia's retreat before Shia protests made his Sunni fundamentalist allies deeply unhappy. Just as had happened under the Umayyad and Abbasid caliphs, these Sunnis thought, the Shia community was proving itself to be the worm in the Muslim apple and a standing threat to the authority of an Islamic state. For their part, the Shia were angered not only by the Islamization laws but also by Bhutto's 1979 execution, and stimulated by Khomeini's example as well as his anti-American rhetoric. Pakistan was becoming the site of a battle between two fundamentalisms: the "red" variety, coming from Iran, and the "green" kind that Zia and the military were promoting with the help of Pakistan's fundamentalist parties. This test of wills quickly became cast as a competition between Shia and Sunni fundamentalisms. Iran sought to avoid the sectarian definition, but in the end Zia, his allies, and Saudi Arabia defined the competition in sectarian terms to their advantage.

Zia knew that Khomeini did not like him. He had gone to Tehran in 1977 to urge a crackdown on revolutionary forces in the streets in meetings with the Shah. Later Khomeini asked for Bhutto's life to be spared and Zia ignored the plea. In their few personal encounters, Khomeini openly showed his disdain for the general and his Islamic idealism. On one occasion Zia took it upon himself to caution Khomeini about confronting the United States, warning that it was imprudent to tangle with a superpower. Khomeini retorted that he would never do such a thing and in fact had always relied on *the* superpower. Zia was baffled at first, but then realized that Khomeini was mocking him, saying that his own superpower was God, whereas Zia's was the United States.[8] Humiliated, Zia decided to take no chances by allowing Iranian influence in Pakistan and soon had his Sunni fundamentalist allies reining in the Shias.

Opposition to the Shias was centered in Islamic parties, and more important in madrasahs associated with Deobandi and Ahl-i Hadith traditions. The ulama in these madrasahs had ties with Saudi ulama and the network of religious charities and educational institutions that had been spawned by Saudi Arabia since the 1960s. Deobandi and Ahl-i Hadith ulama networks extended into Afghanistan and India, where the Shia had responded to Khomeini's rise with much the same assertiveness that they had shown in Pakistan. The Indian and Pakistani ulama thus began to share Saudi Arabia's perception of the Iranian and Shia threat.

The more aggressively Iran tried to influence the Shias of India and Pakistan, the more the Sunni ulama in those countries became determined to respond. After Iran organized Shia youth into student associations and supported the formation of a Pakistani Shia party modeled after Lebanon's Amal, the Sunnis began to form sectarian militias recruited from madrasahs across the country, including those that had been set up in the Pashtun region along the Afghan border to train fighters for the war against the Soviet Union. These militias enjoyed the backing not only of Islamabad but also of Riyadh and even for a time of Baghdad, since all three regimes saw Iranian influence in Pakistan as a strategic threat. Zia tried to take back some of the ground that he had conceded to Shia dissidents by pushing through a constitutional provision that banned insults against the first three caliphs, those Shia bêtes noires Abu Bakr,

Umar, and Uthman. In 1983 the conflict escalated after Sunni militants attacked two Shia places of worship.

Even as tensions mounted, mainstream Islamic parties were refusing to adopt a hard-line sectarian posture. Mainstream Sunni fundamentalists had always preferred to treat Shiism as a misguided interpretation of Islam and had sought to persuade Shias to accept the truth of Sunni views by reinterpreting Shia narratives and doctrines in accord with Sunni readings of Islam and the ideal of Muslim unity. To create their anti-Shia front, therefore, Saudi Arabia and Iraq had to look elsewhere. They turned to self-styled Islamic activists and intellectuals, such as the maverick Israr Ahmad, who was well known for his shocking statements on television and his popular and fiery Friday sermons. Israr was a fundamentalist of a decidedly radical stripe, keener to condemn than to persuade. He was also ambitious and eager to make himself an influential voice in Pakistan's crowded Islamic scene. He took with a vengeance to the task of attacking the Shias, caustically denouncing them with a force and stridency that were new to Pakistani life. So ready was he to insult Shia sensibilities that he held his daughter's much-publicized wedding on Ashoura, as if to show special disdain for his Shia compatriots' solemn observance of Imam Husayn's death.

The other pillars of Saudi policy were those ulama and madrasahs that had close theological and organizational ties to Wahhabi institutions in Saudi Arabia and had benefited from Saudi patronage. Like Israr, these ulama argued that Shias were not worthy of being called Muslims. The traditional Sunni polemic against the Shias as wayward brothers thus gave way to a newly virulent, root-and-branch rejection of Shiism as a gross heresy. Soon tomes with titles such as *The Shias' Revolt Against the Quran* and *Shias Rebel Against Islam* were appearing in bookstores from Karachi to Delhi. Militant Sunnis began to name their sons Muawiya and Yazid, breaking taboos by honoring caliphs who had persecuted and killed members of the Prophet's family. In fact, eulogies for these two Umayyad caliphs soon became an important part of the new anti-Shia discourse. This implied that Sunnis should revere as defenders of the faith rulers who had fought Ali and killed Husayn, facts that are difficult to gloss over for Sunnis, who are dedicated to exact emulation of the Prophet's life. Sunni extremists were particularly harsh in damning Ashoura as a heathen spectacle and a shocking affront to the memory of the rightful caliphs.[9] The attacks even went further, openly condemning the Shia imams as un-Islamic historical figures whom all Sunnis should actively reject.[10]

In 1984 a senior Deobandi leader, Muhammad Manzour Numani, of Lucknow, published a book entitled *Iranian Revolution: Imam Khomeini and Shiism (Irani Inqilab: Imam Khumayni awr Shi'iyyat).*[11] The preface was the work of the popular Indian religious leader Abul-Hasan Ali Nadwi (popularly known as Ali Mian). Nadwi was then one of the most senior religious leaders of India. He was a scholar and the rector of an important seminary in Lucknow as well as a trustee of Oxford University's Center for Islamic Studies. He was also a leader of India's Muslim community, often interacting with politicians on behalf of Indian Muslims and traveling across the Muslim world to represent them. Nadwi was an adviser to the Saudi Islamic World League. Although moderate in his views and a critic of fundamentalism, he nevertheless let himself be prevailed upon to lend his authority to Numani's attack—itself an ominous sign.

Numani saw Khomeini as the face of Shiism and pointed to Iranian excesses as proof that Shiism was beyond the Islamic pale. The book quickly made a stir. Numani and Nadwi were not marginal opportunists but senior Sunni ulama. Their commentary had the quality of a major fatwa. With Saudi financial support, the book was translated from Urdu into English, Arabic, and Turkish for wide circulation across the Muslim world. A copy in either English or Arabic was available to any interested person who requested one at the Saudi Embassy in Washington, D.C. The book made Deobandis central to the ongoing sectarian confrontation in Pakistan.

When I visited Nadwi in 1989, I asked him about the book. I expected him to go into outspoken anti-Shia mode, but to my surprise he grew quiet. He preferred not to talk about the book. When I pressed him about whether it was prudent to equate Shiism with Khomeini and to denounce the Shia faith so strongly, he demurred—it had all come down to the fact that Numani had been his friend, and that political circumstances had dictated the book's production. Moderate Sunnism was being pushed to adopt an unbending position toward Shiism. Nadwi had always been a pragmatic and temperate man. He had traveled to Iran during the Shah's day and until 1984 had not adopted an anti-Shia position. But as he hinted, the Saudi-Iranian rivalry was imposing its own radicalizing logic on sectarian relations.

Numani's book became the gospel of Deobandi militant organizations that in the 1980s mushroomed across Pakistan to press the fight against the Shia. Extremist Deobandi madrasahs trained Taliban and other violent recruits for action in Afghanistan, Kashmir, and elsewhere. Militantly anti-Shia militias such as the Sipah-i Sahaba (Army of the Prophet's Companions) and Lashkar-i Jhangvi (Jhangvi's Army) hailed from the same madrasahs and maintained close ties with Taliban and terrorist organizations such as Jaish-i Muhammad (Army of Muhammad), which was active in Kashmir and is responsible for acts of terror such as the kidnapping and savage videotaped murder of the *Wall Street Journal* reporter Daniel Pearl in January 2002. Sipah and Lashkar have cadres who trained in the Afghan camps maintained by al-Qaeda before the

U.S.-led destruction of the Taliban regime following 9/11. Ahmad Ramzi Yusuf, who built the vehicle bomb that damaged the World Trade Center and killed six New Yorkers on February, 26 1993, is also alleged to have instigated a bomb attack the following year on the Shia shrine of Imam Reza in Mashad, Iran.[12]

Sipah and Lashkar, which later became a part of the al-Qaeda network in Pakistan, attacked Shia targets. As in Baghdad and Najaf, Sunni extremist bombing campaigns have targeted Shias in their holy places and mosques, especially during times of communal prayer, when the symbolic significance of the violence is most obvious and when the buildings are most crowded with potential victims. Violent extremists in the Shia ranks responded in kind, touching off a classic vicious circle of outrages and vengeance attacks. Bombings and assassinations since the 1980s have scarred both the Sunni and the Shia community. Since 1989 more than nine hundred clashes between the two groups have claimed more than four thousand lives.[13] One "war" in the country's wild North-West Frontier Province raged for five straight days in 1996 and saw the combatants using mortars, rocket launchers, and antiaircraft missiles against one another. When it was over, about two hundred people were dead. From January to May 1997, Sunni terror groups assassinated seventy-five Shia community leaders in a systematic attempt to remove Shias from positions of authority. The strife was a factor in the destabilization of tenuous but at least incipiently democratic civilian governments in the 1990s—a decade that ended with a military coup by the current ruler, General Pervez Musharraf.

Sunni extremists eventually got the upper hand in this struggle as they became tied to the broader network of Deobandi extremists who were fighting alongside the Taliban in Afghanistan and spearheading the jihadi campaign in Kashmir. In Afghanistan and

Kashmir, Sunni gunmen and bombers fought foreign enemies; in Pakistan they fought Shias. As the same seminaries produced Taliban cadres, jihadis dedicated to striking in Kashmir, and anti-Shia extremists, the lines between the jihad within (against Shias) and the jihad outside (in Afghanistan and Kashmir) became blurred. When Sunni jihadis came home from Afghanistan or Kashmir, they often turned their attention to the Shia. Anti-Shia activism helped recruit fighters for the war in Afghanistan and the campaign in Kashmir, and those conflicts in turn trained anti-Shia militants who immersed Afghan and Pakistani cities in sectarian violence.

There are organizational as well as ideological ties that bind Sunni sectarians, Arab and Asian alike, with Sunni Arab extremists. While outside the Muslim world the violent anti-Westernism of the Taliban and al-Qaeda appears most prominent, there can be no question that intense hatred of Shias and Shiism is an important motive for both these Sunni terror groups. The Taliban, al-Qaeda, and various Pakistani Sunni extremists fought side by side during the Afghan internal strife of the 1990s. Indeed, most of the murders of Shias at Mazar-i Sharif and Bamiyan appear to have been committed by Pakistani killers from Sipah-i Sahaba, who nearly started a war with Iran when they overran the Iranian consulate in Mazar-i Sharif in 1998 and slaughtered eleven diplomats.

Iran was not able to match the scale of Sunni militancy that stretched from the battlefronts of central Afghanistan to the mountain peaks of Kashmir and the urban centers of Pakistan, rooted in thousands of madrasahs and bankrolled by millions of dollars from Saudi patrons. By the mid-1990s Iranian financial support for Shia activism had dried up. Moreover, the Shias understood that given their numbers, this was not a conflict they could win, and as the Sunnis became more militant, the Shias would only suffer more. Sensing their advantage, however, the Sunni extremists became bolder and more ruthless. In the 1990s they began to demand that Shias be declared a non-Muslim minority. They could live in Pakistan but could not call their places of worship mosques and would have to accept the laws that govern non-Muslim minorities.

The Shia of Pakistan have not yet been officially declared a non-Muslim minority, but they have clearly lost their bid for power. By the 1990s the awakening that followed the Iranian revolution was subdued. Sectarian violence became a part of life, and has in fact become more prevalent in response to the growing Shia-Sunni rivalry in Iraq. Lashkar-i Jhangvi now openly identifies Shias as "American agents" and the "near enemy" in the global jihad against America. The extremist group has declared that Shias in Pakistan will pay for Shia support for the United States in Iraq and Afghanistan—where the main Shia parties have joined the American-backed government of Hamid Karzai. Assassinations and bombings have become depressingly common since 2003 and are now mostly cases of Sunni attacks on Shias. The extremist face of Sunnism has proven itself capable of reacting to the Shia challenge, using violence but also theology and religious ideology to roll back Shia gains.

What happened in Pakistan is a window on what will follow in Iraq and everywhere else when the balance of power between Shias and Sunnis established in earlier periods of Islamic history comes into question. The Sunni extremists of Pakistan have a counterpart in Iraq in Abu Musab al-Zarqawi and his army of suicide bombers. In Iraq or Bahrain, given their numbers, the Shias may well win, but their gains will lead to violence and will stoke the fire of Sunni extremism.

Chapter 6

THE TIDE TURNS

In March 2003, as U.S. troops pushed north from Naseriya, the little-known supreme leader of Iraq's Shias, the grand ayatollah Sayyid Ali al-Husayni al-Sistani, told his community not to resist the American march to Baghdad. Shortly thereafter, when U.S. Marines drove into the heart of the holy city of Karbala at midnight, they found it quiet and dark, save for the luminescent golden dome of the shrine of Imam Husayn—a scene of serenity and beauty that dazzled many of the young American fighting men. The only face of Shiism that revealed itself to American troops as they entered one of Shiism's holiest cities was a distinctly quiescent and even spiritual one. The deputy secretary of defense, Paul Wolfowitz, interpreted the ayatollah's decree as a good omen for the United States. He told the Congress that there was now a "pro-American" fatwa in place; the war in Iraq, he suggested, was already realizing the Bush administration's wish: the Muslim world was changing even before the Marines reached Baghdad.[1]

Sistani's decree, however, was less a favor to America than a first step in claiming Iraq for the Shia. Unbeknown to many Americans at the time, this was indeed the beginning of a major change in the region. The fall of the Saddam regime was the end of Sunni rule over Iraq, and that changed the balance of power between Shia and Sunni. In March 2003, the United States not only changed the regime in Iraq but also challenged the regime—call it "the Sunni ascendancy"—that had long dominated the region as a whole. In fact, the most important outcome of war in Iraq has been that one of the three most important Arab-majority countries officially became the first state in the Arab world to be ruled by a democratically empowered Shia majority. The United States hoped to usher in a new era in Middle Eastern history—to build a Middle East that would be democratic, secular, and economically prosperous. The toppling of Saddam and his Sunni-minority regime portended first and foremost a Middle East in which Shias would wield greater power and thereby reshape regional alliance structures, cultures, and political institutions. The growing prominence of Shias would likely influence how this new Middle East would define itself more than the values that U.S. leaders hoped for. And if the region one day draws nearer to those U.S.-supported values, moreover, it will almost certainly do so in a distinctively Shia way.

The dynamism of the Shia revival revealed itself first at the cultural and purely religious levels. Saddam's fall opened up Iraq's Shia holy cities and centers of learning to a degree not seen in years or even decades. Hundreds of thousands of pilgrims visited Najaf and Karbala, generating commercial links and strengthening transnational Shia religious and cultural ties from Lebanon to Pakistan.

In May 2003, just after the fall of Saddam, Iran's then president,

Seyyed Muhammad Khatami, traveled to Beirut. Local Shias gave him a hero's welcome, lining the streets to cheer his motorcade. A speech he gave at a stadium drew fifty thousand people. Khatami has personal ties to Lebanon; by marriage he is related to Abdul-Husayn Sharafuddin Musawi, who was the religious leader of the Lebanese Shia in the 1950s. In Beirut, Khatami visited the family of Imam Musa al-Sadr and talked of Iran's cultural ties with Lebanon. He said nothing explicitly about a Shia political resurgence, but then again, he hardly needed to. It was all around him and obvious. Not since Egypt's Nasser, the Paladin of Arab nationalism, had inflamed Lebanese passions in the late 1950s had the leader of another country received such a jubilant welcome. The symbolism of Khatami's triumphal visit—that of transnational Shia ties asserting Shiism's power where once Arab nationalism commanded this kind of sentiment—was designed to signal a new dawn in Middle East politics, and to emphasize that Iran would be riding the crest of the Shia revival.

The opening of Iraq also produced a new leadership for the Shia in the person of Ayatollah Sistani. Heir to the mantle of his mentor Ayatollah Khoi, Sistani emerged as the undisputed leader of Iraq's Shias and was quickly recognized as such by Shias from Lebanon to Iran to Pakistan. He received the adulation of millions of people, and, more important, their religious taxes and contributions—a monetary vote of confidence that showed the high regard in which so many held this low-key, even retiring senior cleric, known for his modest way of life and profound learning. Sistani's representatives, who collect funds on his behalf and transmit his views on religious and political issues to the faithful, have gained in standing in various Shia communities outside Iraq, including Iran.

Sistani is from the old school. He is first and foremost a scholar, intelligent and well read, with a keen appreciation for history and a gift for seeing the big picture. He rose in the ranks in Najaf owing to the quality of his scholarship. Although born and raised in Iran— he hails from a clerical family in the great shrine city of Mashad— he never mixed in Iranian clerical politics. Over the years Sistani has sponsored many charitable activities in his home country, but he never commanded a large following there until Saddam's fall. Before 2003 he was not widely known in Iran, and none of the noted clerics in Qom claimed to be his follower. Only a small group of diehard followers of Ayatollah Khoi knew him and shifted their allegiance to him after Khoi had died.

Much like Khoi, Sistani sees the ulama mainly as teachers and defenders of the faith—roles that are filled not by an Islamic government but by protecting and promoting Shia piety under whatever government Shias may happen to have. Sistani is knowledgeable and adept in the minutiae of Shia religious law and can also hold his own in matters such as secular constitutional theory. From the outset he proved himself particularly good at grasping the varying implications of different approaches to a post-Saddam Iraqi constitution. To press his point of view, moreover, he skillfully deployed Islamic as well as secular democratic arguments. His persona and growing popularity were particularly important in strengthening allegiance to the faith at the popular level, and helped to spawn new networks of people and organizations around the authority of the clerical leadership in Najaf.

Sistani's ability to exert such influence began with his record of never having entangled himself in Iranian politics. He had profound theological and political differences with his fellow clerics who were ruling Iran, but he never tried to promote a rivalry between Najaf and Qom. He rose above disagreements between Muhammad Husayn Fadlallah and Iran's clerical leaders; he said nothing about confrontations between reformists and conservatives in Qom, even after the reformist Ayatollah Hossein Ali Montazeri sought to associate himself with Sistani, or between various Shia voices in Lebanon. Based on Sistani's approach, it proved possible to build a regional consensus among Shia political forces. Even Iran more or less accepted the consensus in hopes that it might become a vehicle for Iranian power. Shias from Lebanon to Iraq, the Gulf, and Pakistan looked to Shia regional power to protect and further their particular communal interests.

In Iraq, Sistani put forth a simple model of government on which everyone could agree. He took his stand on the principle of majority rule and demanded an accountable and representative government that would reflect and protect Shia identity. The two parts of this formula reinforced each other. Accountable and representative government would mean empowering Shias; and Shia identity meant entrenching that power in state and society. What Shia identity meant was open to question. For some it meant enshrining Shia law in the constitution, and for others providing space for Shia piety and popular practices to define society and culture. In matters of religious law Sistani is conservative; the form of Shia law that he prescribes is unaffected by modernism.[2] Yet the scope and nature of Shia law in Iraq's state and society was a matter that he believed would best be settled later. This was an important departure from other models of government in the region. Sistani parted ways definitively with anything like an Arab dictatorship, such as the Ba'thist one that the U.S.-led coalition had come to destroy. Nor was he a Khomeini-style would-be theocrat or a fundamentalist dreaming of "the Quran as constitution," as Sunni extremists are wont to do. He limited the role of Islam to providing values and guidelines for social order (nizam al-mujtama). While the world little noted the significance of his innovation, he had quietly but surely brought to the broader Middle East a new approach to politics that stands as

the most compelling and most credible challenge that fundamentalism and other forms of authoritarianism have ever had to face.

Sistani was careful not to position himself as pro-American and
was not shy about confronting U.S. authorities when his goal was
threatened. He clarified his position early on in a fatwa regarding
the extent of U.S. authority in determining Iraq's future:

> The Occupational Authority in no way has the authority to
> choose members for the drafting committee of a Basic Law. In
> no way does any authority exist for such a drafting committee
> to represent the lofty interests of the Iraqi people or to trans-
> late into law the wishes and basic identity of the Iraqi people,
> the pillars of which are the glorious faith of Islam and soci-
> ety's values. The current [American] plan discussed is funda-
> mentally unacceptable. Accordingly, popular elections are
> necessary so that each Iraqi who is of voting age can choose
> his representative for a constituent assembly. And then any
> Basic Law written by this assembly must be approved by a
> national referendum. It is incumbent upon all believers with
> their utmost commitment to demand this, and asserting the
> truth of this path is the best way that they can participate in
> this process.[3]

Yet despite pressure from the street, Sistani never trafficked in
anti-Americanism either. Early on he sought—with much success—
to draw lines around what the United States could do politically in
Iraq, but always in the name of democratic principles forcefully, per-
sistently, and nonviolently advanced. He argued that United States
should avoid taking any steps that would foreclose Iraqis' future constitutional and political options, since to do anything else would be
undemocratic. This may have been a shrewd piece of tactical jujitsu
meant to handcuff U.S. authorities with their own democratic rhet-

oric. Yet Sistani's choice of strategy and the reasons that he gave for rejecting a steering American hand were significant. There were no fiery invocations of divine wrath or Khomeini-style denunciations of the United States as the "Great Satan," but only calm arguments (sometimes backed by impressively large but peaceful street demonstrations) about pragmatism, rights, democracy, and self-determination. Sistani's moderate and levelheaded style would set the tone for the Shia ascendancy in Iraq—and in the region.

In order to maintain his credibility with Iraqis, Sistani avoided engaging the United States too directly. He refused to meet with any American officials but authorized his son and other senior Shia ulama to do so. He proved adept at frustrating America's transitional proconsul, L. Paul Bremer, by challenging U.S. plans to hand power to Iraqis such as Iyad Allawi and Ahmad Chalabi, whom Sistani felt were at odds with his vision of a Shia Iraq. When Bremer announced that the first elections would use the caucus format, Sistani insisted on a one-person, one-vote standard, arguing that a constitution devised by any other means would be "illegitimate." To reinforce his point, he brought large and orderly crowds into the streets of Baghdad for five consecutive days until Bremer backed down. When Bremer asked to meet the ayatollah to discuss their differences, Sistani's crisp response was "Mr. Bremer, you are an American and I am an Iranian. I suggest we leave it up to the Iraqis to devise their constitution."[4]

This was a pragmatic vision that was a world apart from Khomeini's revolutionary idealism or the combative politics of Hezbollah. It was a practical engagement with the United States based on realizing Shia interests. So long as U.S. policy and presence in Iraq served Shia interests, Sistani would deal with the United States. His greatest success was to convince various Iraqi Shia factions, as well as Iran and Hezbollah, of the wisdom of this approach. He argued that anti-American opportunism and zealotry would not serve the Shia. When the renegade Muqtada al-Sadr deviated from this strategy to confront the United States, he found some support from Iran's Revolutionary Guards and former president, Ali Akbar Rafsanjani, who praised his anti-Americanism—but mostly to distinguish Muqtada's followers from the Sunni insurgency in al-Anbar Province to the north and west.[5] In general Sadr aroused very little sympathy for his cause among other Shia forces. Iran's dissident Ayatollah Montazeri criticized the Mahdi Army for violating the sanctity of shrine cities by agitating in Najaf, Karbala, and Kufa.

Sistani prudently did not seek to become the paramount source of authority among the Shia, but rather strove to be an honest broker and bridge-builder who could link various political voices and communities. He did not attempt to add line or color, but only to provide the canvas on which the Iraqi Shia community could paint its future. He did not try to produce an ideal "Islamic" state, but merely to give constitutional and elective political power to Shias in accord with their numbers and the principle of majority rule. The political uses they would make of that power were a topic for a later day. Such a Shia consensus would gather under its umbrella theocrats and democrats, pietists and secularists, clericalists and reformers. All could agree that the Shia should have more say, and then it would be up to each group to argue, lobby, organize, and make alliances both within and outside the community in order to see its preferences enacted as the blueprint of the new, post-Saddam Iraq. This was a role that senior ulama had traditionally played, and under Sistani's leadership would play once again.

For Sistani, Shia revival at the regional level meant building on an identity common to millions of Iraqis, Iranians, Lebanese, Pakistanis, and Afghans in order to reap the gains in political capital that such a shared identity could entail. From the point of view of

Sistani and his grand project, the shifting turf wars involving Sadr, the Supreme Council for Islamic Revolution in Iraq (SCIRI), and al-Da'wa were mere distractions, and predictable ones at that. Power struggles over who would pick up the post-Saddam pieces of the new Iraq were inevitable.

The draft constitution for Iraq that was approved in a referendum in October 2005 showed Sistani's imprint and also that of the Iranian constitution of 1906, in accepting principles of representative government but stipulating that no law should contradict "the tenets of Islam's jurisprudence." This was neither Khomeini's creed nor anything resembling his notion of Islamic government. Sistani's success in Iraq promised to demote Khomeini's movement to the status of an aberration in Shia history, a brief departure from the norm in the political attitudes of the grand ayatollahs. Iraqi constitutional developments are not providing Iranians with a democratic model—the scope and depth of discussions about democracy in Iran, to say nothing of the population's familiarity with the mechanics of elections and so on, is already far ahead of what one finds in Iraq. Instead, Iraq's influence on Iran appeared in the form of a newly rediscovered Iranian regard for the quietist model, which is reflected in renewed interest in the constitution of 1906 and the balance between religion and politics that it struck.

Sistani relies on an extensive network of representatives (wakils), who promote his views in large and small ways in neighborhoods, mosques, bazaars, and seminaries from Kirkuk in the north to Basra in the south. Through these representatives, he shapes Shia public opinion. Sistani does not abuse this influence by endorsing specific politicians or programs but sets the general tone for Iraqi Shia politics. His impact has arguably been most evident in preventing the Shia from responding to the atrocities committed against them almost daily by Sunni extremists. Sectarian war is a trap, he warns—

one the Shia should avoid on their march to empowerment via elections and that rarity in the political history of the Middle East, majority rule.

Frustrated by the scale of violence against the Shia, in November 2004 the prominent Shia politician and scion of a notable clerical family Muhammad Bahrul-Uloum went to Sistani. Standing before the ayatollah, he angrily struck his cane on the ground and said, "We're not going to have our families attacked by terrorists. Everything has its limits. Once that limit is passed, all that is left is God and your weapon." He asked Sistani to call on Shia militias to fight back. Sistani replied quietly, "Please don't do this. Please be civilized. We don't want to start a civil war. This is the most important point."[6] Bahrul-Uloum bowed to Sistani's wish. During the ensuing months of bombings and bloodshed—and even in the aftermath of the destruction of the Shia Askariya shrine in Samarra in February 2006—Sistani repeated his counsel. Shia clerics and preachers in turn repeated his words in their sermons across Iraq, and once again most Shias heeded his call—even after the shock of the Samarra bombing. After every bombing, Shia mosques associated with Sistani would tell their congregations that it was not their Sunni neighbors who were killing them but foreign "Wahhabis."

Bremer and the administration in Washington eventually learned to live with Sistani, and to even view him as an asset. Sistani represented a very different kind of ayatollah from the one Americans had come to know in Iran. His case reminds us how important leadership remains, how greatly realities on the ground matter, and also how ready and willing the Shia have become to make themselves a stronger and more assertive set of players than ever before in shaping the future of the Middle East.

———

At a more fundamental level, the Shia revival refers to a consensus among Shia governments and movements that gains made in Iraq should be protected and entrenched. The outcome of the war has benefited Shias not only in Iraq but across the region. Shia revival does not mean the advent of "pan-Shiism." But it does have several implications. First, stronger cultural and religious ties will continue to form among the various Shia communities in the Middle East, and a consensus will solidify around the need to defend their political power. Second, the example of Iraq will spur a "demonstration effect" in Shia communities beyond Iraq to begin to demand more say in how they are governed within their own countries. Third, these gains in power and assertiveness will reinforce inter-Shia cultural and religious ties, and these ties will in turn sustain the gains in power.

The Shia revival is not associated with any single form of government. It portends neither the spread of Iranian-style Islamic republics nor the prospect that Iraq will become a political model for government in Bahrain or Lebanon. Iraq's significance lies not in detailed questions of governance but in the lesson that Shias can demand more and get it. Iraq has set in motion a chain reaction that will play out differently in Lebanon, Bahrain, and Saudi Arabia, but the overall result will almost certainly be greater Shia power and more manifest cultural and religious ties across the crescent from Lebanon to Pakistan.

Expecting to have more rights and powers under the emerging order, Shias have welcomed both the fall of Sunni domination and the rise of prospects for political change. This makes them in principle more likely to work with the United States. Greater democracy serves Shia interests across the region, and hence Shia revival is favorably disposed toward democratic change. The Shia universe of discourse is now the site of the entire Muslim world's most interesting and thorough debates about Islam's relationship with democracy and economic growth, and indeed about Islam's situation vis-à-vis modernity. In heavily Shia Lebanon, Iraq, and Iran, popular political discourse and debate are far more concerned with modernity and democracy than is the case in Sunni-dominated countries.

The Shia, in other words, are both an objective and a subjective democratic force. Their rise in relative power is injecting a robust element of real pluralism into the too-often Sunni-dominated political life of the Muslim world, and many Shias are also finding democracy appealing as an idea in itself, not merely as an episodically useful vehicle for their power and ambitions.

In Iran, the theocratic character of the Islamic Republic obscures the reality that electoral considerations play an important role in politics.[7] Since the Shah's fall in 1979, there have been nine presidential and seven parliamentary elections. Although the elections are open only to candidates approved by the clerical leadership, the campaigning and voting are taken seriously by the population. In 1997 a reformist cleric, Muhammad Khatami, won the election in a landslide after the country's supreme leader, Ayatollah Khamenei, openly endorsed Khatami's conservative opponent. Iran is the only country in the Middle East where a former head of state has stepped down from power at the end of his constitutionally mandated term of office and continues to live peacefully in his own home. The undeniable and serious flaws in their country's electoral process have not prevented Iranians from learning about democratic practices and internalizing democracy-friendly values. Indeed, the debate over democracy has been near the heart of Iranian politics for a decade now.

The years since the early 1990s have also been a time of intense discussions about religious reform in Iran. A group of Shia intellectuals, including some clerics, have questioned the authoritarian bent of Khomeini's *velayat-e faqih* and argued for both limiting the powers of Iran's clerical leaders and reconciling religion with democracy. Leading voices in this regard, such as Ayatollah Montazeri (once Khomeini's heir-apparent), Montazeri's student Mohsen Kadivar, and the lay intellectual Abdol-Karim Soroush, have challenged the assumptions that undergird Iran's theocratic constitution, and in Soroush's case have even raised questions about certain foundational doctrines of Shiism itself. Many in the West still hope that the opening of Iraq might help to amplify such voices in Iraq's neighbor to the east.

One-time rivals Amal and Hezbollah have lately been acting as a united political platform in Lebanon. Amal and Hezbollah have been active in parliamentary politics since 1992. They have contested national and municipal elections—often sharing a ticket with Christian or Sunni politicians—and Amal's leader, Nabih Berri, has been speaker of the parliament for the past decade and a half.[8] In the 2005 elections an alliance between the two Shia organizations won four fifths of the Shia vote, giving them a strong voice in the parliament.

Also in Lebanon, Hezbollah's 1980s "oracle," Muhammad Husayn Fadlallah, has over the past decade taken a more moderate tack.[9] He has distanced himself from the Khomeini legacy and now argues that no Shia religious leader, not even Khomeini and definitely not his successor, Ayatollah Khamenei, has a monopoly on the truth. Like all other believers, says Fadlallah, leaders are fallible and open to criticism. Fadlallah has also deviated from Hezbollah and Iran's positions on a host of other social issues, including the role of women in society and politics. He first endorsed Sistani, rather than Khamenei, as the source of emulation for Shias in matters of religion, and then claimed that role for himself.[10] For the past decade Fadlallah has been holding meetings once a month at the mosque attached to the shrine of Zaynab in Damascus. Shias from Lebanon, Iraq, and especially Kuwait, the United Arab Emirates, and Saudi Arabia—many with secular leanings—go to these sessions. Fadlallah combines progressive social views with anti-American rhetoric and criticism of Iranian and Hezbollah theocracy. Iran's regime has bitterly denounced him, and some of the attacks emanating from Qom, Iran's religious capital, have caustically questioned his religious credentials. Fadlallah's case, along with those of Montazeri and his fellow Iranian reformists, highlights how much things have changed since Khomeini's death and reveals how strongly the debate over ideology, politics, democracy, and reform has gripped the Shia world.

The Shia revival has also been defined by the desire to protect and promote Shia identity. This has meant confirming the place of Shiism in Iraqi and Lebanese politics—often by emphasizing the role of piety and law in society and politics—but also strengthening ties between the Shia masses and their religious leaders and institutions, between Shia communities, and between those communities and their centers of learning in Najaf and Qom. The opening of Iraq has made all this far more possible than it was before, and has also showed how cultural revival can translate into political power. As a result, Shias have attempted to consolidate their gains in Iraq by strengthening their identity and culture.

Many in United States predicted that with the opening of Iraq, the historic rivalry between Khoi and Khomeini would lead Najaf to challenge Qom and lead the charge against the Islamic Republic in Iran.[11] That has not come to pass—at least not yet. In fact, ties between the two have been strengthening. The rise of Najaf has instead had a more palpable impact on those Shia-minority communities in Lebanon and across the Persian Gulf that have traditionally looked to Iraq for religious leadership and political support. An ascendant Najaf will probably be a thorn in the side of Kuwait, Riyadh, Manama, and Islamabad more than of Qom. Meanwhile, other debates and rivalries will matter more. Disagreements between Muhammad Husayn Fadlallah and the Iranian leadership, along with calls for reform and democracy within Iran, continue to shape arguments among the Shia.

Disagreements only intensified after Saddam's fall. There was unhappiness in the ranks of Hezbollah with Ayatollah Sistani's call for Shia clerics to remove themselves from politics. Hezbollah also disagreed with SCIRI and its militia, the Badr Brigade. Hezbollah has always followed Khomeini's policy of downplaying sectarian differences with Sunnis by focusing attention on the fight with the United States and Israel, an approach that is also followed by Muqtada al-Sadr as he mixes Shia, nationalist, and anti-American politics to define his role in Iraq.[12]

After Saddam, various claimants to power emerged among the Iraqi Shia. These contenders put forward varying conceptions of how Shia power should express itself and how the community should seek to mold its future and the future of its country. These factions exchanged words in the press and also, more alarmingly, gunfire in the streets of Baghdad, Najaf, and Basra.

Shias, in short, are far from a political monolith. They are under the control of no single authority, and no one person or entity is dictating their views of the future. Competition over power and authority will probably only multiply their differences, first in Iraq and then in other parts of the region as well. There will be various claimants to the mantle of Shia leadership, from Fadlallah to Sistani to Khamenei. Different conceptions of Shia theology and politics will emerge, and Shia states and political communities are likely to endorse different ones. The prospect of a monolithic pan-Shia polity or regime model dominated by Iran is remote. In fact, it is evident that Iran is hard-pressed to assert the claim of its supreme leader to a Shia "papacy." Iran will be an influential big brother but not a "heavy father," much less a master.

The pluralism and the contentions within Shia ranks do not mean that there is no basic shared vision of Shia interests or of what the Shia revival means. Shias are surprisingly in agreement over the stakes of what is happening in Iraq. They seem to recognize that regardless of whatever disagreements may come between them, they have a common interest in protecting, entrenching, and furthering the gains that the cause of Shia empowerment has made in the affairs of the new Iraq struggling to be born. It was in this context and in confirmation of Sistani's initiative that conservative Iranian newspapers began to talk of a Nasrallah-Sistani-Khamenei axis, bringing Hezbollah, Iraqi Shias, and the Iranian government together to defend Shia interests. This was a regional Shia project, not an Iranian one. This axis was no different from the "Shia crescent" that Jordan's King Abdullah warned of. What Abdullah saw as a threat, Shias saw as the bedrock of their newfound regional power.

The Shia revival rests on three pillars: the newly empowered Shia majority in Iraq, the current rise of Iran as regional leader, and the empowerment of Shias across Lebanon, Saudi Arabia, Kuwait, the UAE, and Pakistan. The three are interconnected, and each reinforces the others. Together they ensure a greater Shia voice in Middle East politics and are pressing events toward a new power distribution in the region. All this will also mean a more even Shia-Sunni balance of power in the Middle East than has been seen in nearly fourteen centuries.

Chapter 7

IRAQ

The First Arab Shia State

A l-Rashid Street is an old colonnaded road of shops in the heart of Baghdad. At its entrance sits the historic British Residency, where the influential British administrator and diplomat Gertrude Bell, the famous "Daughter of the Desert" and "uncrowned queen of Iraq," once lived and literally drew Iraq onto the map. Bell was a red-haired, Oxford-educated mountaineer and an honored poet with a passion for pearls, flowery hats, and everything Arab. She first went to the Middle East in 1900 and over the next decade crisscrossed the deserts of Arabia six times astride a camel, all along eating from fine china that her caravan lugged across the sandy terrain. When British attention turned to controlling Iraq after World War I, it was Bell, sitting in Al-Rashid Street, who determined the course of history. She conceived of Iraq and groomed its future king, Emir Faysal of Mecca. Bell showed him the country that he would rule, introduced him to local sheikhs, and explained tribal lineages and clan loyalties to him. She had a very clear idea of what Iraq would be and who would wield power in it.

It is said that Bell harbored deep suspicions of the Shia and had little patience for their prickly religious leaders, who she believed had most to do with the revolt against the British at the end of the war and who had always been a thorn in the side of her colleagues in neighboring Iran. The Shia ulama reciprocated, cultivating ample distrust of the British and nursing a bitterness that would percolate through the years. The Shia and their religious leaders did not fit Bell's romantic view of Arabs. She did not know them, at least not as well as she knew the tribal leaders that she visited on her tours of the desert. The world of Najaf was alien to her and would not have any place in the country that she imagined. The new state of Iraq would be entrusted to Sunnis. They would rule it for the following eight decades as a minority with the mindset of a majority, and Shias would look from the outside in, a majority that lived as a minority.

When King Faysal's twenty-three-year-old grandson Faysal II was overthrown and murdered in a July 1958 coup, the Shia enjoyed a brief taste of power, owing to the fact that the coup's leader, Colonel Qasim, whose mother was Shia, had close ties with communists, many of whom were also Shia. Qasim was overthrown in another coup in 1963, and the subsequent rise of Arab nationalism and Ba'thism only further marginalized the Shia. Ba'thism may have been secularist and nationalist on the surface, but at heart it was yet another vehicle for at times brutal Sunni hegemony. Many Shias embraced Arab nationalism, and some were initially prominent in the leadership of the Ba'th Party. But by the time the party took full control of power in 1968, it was led by a group of Sunnis with roots in the tightly knit tribes of Saddam's hometown of Tikrit and its environs. The tribal Sunni leadership was anti-Shia and anticommunist (which by default meant anti-Shia). Thirty-five years of Ba'th rule would prove hard for the Shias, and the Saddam years would be the worst. He relentlessly suppressed and mistreated them. For the Shia, Saddam was Yazid.

The Shia are predominantly a people of the Iraqi south. During Saddam's rule they were ruthlessly assaulted, their cities systematically neglected and starved of services, their magnificent riparian wetlands punitively drained so that they could no longer shelter anti-Saddam rebels as they had in the early 1990s. Many joined an accelerated exodus to Basra, Baghdad, and other Iraqi cities. Some one million Shias who just a generation or less ago could have been found on farms and in villages across the lower Tigris-Euphrates river system now eke out a precarious urban existence in the vast northeast Baghdad slum that was once known as Saddam City and is now called Sadr City, after the murdered Ayatollah Muhammad Sadeq al-Sadr, Muqtada's father.

The Ba'thists banned public celebrations of Shia festivals such as Ashoura and murdered popular religious leaders. It is said that Saddam's henchmen murdered the popular Shia cleric Muhammad Baqer al-Sadr in 1980 in particularly gruesome fashion (allegedly they forced him to watch his sister's rape and then drove nails into his forehead).[1] Ba'th Party thugs also killed many of his followers in the Da'wa movement and chased many more underground or into exile in Iran, where they joined such Shia activists as the cadres of SCIRI. These groups received training and support from Iran to launch a violent but futile anti-Ba'thist insurgency.

Every Shia clerical family of note in Iraq suffered under Saddam and has tales of torture and murder to recount. Saddam killed the grand ayatollah Muhammad Sadeq al-Sadr and his two sons (Muqtada al-Sadr's father and elder brothers) in 1999, and several uncles and cousins and ten brothers of Abdul-Aziz al-Hakim, the current head of SCIRI.

Despite all this the Shia remained generally loyal— that is, until 1991, when Shia soldiers returning from first Gulf war in Kuwait sparked a riot in Basra that quickly spread north to Najaf. The Shia looked to the United States for support, interpreting President George H. W. Bush's call to the Iraqi people to overthrow Saddam to mean American intervention on their behalf. However, Saudi Arabia warned Washington in no uncertain terms that if Saddam were to fall from power, Iran would gain control of southern Iraq. The House of Saud did not wish to see the Shia uprising against Saddam succeed. Riyadh saw the same threat in Shia empowerment in Iraq in 1991 that it sees today. It preferred to keep Iraq under a Sunni dictatorship rather than risk empowering the Shia. Influenced by their ally in the war, the United States balked at involvement in the uprising. U.S. forces stationed in the Euphrates Valley looked on as Saddam sent his dreaded Republican Guards to the south, armed with tanks and helicopter gunships to crush the rebellion.

Large parts of Shia towns were razed, the shrines in Najaf and Karbala were shelled, and tens of thousands of Shias were killed. Bodies were draped across the beams of the shrine of Husayn in Karbala. The brutality was merciless; as one Iraqi general said about a massacre of Shias in Hilla after the 1991 uprising, "We captured many people and separated them into three groups. The first group we were sure was made up of people who were guilty. The second group we had doubts about, and the third group was innocent. We telephoned the high command to ask what we should do with them. They said we should kill them all, and that's what we did."[2] The mass graves from all the killings would be uncovered only after the fall of Saddam. Saddam forced an uncle of Abdul-Aziz Hakim to watch several of his nephews being hanged and then sent him to Tehran to relate the scene to Abdul-Aziz and his elder brother, Baqer, who was then the head of SCIRI. In Saddam's Iraq there were no legal Shia political organizations, and the only leaders to whom the Shia could look for support and guidance were their ayatollahs, who continued to shepherd their community despite the regime's viciousness.

Some fifteen years later, on January 30, 2005, millions of Iraqi Shias went to the polls, not so much to celebrate the rise of democracy in Iraq as to confirm the Shia dominance in it. Ayatollah Sistani had argued for a truce between various Shia factions, forcing them to join hands in the United Iraqi Alliance (also known as the Shia House) and to focus on confirming their power at the polls. Once the prize of Shia majority rule was won, he suggested, then the Shia could quibble over who precisely should rule and under what exact system. But the first item of business had to be protecting and consolidating the basic Shia gains without which no future achievements could be made. Sistani also issued both written and verbal fatwas compelling Shias to vote—going so far as to tell women that they were religiously obligated to vote, even if their husbands had forbidden them to do so.[3] "Truly, women who go forth to the polling centers on election day," he said "are like Zaynab, who went forth to [the field of battle at] Karbala."[4] It was no surprise that every third candidate on the Shia list that Sistani helped to create was a woman.[5]

The Shia House did well in the elections, winning 48 percent of the vote and close to half of the seats in the parliament. Its most religious elements, SCIRI and al-Da'wa, were the top vote-getters. The former even swept Baghdad's municipal seats. Washington now had to learn to deal with the religiously inspired leaders that the Shia had chosen to represent them. The coalition would further confirm its dominant position almost a year later in the December 15, 2005, national elections, winning 46 percent of the seats in the parliament, more than the Sunni and Kurdish blocks put together—

although this time Muqtada al-Sadr's followers would win a lion's share of UIA seats.

In the aftermath of the war, the Shia and their ayatollahs became Iraq's real power brokers. This did not, however, mean a repeat of Iran's experiment with theocracy. The issue in Iraq was not how much Shiism but whose Shiism. As they prepared to take over the country, Shia clerics found themselves deeply divided, more over political than purely theological issues.

Three clerical positions emerged to dominate Shia politics in the new Iraq. The first was the quietist posture. This was the camp of Ayatollah Sistani and the other grand ayatollahs of Najaf, Muhammad Ishaq al-Fayyad, Bashir al-Najafi al-Pakistani, and Said al-Hakim, and included their representatives in various cities and towns across Iraq as well as those Shia leaders in exile who were associated with Ayatollah Khoi, most notably his son Majid al-Khoi, who was stabbed to death shortly after returning to Iraq from British exile in the spring of 2003, possibly at the behest of Muqtada al-Sadr.

The second tendency was represented by Sadr and his supporters in the slums of Baghdad and Basra, but also in Kirkuk and among Turkoman Shias in the north. Although the Sadr movement is fractured and others claim its leadership, Muqtada dominates the movement. His father was a popular cleric during the Saddam era, known for his extensive social work among the Shia urban poor. Muqtada inherited his father's devoted flock and his network of social services, which was particularly strong in the Sadr City area of Baghdad.

Muqtada was not a proper cleric. To begin with, he was too young; his father's legacy gave him charisma and support but not the scholarly attainment and respect that are the real sinews of lasting esteem among the Shia clergy. It did not help that he had failed to finish his seminary education, and that as a youth he was better at playing video games than dealing with the intricacies of Shia law and theology (in his seminary days he was nicknamed Mulla Atari, after the maker of electronic amusements). Like the scions of many other clerical families of Iraq, he found himself catapulted into a position of power and prominence because his father and older brothers had been killed. So weak were Muqtada's religious credentials that he had to rely initially on the authority of one of his father's allies, the Qom-based Ayatollah Kadhim Husayn al-Haeri, until al-Haeri, worried by Muqtada's erratic politics, found it prudent to distance himself.

What Muqtada lacked in religious credentials he tried to make up for with a radical brand of politics exacerbated by his own unstable personality. He preferred fighting his battles in the political arena, and actors ranging from Hezbollah and Iran's Revolutionary Guards to Ahmad Chalabi manipulated him to serve their own ends. Even Sistani, who was a target of Muqtada's rash politics, found the young firebrand cleric a useful tool in dealing with the U.S. administration in Baghdad, since he and Muqtada formed a kind of de facto "good cop, bad cop" team that helped to keep the Americans off balance.

Muqtada's rebel image, mixing Islam and nationalism, and his willingness to challenge U.S. authority, gained him popularity. His movement, however, lacked coherence. It was powerful but chaotic, best characterized as street (or barrio) politics. He had a cultlike following among poor and uneducated Shia youth, and his support in southern Iraq grew after he threw his Mahdi Army into a fight against U.S. forces in 2004. He gained a foothold in that city as well as Basra and, most notably, Karbala, where commerce associated with pilgrims' visits to the shrine of Husayn provided him with funding. His supporters participated in the January 2005 elections, and although his party did poorly compared to the Shia House, he was able to open government jobs to his followers. After a period of bickering with SCIRI and Sistani, Sadr decided to join forces with them in the December 2005 elections. The election results elevated Sadr's status. With control over a large portion of the Shia alliance's seats in the parliament, he became a king-maker—choosing the alliance's candidate for prime minister.

Somewhere in between Sistani and Sadr on the political scale were SCIRI and its military wing, the Badr Brigade. SCIRI's leaders were the Hakim brothers, Baqer and Abdul-Aziz, whose father had been Najaf's leading ayatollah in the 1960s. In the 1980s the Hakims went into exile in Iran, settling in Tehran and Qom. There they organized SCIRI. During the Iran-Iraq war, Iran's Revolutionary Guards formed and trained the Badr Brigade, which fought alongside Iranian troops against Saddam's military. SCIRI and its brigade played an important role in the 1991 Iraqi Shia uprising, for which they paid dearly. After an enormous August 2003 bomb blast by Sunni extremists killed Baqer and another eighty-five people outside the Imam Ali shrine in Najaf, Abdul-Aziz became SCIRI's leader.

Abdul-Aziz cuts an impressive figure.[6] Tall and at first seemingly shy, he has the air of an accidental leader. While close to his slain brother and a veteran of many of the same experiences, Abdul-Aziz had long lived in the more worldly-wise Baqer's shadow. In the summer of 2002, he presented the moderate and appealing face of SCIRI when he traveled to Washington to meet with Vice President Richard Cheney and Secretary of Defense Donald Rumsfeld. Despite some observers' early skepticism that he would be able to assert control over the organization and its militia on his own, he succeeded at this task and put himself firmly in charge. The emissary and adviser became the leader.

Other, nonclerical Shia groups also garnered support. Most notable was al-Da'wa, which had once been the torchbearer for Shia activism and had organized the Shia against Saddam in the 1980s. Al-Da'wa had a religious orientation, but clerics did not run it. Some of its members, including Iraq's first elected prime minister, Ibrahim al-Jaafari, had lived in exile in Iran and Europe; others had stayed in Iraq and continued to agitate against the Saddam regime. There were also secular Shia politicians. Some were Iraqi exiles with close U.S. ties, including Ahmad Chalabi and the transitional prime minister, Iyad Allawi. Others were affiliated with the Iraqi Communist Party, which had always been a mostly Shia outfit.

No sooner had Baghdad fallen to American troops than the various Shia factions began to compete for power. Making much of the foreign origins and ties of Sistani and the Hakims, Sadr argued that he alone among the Shia clerical leaders was an Iraqi Arab, a son of the soil (*ibn al-balad*). As the drama of occupation, reconstruction, and state-building played out through various twists and turns, he and his rivals clashed, shifted positions, and switched alliances as tactical necessity seemed to dictate. The factions disagreed over cooperation with the United States, elections, governance, reaching out to Sunnis and Kurds, the constitution, and federalism.

Sadr mostly went his own way, refusing to accept Sistani's leadership and even challenging SCIRI and the Badr Brigade. More than once the Iranians, the Lebanese Hezbollah, or Ahmad Chalabi stepped in to broker truces between Sadr and rival Shia forces. Eager to strengthen his position by playing the nationalist and anti-American cards, Sadr openly challenged U.S. authority. He hoped at once to appeal to the Sunnis and to undermine those Shia leaders who were cooperating with the United States. Anti-Americanism, he thought, would make him the perfect Iraqi leader—Shia like the country's majority, but acceptable to Sunnis as well.

In summer 2004, Sadr defied a truce agreement with U.S. forces by moving Mahdi Army gunmen into Najaf, where they occupied the shrine of Imam Ali and the vast necropolis and narrow alleys that surround it. U.S. Marines, later joined by troops of the U.S. Army, moved to dislodge him. Pitched battles scarred the holy cemetery around the shrine, and only after American troops reached the walls of the shrine itself—with the prospect looming that U.S.-trained Iraqi commandos would have to storm the sacred site—did Sistani return from a medical trip to London and negotiate Sadr's withdrawal. Sistani had apparently been counting on the United States to remove Sadr permanently from the scene, but he decided to intervene—it is said with the encouragement of Hezbollah, which had close ties to Sadr and did not wish to see the Mahdi Army destroyed—when it seemed that an assault on the shrine complex might rouse an uncontrollable storm of popular anger.

While Sadr was exploring his prospects by throwing his poorly trained militia into pitched battles with U.S. troops, SCIRI was making up for the time lost to its twenty-year Iranian exile by rapidly assembling support in the Shia south, with Iranian and Hezbollah help. A special focus of SCIRI's interest was Basra, where the Badr Brigade quickly became the de facto government. SCIRI's efforts paid off in the form of a strong showing in the national and municipal balloting of January 2005, when SCIRI won six out of eight Shia-majority governorates and came in first in Baghdad, with 40 percent of the vote.[7]

After their victory at the polls in January, SCIRI and al-Da'wa joined with other Shia factions, including Chalabi's group and some of Sadr's followers, to confirm that power had indeed passed into Shia hands in the election's wake. SCIRI quickly set about infiltrating various ministries with its members. In particular, the Badr Brigade became entrenched in the Interior Ministry, ensuring a favorable position for SCIRI in the country's future.

Electoral victory for the Shia as a whole—Sistani's top priority—spawned intensified rivalries among various subgroups. Throughout 2005 the pan-Iraqi debate over a new constitution ran parallel with an intra-Shia debate about the nature of the future Shia state. The Shia government at the center presented a far more pluralist image than did Basra's SCIRI-run city government, which showed great enthusiasm for enforcing religious law, closing cinemas and video shops, harshly punishing prostitutes and alcohol vendors, enforcing a stringent dress code, and expelling Sunnis from the municipality. The prospect of an Islamic republic in Basra raised the ire of many Shias in Baghdad and brought to the fore all those questions that Sistani had postponed for consideration at a later time. Meanwhile, al-Da'wa and SCIRI's municipal administrations solved few social problems while appearing to tolerate a great deal of corruption and nepotism. SCIRI's government in Basra was particularly problematic, not only for its theocratic bent but for its corruption. Its critics saw it as theocracy mixed with thuggery.[8]

Sadr's followers meanwhile reorganized and began to challenge SCIRI in Baghdad and also the south. SCIRI and the Badr Brigade had used control over levers of power to expand their reach into the bureaucracy and security forces. Sadr was keen to keep SCIRI out of his turf and conversely to find his own way back into the thick of Shia politics. He and SCIRI fought turf battles and accused one another of betraying the Shia cause—Sadr for his overtures to the Sunni Ba'thists and SCIRI for its ties to Iran. The fate of the Iraqi constitution that was being negotiated in August 2005 intensified conflict as a resurgent Sadr movement, enjoying greater popularity in southern Iraq, grew closer to Da'wa because of their shared commitment to a centralized Iraqi state, while SCIRI began to demand an autonomous Shia zone in the south under a loose pan-Iraqi federation. These political debates precipitated bloody clashes. They reflected philosophical differences about the shape of the Iraqi state but also the deep-seated fears and angers of various factions within Iraq's Shia population. SCIRI's position reflected the mood of Basra and Shia areas south of Naseriya, where residents tended to believe that Baghdad had long been starving them of resources. These southerners did not trust a strong center and looked at Baghdad as a bastion from which Sunnis could keep a chokehold on their resources and their future. Shias who lived in Baghdad, Kirkuk, Mosul, or even al-Anbar, by contrast, viewed with alarm a loose federal arrangement that would make them minorities in heavily Kurdish or Sunni autonomous regions.

Throughout all this debate and conflict, Sistani tried to stay above the fray. He continued to keep his eyes on the big prize: delivering Iraq to the Shia and protecting Shia identity by ensuring its embodiment in the new constitution and the state arising from it. He did not get bogged down in debates over who was Iranian and who was Iraqi. Most Iraqi Shias were clearly Arabs, but that identity was surfacing in a new way, different from the way in which Arab nationalism and Ba'thism had always envisioned it.

The bombing of marketplaces, police stations, mosques, and open-air religious gatherings meanwhile occurred almost daily, generating a tale of sorrow and rage that would tear Shias and Sunnis apart. On August 31, 2005, about a million Shia pilgrims gathered at the shrine of Kazemiya in Baghdad to mark the anniversary of the death of the seventh imam, who is buried there. The crowd stretched from the mosque across the River Tigris to Sadr City, clogging the bridge over the river. A mortar attack on the crowd early in the day killed sixteen and injured many more. The crowd was on edge when some person or persons on the bridge spread a rumor— Shias believed deliberately—that there was a suicide bomber in their midst. Anxious and fearful, the crowd panicked. In the ensuing stampede, more than a thousand people died; some were trampled to death, while others drowned after jumping into the river. Most of the victims were women and children. The incident showed the extent to which the insurgency could disrupt Shias' lives and turn their commemoration of the death of their imams into a new occasion for mourning. It also underscored the inability of the Iraqi government to contend with the violence, and even more the extent to which the insurgency had succeeded in instilling fear in Shias' hearts and minds.

Urged by Sistani and his clerical network not to respond in kind, Shias showed tremendous restraint. Their patience was taxed, but their sense of distinct identity only grew under the onslaught of Sunni terror (a good deal of which was the work of non-Iraqis, such as the terror group run by Abu Musab al-Zarqawi, the Jordanian Salafi who masterminded the insurgency's most violent excesses). Attitudes on the street hardened, as did Shias' determination to stay in charge of their own destiny. Even where relations between Shia and Sunni neighbors remained friendly, distrust of Ba'thists and the Wahhabi influence on Sunni clerics intensified.

Increasingly, Shias saw Sunnis as vicious brutes and ridiculed their historical claims to grandeur. In Basra and other places in the south, Sunnis came under attack. Targeted killing of Sunni clerics and community leaders served notice to others to move away. These acts, which some blamed on the Badr Brigade, reflected the mood on the street. Anger and prejudice were rising on both sides of the sectarian divide. The manner in which Shia identity was taking form was directly tied to the intensity of the sectarian conflict.

This became clear when a bombing attack on the Shia Askariya shrine (where the tenth and eleventh imams are buried, and wherefrom the Twelfth Imam went into hiding) brought sectarian conflict into the open. Hundreds died as angry Shias and Sunnis attacked mosques, killed clerics, and abducted and murdered civilians. Despite calls for calm the violence continued to rage, exposing the deep sectarian fissures that were shaping Shia identity and politics.

As American tanks rolled across the plains of Iraq, the majority that Gertrude Bell had wished away began to act its part. No sooner had statues of Saddam tumbled across Baghdad than the scope of change became apparent. Pictures of imams and ayatollahs were ubiquitous on walls from Basra to Baghdad, and the bazaars and alleyways of Karbala and Najaf came alive with pilgrims who came from near and far to visit the Shia shrines. Change was also evident in the composition of the Iraqi Interim Governing Council (IGC), the transitional governing body that the U.S.-led Coalition Provisional Authority had set up as a first step toward handing over power to Iraqis. Thirteen of the IGC's twenty-five members were Shias, as was its first head, Ibrahim al-Jaafari. As Iraq's Shia vice president, Adel Abdul-Mahdi, put it, "The Shia could now raise their head; they could represent Iraq."[9]

While many hailed the Shias' prominence on the IGC and saw it as a mark of greater pluralism, Sunnis took it as an ominous sign. Sunni leaders in suits and clerical robes alike objected vigorously. After the United States began "de-Ba'thification" of government agencies and summarily disbanded what was left of the Saddam-era Iraqi military, Sunni concern turned to alienation and anger. Many saw "de-Ba'thification" as another name for "de-Sunnification." The championing of the policy by once-exiled Shia politicians such as Ahmad Chalabi and Abdul-Aziz Hakim only heightened this angst.

Sunnis associated growing Shia power with Iran. Sunni leaders, especially those with Ba'thist ties, even accused the Shia point-blank of being tools in a nefarious Iranian campaign to subjugate and control Iraq. Hazem Shaalan, who served as defense minister in the interim government of the secular Shia prime minister Iyad Allawi, called Iran Iraq's enemy number one and claimed that Tehran was responsible for most of the violence in the country. Shaalan hoped to prevent emerging ties between Iraq's Shias and Iran from determining the course of Iraqi politics. This became clearer when he characterized the election list of the Shia-dominated United Iraqi Alliance (UIA) as the "cat's paw of Iran."[10] Shaalan's views were a reflection of the way that many Iraqi Sunnis and some secular Shias saw the UIA and the government that it would form after winning the January 2005 elections. It was not only openly Shia but was led by men who had maintained close ties with Iran since the 1980s. Many Sunnis spoke of it with bitter derision as "the Safavid government."

When, during the ensuing constitutional debates, elements of the UIA called for federalism and a Shia autonomous zone in the south, Sunnis were quick to dismiss the idea as an Iranian plot to dismember Iraq.[11] All this underlined the strikingly different notions of identity, and also perceptions of the Iran-Iraq war, that were at play among the Sunni and the Shia. Whereas Sunnis emphasized the Arab-Iranian and Iraqi-Iranian divide and still saw Iran through the blood-coated lenses of the 1980s, Shias felt an attachment to the religious identity that they shared with Iranians, who were their only source of support in the aftermath of their ill-fated 1991 uprising. They saw the war as Saddam's sin, in which Shias from both sides of the border were caught up as combatant-victims.[12] In the minds of Iranians and many Iraqi Shias, the Iran-Iraq war became the Iran-Saddam war. Shia soldiers on both sides fought for faith and country, but they were wrapped into a Sunni dictator's war of ambition and fear. With Saddam gone, the memory of the war unites rather than divides Shias in the two countries.

That Shias would vote for leaders such as Ibrahim Jaafari and Abdul-Aziz Hakim, who had spent the war years living in Tehran and whom many Sunnis saw as traitors, showed the widening gulf between the two communities. This became more evident after Prime Minister Jaafari opened diplomatic ties with Iran and expressed regret for Iraq's conduct during the war.

Outside the precincts of government, Muqtada's popularity grew in the months following the U.S.-led invasion, but not because of his anti-Iranian posturing. In fact, his superficial nationalist rhetoric belied his actual interest in drawing Iranian money and support.[13] Iranian birth and citizenship did not diminish Ayatollah Sistani's broad support among Iraq's Shias, and despite close ties with Iran, SCIRI was able to deepen its support in Baghdad and the south. At the same time, Iyad Allawi, who campaigned in the January elections as a bridge-builder, reaching out to Sunnis, did poorly; by some estimates his support was even weaker than his numbers suggested.[14] Almost a year later in the December 2005 elections his popularity would plummet even further. All this showed that amid the raucous accusations of Iranian influence-peddling in Iraq, for the country's Shias the enemy was not external—not Iran—but rather internal. The problems, as Shias saw them, were Ba'thism and Salafi-style extremism, which could easily foster tactical alliances and which were casting a grim double shadow over Sunni politics.

Iraqi Sunnis' attitudes were from the outset shaped by their belief that they would be able to get back on top. Many Sunnis clung to the illusion that the Shias' majority status within the country was a myth spread by America. One Sunni talking point, repeated by no less a figure than Jordan's King Abdullah as well as then Defense Minister Shaalan, was that Iranians were crossing the border into Iraq in order to inflate Shia numbers.[15] The insinuation was that many, if not most, Shias were not actually Iraqi at all—that Iraq was being turned into a Shia state by force and fraud.

The currency of such beliefs among Sunni Arabs was important in driving the Sunni decision to boycott the January 2005 elections—a choice that the weight of Sunni opinion later came to recognize as a mistake. Many Sunnis at the time, however, were still overestimating their own share of Iraq's population and so believed that sitting out the January vote would hold turnout below the final mark of almost 60 percent. The same belief was also at play when Sunni members of the committee charged with drafting a new constitution first rejected the final draft in the summer of 2005 and then agreed to putting it to a vote—only after securing guarantees that key clauses could be renegotiated later. They expected to be able to sink this draft in the referendum that would have to sanction the constitution. The Sunnis would then, they hoped, have a noticeably greater say in the new parliament that would have to be elected to restart the process. Despite large Sunni turnout, the referendum approved the constitution. The results showed the universal Sunni disdain for the constitution but failed to derail it, disappointing Sunnis by confirming that there are fewer Sunnis in Iraq than they had estimated. This point became irrefutably clear in the December 2005 national elections. The Sunni turnout was high but Sunni parties still lagged behind the Shia coalition in the final tally of the vote by a margin of more than two to one. Parties that had led Sunnis into the political process now stood accused of having only confirmed their minority status. Having exposed Sunni weakness, all the Sunni parties could do was challenge the election results.

Sunnis also believed, perhaps with some justification, that Shias would not be able to rule Iraq without their cooperation. Otherwise a Shia government would work only if propped up by Iran and the United States. Accusing Shias of ties with Iran was designed to isolate them politically and sully their relations with the United States, and also to underscore the fact that they could not rule without for-

eign support. This strategy required attacking the country's infrastructure, along with international agencies and humanitarian
groups, to weaken the government and prevent it from providing
basic services to the population. Attacking the Shia government and
its security forces directly would further emphasize its inability to
provide security.

Iraqi Shias had joined the new security forces in droves. They
were encouraged to do so by their leaders; even Ayatollah Sistani
openly encouraged Shia youth to join, which they continued to do
in the face of the raging violence. The Shia saw the new state as
their state. There was no reason for them to resist state-building; to
the contrary, they had everything to gain. Thus the Sunni attacks—
killing recruits standing in queues to join the police and security
forces, bombing police stations, and kidnapping and killing police
and security forces—were not just (or even primarily) acts of resistance against American occupation but efforts to impede the emergence of a Shia-dominated nation.

Sunnis viewed Iraqi security forces as Shia—and at times
Kurdish—militias and interpreted their security operations in Sunni
towns as sectarian provocations. For Sunnis, the Badr Brigade, many
of whose cadres had joined the Interior Ministry and the security
forces and were accused of abusing Sunni prisoners in government-
run detention centers, looked much like Lebanese Shia militias such
as Amal and Hezbollah, and prospects of its assumption of power
evoked images of the bloody civil war that tore at Lebanon from
1975 to 1990. The Badr troops appeared to be the most anti-Sunni
element in Iraq's Shia politics, and Sunnis held it responsible for
attacks on their mosques and clerics. In July 2005, Abu Musab al-
Zarqawi formed the Umar Brigade to confront the Badr forces
directly.[16] The choice of name—of the second caliph, hero to
Sunnis and villain to Shias—was to inflame sectarian passions on

both sides. The new brigade targeted Shias, and especially the members of the Amiri tribe (many of whom live in Sadr City), to which the Badr Brigade's commander Hadi al-Amiri belongs.

Suicide bombings throughout 2005 continued to be aimed at Shias for the most part, killing policemen, construction workers, clerics, community leaders, government officials, pilgrims, and men, women, and children at work, at play, at prayer, and in markets, hospitals, and offices, and on streets everywhere. These actions were designed to intimidate the Shia and sap their confidence. In addition, hundreds more ordinary Shias were murdered in what has appeared to be random violence. Some were shot at home or in the street. Others were abducted and found floating in the Tigris, their hands bound and throats cut. Throughout 2005, each dawn revealed bodies dumped by the roadsides or on garbage heaps. Some were killed alone or in small groups. Others were killed in large numbers. The deaths were a testament to the Sunni resistance against the Shia revival and the deepening of the sectarian divide.[17] The violence drew on the Sunnis' long-held belief that when intimidated, the Shia always back down. That was how the Abbasids dealt with Shia unrest, how Saddam ruled over his Shia majority, and how Pakistan's Sunni extremists ended the challenge from their Shia minority. Sunni responses to the Shia challenge have always been displays of force and power. The insurgency strove to show the Shia—and the United States—that the Sunnis could keep the violence going forever, in the belief that this would eventually force the United States to abandon the Shia, thereby paving the way for the return of some form of Sunni rule.

The attacks were also meant to show the Shia that their chosen government and their venerated religious leaders were feeble and incapable of protecting them. Nor was the United States able to provide the security the Shia yearned for. Shias were not safe in their markets, homes, mosques, police stations, or, symbolically, at the large religious gatherings that were banned under Saddam and were now commemorated by millions as a mark of Shia empowerment.

For many Iraqis, what was unfolding in the country in the summer of 2005 was no longer just an insurgency but a civil war. As suicide bombers killed and maimed, attacked shrines and mosques, provoking retaliations and chaos on the streets, the country began slowly to come apart. In the midst of the violence, the fuss over democracy, development, and writing constitutions did not answer the fundamental question: How would the new Iraq give the Shia majority not only de jure political control but also de facto protection from violence? Without Sunni acquiescence to the new reality, it would not be easy to achieve both goals.

It was in this context that many Shias in the south, secular as well as those associated with SCIRI, abandoned commitment to a strong central government and demanded autonomy for Shia regions in the south under a federal constitution. The violence perpetrated against them made the notion of an Iraqi nation a distant dream, with no reflection in the hatred and violence that faced them. If the United States and Iraqi forces could neither crush nor mollify the insurgency, and if Sunnis were unwilling to accept Shia rule over Iraq, then perhaps Shias would need to think about Iraq differently.

The Sunnis found federalism threatening, not only because the Shia—and the Kurds—would have sole control over oil revenue, but because it challenged their conception of a unitary Iraq. If there was to be no strong center in Iraq, then there would be no basis to the Sunni claim that without them it would not be possible to govern the country.

By the summer of 2005, the insurgency consisted of as many as forty groups, but its most important and potent elements were former Ba'thists as well as extreme Salafis and other jihadis.[18] These two defined the force and ideology of the insurgency, and the thrust of their campaigns, which became increasingly entwined as the insurgency unfolded between 2003 and 2005, was directed at forcing the United States to leave Iraq but also to stop the Shia from inheriting it.[19]

It was left to the insurgency's most extreme element, the Iraqi and foreign fighters gathered around Abu Musab al-Zarqawi, to erase any doubt in Shia and Sunni minds that the issues on the table were not power-sharing, pluralism, and democracy but which sectarian community would rule over Iraq. Zarqawi put religion front and center in the conflict. In February 2004 he described his view of the conflict in an open letter. Its anti-American tone and its call to jihad were not surprising—they fit in the mold of extremist propaganda and al-Qaeda's communiqués. What was new was what Zarqawi said about the Shia and the sectarian focus of his insurgency. The letter is worth quoting:

> [The Shia are] the insurmountable obstacle, the lurking snake, the crafty and malicious scorpion, the spying enemy, and the penetrating venom. We here are entering a battle on two levels. One, evident and open, is with an attacking enemy and patent infidelity. [Another is] a difficult, fierce battle with a crafty enemy who wears the garb of a friend . . . but harbors ill will . . . These are a people who added to their infidelity and augmented their atheism with political cunning and a feverish effort to seize upon the crisis of governance . . . whose features they are trying to draw . . . in cooperation with their hidden allies the Americans.
>
> Their religious and political 'ulama have been able to con-

trol the affairs of their sect, so as not to have the battle between them and the Sunnis become an open sectarian war, because they know that they will not succeed in this way. They know that if a sectarian war was to take place, many in the [Islamic] nation would rise to defend the Sunnis in Iraq . . . Our combat against the Americans is something easy . . . Crusader forces will disappear tomorrow or the day after. The police, which [are] made up of the Shi'i filled out with Sunni agents, is the real danger that we face. They [Shi'is] are more cunning than their Crusader masters . . . As the days pass, their hopes are growing that they will establish a Shi'i state stretching from Iran through Iraq, Syria, and Lebanon and ending in the Cardboard Kingdom of the Gulf . . . Targeting and hitting them in [their] religious, political, and military depth will provoke them to show the Sunnis their rabies . . . and bare the teeth of the hidden rancor working in their breasts. If we succeed in dragging them into the arena of sectarian war, it will become possible to awaken the inattentive Sunnis as they feel imminent danger and annihilating death at the hands of these Sabeans [pagans] . . . Most of the Sunnis are aware of the danger of these people . . . Awaking of the slumbered and rousing of the sleeper also includes neutralizing these [Shi'i] people and pulling out their teeth before the inevitable battle, along with the anticipated incitement of the wrath of the people against the Americans, who brought destruction and were the reason for this miasma.[20]

Zarqawi wove together a number of themes: Sunni political concerns in postwar Iraq, the legacy of Shia-Sunni rivalry over the centuries, the future of Islam and that of Sunnis in Iraq. The rationale for insurgency here thus related the past to the present and tied the theological to the political and antioccupation nationalism to anti-Shia sectarianism. Zarqawi evoked the memory of Ibn Taymiya, many of whose anti-Shia fatwas were cited in the letter, and repeated many well-known (as well as forgotten) Sunni polemics against the Shia to drive a theological wedge between the two communities.

For Zarqawi, the aim was to start a civil war. This would not only confound state-building but also weaken the Shia position and force the United States to leave Iraq without a positive political outcome. In September 2005, after U.S. and Iraqi troops launched a major offensive against insurgent forces along the Iraq-Syria border, Zarqawi retaliated with three days of mayhem, during which suicide bombings and assassinations killed and maimed hundreds of Shias, including clerics and government workers. The attacks were followed by a posting on an al-Qaeda–affiliated website that called for a "full-scale war on Shiites all over Iraq, whenever and wherever they are found."[21]

Zarqawi's extremist posture also found reflection in the angry rejection of occupation and Shia empowerment by Iraq's Sunni clerics, especially those who gathered in the more militant and also broadly popular Association of Muslim Clerics (Hay'at al-Ulama al-Muslimin). The association was important in giving the insurgency religious sanction. In particular, some of its leaders, such as Ayyash al-Kubaisi, openly endorsed the insurgency as a legitimate jihad. The association also reflected the sectarian bias of the insurgency's Salafi sentinels. Some of its ulama had maintained ties with Saudi Arabia, from which they received financial and moral support. Some of the association's leaders who had recently returned to Iraq after the fall of Saddam, such as its spokesman, Muthanna Harith al-Dhari, who was also an important link between the association and the insurgency, had studied in the kingdom.[22] These ulama favored Hanbali law, associated with Ibn Taymiya and Wahhabism (and thus a strong anti-Shia posture), over the Hanafi law that has long been the traditional creed of Iraq's Sunni Arabs.

The Shia understood the rage and the roots of the violence that was perpetrated against them. As one Shia cleric put it, "The killers of today are the same killers as yesterday."[23] Still, Shia leaders and their flock, victims and bystanders, all repeatedly chose to blame outsiders for the violence against them. It was almost as if there was great fear in identifying neighbors and countrymen as those responsible. But even if this were true, and if the Shia genuinely believed it, then the question would remain: Who were these outsiders? They were Jordanians, Syrians, Egyptians, and most of all Saudis— all Sunni extremists who had come to Iraq to fight Americans and kill Shias. Their national identity would cast them as outsiders to Iraq, but they were still Sunni Arabs. They shared Sunni religious, Arab ethnic, and in some cases even tribal identities with Iraq's Sunni insurgents, and shared in a Salafi ideology that guided their actions.

The notion of insider and outsider had little meaning when broader identities such as Shia and Sunni, Arab and non-Arab were defining the conflict. This point was made clear by Ayatollah Ahmad al-Safi, a close aide of Ayatollah Sistani's and his representative in Karbala. Safi reacted to the Kazemiya stampede by calling on the ulama of al-Azhar in Egypt—symbolizing the Sunni world—to break their "negative" silence and condemn the insurgency, just as he called on Shias to maintain their "positive" silence and refrain from responding in kind to the violence.[24] Other Shia leaders more directly criticized the country's Sunni clerics for not forcefully denouncing the insurgency's anti-Shia violence.

When Zarqawi declared a "full-scale war on Shiites," the association's Abu Bashir al-Tartousi objected, criticizing this brazen call to arms in a tract entitled "About Sectarian War in Iraq."[25] Tartousi argued that Shia civilians did not bear responsibility for the actions of the Shia-led government or U.S. forces and should not be the object of war. However, he prefaced his criticism by validating the general thrust of Zarqawi's sectarian rhetoric, saying that "although sectarian war in Iraq *may* have been provoked and sparked by the Shia, perceived to be major allies of the occupation forces; and although it is the right of the Muslim mujahid [one who undertakes jihad] to defend himself, his honor, and his cities against the crusader invaders and whoever is allied with them, killing according to sectarian affiliation is not justified by Islamic Law." Tartousi saw the victims as responsible for the violence. The insurgents were justified in their anger at the Shia and should merely refrain from "taking justice into their own hands." It was a matter not of the Shias' guilt—Tartousi took that for granted—but of the kind of justice that they should face and from whom.

Tartousi was also less concerned with the morality of killing Shia civilians than with its implications for the success of the insurgency. He wrote in detail on this theme: "Sectarian war is [in] the crusader's interest, aimed at dividing the efforts of the mujahideen . . . [and] gives grounds for a longer occupation . . . and causes the legitimate Iraqi resistance to lose its credibility in the eyes of the Islamic world." Tartousi's argument was also reflected in the veiled criticism of Zarqawi by Saudi Arabia's most senior cleric, Sheikh Abdulaziz al-Sheikh, who objected to sectarian war because it would "serve the aims of enemies conspiring against Islam."[26] This hardly amounted to the kind of condemnation that the Shia had demanded from Sunni clerics.

Unrepentant, Zarqawi sharply rebuked the Sunni ulama and reiterated his call to war.[27] However, he qualified the "war on Shia" to "war on all collaborators with the occupation."[28] He named a few Shia groups that he would no longer target, including the Sadr group and its Mahdi Army, which had opposed the occupation. Since Zarqawi had always justified his anti-Shiism in terms of the Shia complicity in fall of the Saddam regime, he was willing to call a truce with those Shias who would join the insurgency or stop working with the government. Although the olive branch to Sadr was important, the truce clearly did not extend to the large number of Shias who voted in the January 2005 elections and continued to support the UIA government and join its security forces. In fact, pronouncements by Zarqawi's supporters named SCIRI, al-Da'wa, and Ahmad Chalabi's Iraqi National Congress as legitimate targets for attacks, along with Iyad Allawi's Iraqi National Accord Party and the two Kurdish parties that were part of the government.[29] All this hair-splitting between Sunni extremists and Sunni ulama did not amount to a sectarian truce. In fact, it put the burden on Shias to prove that they were not "collaborators," which they could do only by joining the insurgency and succumbing to Sunni domination. Giving the attacks on Shias a nationalist cover thus served as the mantra for sectarian politics in Iraq.

Chapter 8

THE RISE OF IRAN

In May 2005 the Iranian foreign minister, Kamal Kharrazi, arrived at the checkpoint in the small town of Mehran on the Iran-Iraq border. He got into a car and unceremoniously drove one hundred miles west to Baghdad to meet with the newly elected prime minister of Iraq, Ibrahim al-Jaafari. Kharrazi's trip came fresh on the heels of U.S. Secretary of State Condoleezza Rice's brief stop in Baghdad only forty-eight hours earlier, also to congratulate Mr. Jaafari. The timing of the trip was symbolic, and so was the fact that Kharrazi had driven across eastern Iraq in a car without concern for the violence that raged across the country. Throughout his stay in Iraq, Kharrazi never donned a bulletproof vest, and his demeanor and schedule somehow did not betray concern with security. Asked about future relations between Iran and Iraq while bantering in Persian with Iraq's Kurdish foreign minister, Hoshyar Zebari, Kharrazi told a gathering of journalists, "The party that will leave

Iraq is the United States, because it will eventually withdraw. But the party that will live with the Iraqis is Iran, because it is a neighbor to Iraq."[1] Kharrazi had not gone to Baghdad merely to embrace the new Shia-dominated government, led by a man who had spent years of exile in Tehran and had maintained his ties with Iran. He had gone to serve notice to the world that Iran had regional claims and to demand that its status and interests be recognized. Iran was on the rise, and where better to make that point than in Baghdad, where the future of the region hung in the balance?

The Shia ascendancy in Iraq is supported by and is in turn bolstering another important development in the Middle East: the emergence of Iran as a regional power. The Shia revival is inevitably intertwined with the rise of Iran. With almost 70 million people, 90 percent of whom are Shia, Iran is the largest Shia country. It has enjoyed close ties with the other pillars of Shia revival in the Middle East—powerful political forces in Lebanon and Iraq—as well as with the economically influential Shia communities in the Persian Gulf, many of whose members are Iranian in origin. The Shia revival may have begun in Iraq, but Iran benefits from it and will also play an important role in leading it and defining it.

The Islamic revolution is today a spent force in Iran, and the Islamic Republic is a tired dictatorship facing pressures to change. The victory of hard-line candidate Mahmoud Ahmadinejad in the 2005 presidential election cannot conceal the reality that grassroots concerns about democracy and economic reform are the key defining factors in Iranian politics as a whole today.[2] Iranian society often appears to be gripped by contradictions: a theocracy coexists with limited democratic practices; a secularized middle-class youth culture shares the public sphere with a sizable share of the populace that still puts its trust in Khomeini and his legacy. Daily newspapers run full-page discussions of debates between French philosophers over the meaning of "postmodernist discourse," yet the country continues to languish under the Islamic Republic. The pull of modernity and reformism is strong, but so is that of tradition and conservatism. Despite the influence of the latter two forces, however, Iran more than any other society in the Muslim world is a place where fundamentals are under scrutiny and open to questioning and new thinking.

No other country in the Muslim world is so rife with intellectual fervor and cultural experimentation at all levels of society, and in no place in the Muslim world is modernity and its various cultural, political, and economic instruments examined as seriously and thoroughly as in Iran. The cultural dynamism of the country will also be a force that will define the Shia revival. The hundreds of thousands of Iranian pilgrims who travel to Iraq along the highway from Mehran to Najaf are also a conduit for ideas, investments, and broader social and economic ties. They visit shrines and clerics but also fill the bazaars of shrine cities, and many buy property in anticipation of a boom in pilgrimage and business. The outcome of debates in Iran will bear on the character of the Shia revival and are being influenced by forces that the changes in Iraq have unleashed.

In many regards Iran presents the modern face of Islam. Persian is now the third most popular language on the Internet (after English and Mandarin Chinese), where one can surf more than 80,000 Iranian blogs.[3] Iranians are actively engaged in discussions about Western thought. There have been more translations of Immanuel Kant into Persian in the past decade than into any other language (and these have gone into multiple printings); one of them is by the current conservative speaker of the Iranian parliament. In some areas of mathematics and physics, such as string theory, Iranian research centers rank among the best in the world; and Iranian cinema has in recent years become a powerful force, with films such as Abbas Kiarostami's existential drama *A Taste of Cherry* attracting global notice.

This cultural dynamism has even left its mark on the Iranian religious establishment. Since the Khomeini revolution, Shia centers of learning in Iran, especially in the city of Qom, have prospered. There are large new libraries in Mashad and Qom, each housing millions of books and manuscripts, electronically catalogued with searchable databases and the latest technology for retrieving and maintaining them. A visitor to the Library of the Shrine of Imam Reza in Mashad or the Ayatollah Marashi Library in Qom cannot fail to be impressed by the size of the collections, the scale of the services provided, and the care that has been given to infrastructure and the use of technology. The achievement is as much in furthering Shia studies by making rare manuscripts and archaic texts available to eager clerics and seminarians as it is in promoting library science by creating the means to manage such vast collections. Ancient manuscripts commingle with computer terminals and high-tech restoration and preservation labs. The vast libraries are full of turbaned seminarians, some buried in theological texts, others absorbed in managing the collections on their computer terminals.

The Marashi Library was established by Shahabeddin Marashi Najafi, a contemporary of Khomeini's who was one of the five grand ayatollahs at the time of the Islamic revolution. He had lived all his life in Qom and loved books. Even as a seminarian in Najaf he would save his stipends and a portion of his income from preaching—at times accepting a book in place of payment for his services—to buy manuscripts. His collecting became more prolific as he grew in seniority. By the time of his death, in 1990, he had accumulated some 35,000 manuscripts in addition to a vast number of books, which are now housed in the library. Marashi asked to be buried with his books, and so at the entrance to the library there is a small shrine to this clerical bibliophile, and visitors often say a prayer for his soul as they come and go.

The library houses unique treasures of Islamic and Shia theology, law, and history. When, almost a decade ago, the sultan of Brunei sought to prove that his family roots go back to the Prophet of Islam, he asked the Marashi Library to investigate. Researchers there combed through rare manuscripts to laboriously construct the sultan's genealogy and tell the story of a bloodline that stretched through Arab traders and itinerant Sufi missionaries and ulama over fourteen centuries from Arabia to Borneo.

The library sits amid a cluster of seminaries, some old and some founded since 1979. Both the old and the new now have impressive façades of white brick interlaced with blue tile and are topped by imposing domes. Qom now displays a grandeur befitting the leaders it produces and the country that they rule. The seminaries attest to the clerical control of Iran; they are associated with different clerics and traditions; and a few are specifically associated with Iraqi clerics who settled in Qom to escape persecution and who still live there. These wielded a great deal of influence in the 1980s, as they helped Tehran quickly build its ties with Lebanon's Shia, who have deep connections with Najaf. Together the city's many seminaries, whose architectural styles vary despite the relative uniformity of their façades, are somewhat reminiscent of Oxford and Cambridge in England, with their various colleges, libraries, chapels, and quadrangles. Some of Iran's most powerful men live in them, especially the one known as Haqqani. A kind of Ecole Nationale d'Administration for the Islamic Republic, it has produced a corps of alumni who now form the backbone of the clerical management class that runs Iran's key political and security institutions. During election campaigns, candidates troop to the city to pay homage to its religious leaders and receive their blessing.

None among the city's clerical oligarchs is more powerful and influential than Ayatollah Muhammad Taqi Mesbah-Yazdi, a hardline conservative with a top post at the Haqqani and uncompromising views on Khomeini's theory of Islamic government. Mesbah-Yazdi is the strident face of Qom, its ingrained conservatism and deep attachment to the values of Khomeini's revolution and the power that it bestowed on the clergy. He is the most conservative among Iran's clerical elite and the favorite of Iran's Revolutionary Guards as well as the irregulars and vigilantes who do the bully-boy work of the Islamic Republic. During the heyday of reformism, from 1997 to 2005, he encouraged these forces to stop agitation for change by any means. During the 2005 presidential election cycle, he was the only cleric to issue a fatwa supporting the one-time Revolutionary Guard Mahmoud Ahmadinejad. After the election he cavalierly declared that Iran now had its first true Islamic government and there was no need for any more elections. After all, elections had at the outset of the revolution been a concession to secular forces. They were incompatible with theocracy, and as such, "Islamic republic" was a contradiction in terms that should be replaced with an unadulterated "Islamic government." While many Iranians yearned for a democratic future, Mesbah-Yazdi was looking to the Taliban for his.

Over the years, Mesbah-Yazdi has trained many students in Qom. None have become scholars of note, but many who studied with him at the Haqqani came to occupy sensitive administrative and security posts. For Mesbah-Yazdi, Qom's mission is no longer just to produce Shia men of learning but to produce the country's political and bureaucratic elite—the guardians of the revolution.

There are, however, larger forces at play in this religious seat of learning. The imperative of ruling a modern country has pushed Qom to step beyond its time-honored traditions to chart new paths for Shia learning. After the events of September 11, 2001, the world became obsessed with reforming Islamic education. Madrasahs in the Sunni world, from Indonesia and Malaysia to Bangladesh, Pakistan, Saudi Arabia, and on to Nigeria, were blamed for Muslims' excessive conservatism and, worse, growing extremism and violence. "Madrasah reform" became the mantra of the U.S. government and the primary goal of aid agencies; and Muslim governments from Indonesia to Nigeria, especially in Pakistan, pledged to reform the curricula of their religious institutions. Few have noticed that while the rest of the Muslim world has been grappling with introducing English and science to religious schools, seminaries in Qom have made great advances in incorporating many aspects of modern education into their curricula. Most now teach their students modern social sciences and Western thought. The Mofid University has gone further, by opening degree-granting programs in social sciences and the humanities to those with seminary educations. It has become customary for badly paid professors from Tehran's universities to make the long trek to Qom to teach in the city's various seminaries and educational institutions.

Qom today is home to about three hundred seminaries, easily the largest constellation of such institutions in Iran. There are some fifty thousand seminarians in the city, from seventy countries—and not all these students are Shia. Six thousand Shia seminarians come from Pakistan alone, even though relatively few Pakistani Shias look to the religious authority of any Iranian ayatollahs. There are even seminaries for women. The Jamiat al-Zahra and Jamiat Bint al-Huda train young Shia women from Iran, Pakistan, and the Arab world in theology, law, and history. Their alumni go back to their countries to teach in Shia schools for women. Qom is today training the next generation of Shia community and religious leaders from across the Middle East and South Asia.

These students spend years in Qom, learning Persian, Arabic, religious sciences, jurisprudence, theology, and philosophy. In effect they apprentice themselves to senior clerics, mastering rhetoric and legal disputation, logic, and oratory. In the process, students rise through the ranks to petty cleric and senior student before they receive permission to join the ranks of the ulama. Long stints of study in Qom allow them to forge cultural ties with Iran and also to learn much about the country. If in the 1980s seminary education went hand in hand with indoctrination in revolutionary thinking, today's crop of divinity students reads about reformist debates, election campaigns, and the problems facing religious leaders in governing a modern state and economy. Time spent in Iran no longer imparts only the spirit of Islamic revolution to seminary students, but is more likely to wind up exposing them to reformist and democratic thought.

Qom is today a wealthy city. It has all the trappings of a major center of learning. For much of the past two centuries Najaf was the premier seat of Shia religious learning, but the recent decades of dictatorship, persecution, war, and turmoil have been hard on Najaf. As Qom has prospered during the reign of the ayatollahs, Najaf has declined. Although most of the senior ulama today reside in Najaf, in terms of civic wealth and infrastructure as well as quality, number, and variety of seminaries and students, the city pales next to Qom. The strife that has marked the post-Saddam period has further damaged Najaf's attractiveness to students and scholars. It is therefore unsurprising that Ayatollah Sistani chose Qom as the headquarters for his Internet operation, sistani.org. The combination of religious and technical skills that he was looking for simply could not be found in Najaf, where he continues to maintain his own modest home on a narrow downtown street and do much of his writing on a manual typewriter.

Almost a decade ago, in May 1997, an overwhelming majority of Iranians defied the advice of the country's clerical leaders to elect a reformist to the presidency. Muhammad Khatami's sweeping win seemed to some like Iran's "Prague Spring," a thawing of freedom under the warm sun of cultural revival, a victory for the people, and the beginning of the end of the repressive republic that Khomeini had built. The outside world came to see Iran through much the same lens through which it had viewed eastern Europe and Latin America a decade earlier—as the home of a restless populace that was finally about to throw off tyranny's yoke and embrace democracy's fresh opportunities. Iran's democratic inklings were seen as the beginning of a genuine secularism, for the first time bubbling from below rather than imposed from above.

There was secularism in Iran among the suppressed intellectuals and the middle class, which had had enough of religion and wanted Islam banished from public life. As one student activist told National Public Radio, "We are fed up with being forcibly taken to heaven." There was also a more pragmatic and less exasperated secularism that expressed esteem for and even belief in religion but sought to separate it from politics, giving each its own separate domain, somewhat on the model of the no-establishment clause found in the First Amendment to the U.S. Constitution. The demand for secularism of both sorts showed the extent to which the population had tired of Khomeini's republic, of clerical rule, and of living by Islamic law.

It is, however, a mistake to confuse hostility to the Islamic Republic and its clerical rulers with a turning away from Shia piety at the popular level. In fact, unhappiness with the Khomeini-crafted regime has led many Iranians to go back to Shiism as they knew it before Khomeini. This yearning for an older and less politicized faith also helps to explain why the modest, deeply learned, and plain-living Sistani has so quickly become popular in Iran.

What happens on Tuesday nights near Qom offers another window into the spiritual longings of modern Iranians. Not far from the seminaries, on the city's outskirts, stands a small mosque called Jamkaran. Local belief has it that the Twelfth Imam once appeared and offered prayers at this mosque. Its symbolism is somewhat like that of the shrine of Fatima in Portugal, where many Catholics believe the Virgin Mary appeared six times to three children in 1917. The Jamkaran mosque was long a sacred place, but not a well-known one until recently. Sometime during the past decade—the decade of reformist hopes and disappointment—its reputation spread. People, especially young people, now go to the mosque from near and far. On Tuesday evenings, thousands throng there to pray, and many serve in its vast kitchen devoted to feeding the poor. The popularity of the mosque was not lost on the newly elected Ahmadinejad, who was quick to commit government funds to its restoration as he outlined his populist agenda.

At the rear of the mosque is the "Well of Requests." It marks, it is said, the precise spot where the Twelfth Imam once became miraculously unhidden for a brief shining moment of loving communion with his Creator. The well is covered by two small metal grids. Covering the grids are small strings knotted around the metal bars. Much like a votive candle burning before an Orthodox icon or Catholic statue, or a prayer written in Hebrew on a scrap of paper and placed between the ancient stones of Jerusalem's Wailing Wall, each bit of string represents a human soul's humble plea for God's divine mercy. Every morning Jamkaran's custodians cut away the strings. By afternoon the bars are covered with more. The mosque's entrance features giant photographs of Khomeini and his successor, an ironic feature of the décor, given how strongly the Islamic Republic's founder disliked the kind of piety that Jamkaran embodies.

Going to Jamkaran on a Tuesday night makes it hard to see Iran as anything but deeply Shia, closely attached to the stories and beliefs that have sustained the faith over the centuries and account for its spirituality. So close to the Islamic Republic's seat of power in Qom and even under the watchful eyes of Khomeini's and Khamenei's portraits, and despite Ahmadeinejd's appeal to its popularity, Jamkaran has become as powerful a symbol of Iran's rejection of Khomeini's brand of Shiism as the reformist voters who challenged the Islamic Republic at the polls.

Events in Iraq have only increased this tendency. The opening of the shrine cities has been an emotional event for Iranians, and many regard Ayatollah Sistani as the religious leader they had unconsciously been yearning for. Sistani has brought back respect for the ulama in Iran, washing away the cynicism that had developed toward Iran's clerical rulers, whose reputation for corruption has become legendary. Since Saddam's fall, many Iranians have begun giving their religious taxes and donations to Sistani's representative in Qom, where Sistani enjoys great popularity and influence among the city's merchants and in its teeming bazaars, or directly to his office in Najaf. Many who go to Najaf return home as Sistani's followers. Some three decades ago, in 1975, after the Shah and Saddam signed a peace treaty, Iranian pilgrims flocked to Najaf and Karbala. Many returned as devotees of Ayatollah Khomeini, who then lived in exile in Najaf. They funneled money to him and brought back his messages in the form of pamphlets and audiocassettes. Sistani and his quietist message now command the allegiance of the new wave of pilgrims who go to Iraq.

The hundreds of thousands of Iranians who now visit the shrine cities of Iraq, much like the twelve million who visit the shrine of Imam Reza in Mashad every year, show that the Islamic Republic may have lost steam but Shiism is still thriving in Iran. The piety of the everyday folk who trek to Jamkaran and Karbala binds them to their coreligionists in the Arab world and South Asia, and that will sustain the Shia revival and do much to determine its political force and valence.

Just five years ago, Iran was flanked by hostile Sunni regimes—the Taliban-Pakistan-Saudi axis to the east and Iraq to the west. Iranians have welcomed the collapse of the Sunni wall around them since 2001 and see the Shia revival as the means for preventing its return. In fact, the post-9/11 U.S.-led destruction of the Taliban and Saddam regimes has freed Iran to expand its regional influence at a time when the country's vibrant cultural and economic scene demands greater expression. In many regards, the years since 2001 have been for Iran a "Prussian moment," comparable to the era of growing influence for Berlin that Otto von Bismarck managed to engineer across the German-speaking world in the mid-nineteenth century. The Shia revival will further bolster expansion of Iran's regional influence and its claim to "great power" status. This in turn is tied to Iran's nuclear ambition, which aims both to protect and to perpetuate the country's regional role.

Zulfiqar Ali Bhutto once dubbed Pakistan's atomic bomb the "Islamic bomb," as the counterbalance to the "Hindu bomb" of India. In the 1990s, Pakistan's nuclear capacity gradually took the shape of a "Sunni bomb," as it sat in the middle of the Saudi-Pakistani-Taliban axis on Iran's east. It was an open secret then that Saudi Arabia, Iran's perennial nemesis, was a major financial backer of the Pakistani nuclear program, no doubt with the kingdom's security interests and regional ambitions in mind.[4] It was in worrying about that axis—and the threat from Ba'thist Iraq—that Iran first became interested in a nuclear arsenal. An Iranian nuclear capability would have helped Iran to contain the Sunni pressure and even reverse the balance of power to its own advantage. The prospect of a nuclear Iran will now ensure that the post-2001 strategic gains will not be reversed. An Iranian bomb will also be a Shia bomb, confirming Shia power in the region and protecting Iran's larger footprint.

Iran's position also depends on the network of Kalashnikov-toting militias that form the backbone of Shia power represented by the web of clerics and centers of religious learning. From Hezbollah in Lebanon to the Badr Brigade and Mahdi Army in Iraq, the Baseej volunteer force in Iran, and the Army of Muhammad (Sipah-i Muhammad) in Pakistan, Shia militias project Shia power and enforce the will of the clerics. All these militias have been organized, trained, and funded by Iran's Revolutionary Guards—itself a Shia militia before it grew into a full-fledged military force. They are links in a chain that represents the muscle of the Shia.

In Iraq, Iran's primary objective is to ensure that Ba'thism and Arab nationalism—Sunni rule in an altered guise—do not return to power. The more violent the Sunni insurgency becomes and the more Shias it kills, the more determined Iran grows. The moderate grand ayatollah Yousef Saneie, who lives in Qom, reacted to the growing ferocity of suicide bombing during the summer of 2005 by saying that the suicide bombers are "wolves without pity" and "sooner rather than later, Iran will have to put them down."[5] The higher up one goes in Iran's government, the stronger this feeling becomes. Iraqi clerics who escaped Saddam's rule are a notable force in Qom. Their seminaries have trained Iranian and Iraqi seminarians, and some of their most notable scholars have become leaders of the Islamic Republic. The powerful head of Iran's judiciary, Ayatollah Mahmoud Hashemi-Shahroudi, is an Iraqi—a student of Muhammad Baqir al-Sadr's—and speaks Persian only with difficulty.

At the height of the Iran-Iraq war, the Revolutionary Guards found enthusiastic volunteers among the children of those Iranians whom Saddam had expelled from Iraq in the 1970s as part of his

Arabization campaign. Eager to fight Saddam and Ba'thism, these young people joined the war effort, and many rose through the ranks. Today some of these "returnees from Iraq" (*moavedin-e Iraq*), as they are called in Iran, such as the one-time deputy commander of the Revolutionary Guards and senior adviser to the supreme leader General Muhammad Baqer Zolqadr, are among the most powerful men in Iran. These leaders view Arab nationalism as anti-Iranian and see an Iraq defined by Shia identity as friendlier to Iran. They are committed to restoring Iran's cultural and religious presence in Shia Iraq and to erasing the impact of Ba'thism. They hope that things can go back to the way they were when large communities of Iranian clerics and merchants lived in Najaf and Karbala and Shia identity tied Arab and Iranian Shias together in ways that secular nationalism could not touch. For these leaders, whatever ideological differences they may have with Ayatollah Sistani pale before the symbolism of an Iranian cleric dominating the religious scene in Shia Iraq.

Many among those who were expelled by Saddam decades ago —including the senior denizen of Qom and a teacher of the Haqqani seminary, Ayatollah Muhammad Ali Taskhiri—have returned to Iraq to rebuild an Iranian presence, laying claim to property they lost—which was often given to Sunni families.[6] On their heels have come Iraqi Shia exiles who escaped Saddam's repression in the 1980s and 1990s. These "Iranian exiles" (*al-jaliyya al-Iraniya*) have eagerly joined Iraqi political life. They can be found in municipal and provincial assemblies, mosques and seminaries, and in government offices in virtually every Shia town from Basra to Baghdad. It is often through them that Iran channels its spending on clinics, schools, and social work. The returnees, Iranian or Iraqi, represent Iran's influence in Iraq and strengthen ties between the two countries.

Many more in Iran's leadership, including President Ahmadinejad and a large number of senior Revolutionary Guards officers, are veterans of the Iran-Iraq war; some fought in its most ferocious battles, such as the fight over the Faw Peninsula, when Saddam used chemical weapons. They see Iraq's pacification under a Shia leadership as a strategic objective: what they were not able to win in the Iran-Iraq war, they can now get courtesy of coalition forces and the Shia government in Baghdad. When the Kurds celebrated the inauguration of their National Assembly in Erbil on June 4, 2005, the Iranian envoy captured this sentiment by saying, "This is a great day. Throughout Iraq, the people we supported are in power."[7] He was referring to Iraq's Kurdish president, Jalal Talebani, but also to the Shia leaders who had taken over power in Baghdad. The Iranian public too looks to a Shia Iraq as a source of security, often commenting that "Shia countries do not go to war with one another."

The Iranian presidential election of 2005 also brought to power a leadership that is more keenly aware of the Shia-Sunni divide. President Ahmadinejad, a number of ministers, and some Revolutionary Guards commanders, as well as Mesbah-Yazdi and his potent network of Haqqani alumni, all have ties to the wing of the Islamic Revolution that was most staunchly committed to core Shia values and felt itself more anti-Sunni, and in particular anti-Wahhabi, than the norm. Since Ahmadinejad's election, the tenor of propaganda against Iran's Sunni minority, seen as potential Saudi clients and allies for Iraq's Sunni extremists, has grown more strident. Elements of the Iranian regime are even producing anti-Sunni polemics in Arabic for dissemination beyond Iran.[8]

Unlike Khomeini, with his agenda of subtly steering Shiism closer to Sunnism, these conservative leaders wanted the revolution to empower Shiism and entrench its identity. Their rise to the helm in Iran will make Shia revival and contending with Sunni resistance to it more central to Iran's politics and its regional ambitions. The

2005 presidential election mobilized and gave voice to those Iranians who feel most drawn to the Shia revival and resent the Sunni backlash against it most keenly. The throngs who voted for Ahmadinejad come from humble religious backgrounds. Regardless of what they feel about politics, they are deeply attached to the core values and piety of Shiism, which is in turn tightly bound with the shrine cities of Iraq, and they are offended by the tenor and ferocity of sectarian violence.

The conservative leaders who have risen to the top in Iran share these feelings, and their language of power echoes the mood on the street. Still, Iran's leaders also understand that Iran can achieve great-power status only if it can reduce Sunni resistance to Shia revival. For this reason they have taken a page from Khomeini's strategy of focusing attention on the United States and Israel to divert attention from the sectarian divide.

Chapter 9

THE BATTLE FOR THE MIDDLE EAST

Salt is an ancient Jordanian town, a short twenty minutes' drive north of Amman. Salt was a trading center, once the most important settlement between the Jordan River and the desert lands to the east. In the Ottoman period, it was the capital of the Balqa region, which covered roughly the same territory as modern Jordan. It is a picturesque little town, with narrow streets and charming houses that have tall arched windows in the style of the late Ottoman period. During its heyday, Salt was a cosmopolitan, tolerant place where Muslims and Christians lived together in peace.

This town of many churches showed a different face in March 2005. During that month there was a much-publicized wake for a native son of Salt, Raed Mansour al-Banna, who had died on February 28 hundreds of miles to the south, in the Iraqi city of Hilla, some sixty miles south of Baghdad. Raed was the suicide bomber who killed 125 Shias and wounded another 150 in one of the worst suicide bombings in postwar Iraq. His bomb had killed new recruits who were lined up waiting to join the Iraqi security forces. The government building that Raed targeted was next to an open-air market, so his bomb killed many women and children as well. Even by the standards of the gruesome violence that various "irreconcilables" were using to stop progress in post-Saddam Iraq, the massacre in Hilla was a brutal and shocking act of terror.

Salt, however, seemed to feel proud of its son. Many of the town's young men had done much as Raed had, going over the border during the previous two years in order to gather behind their countryman, Abu Musab al-Zarqawi, as their *amir* (commander) and fight for him against Americans and Shias.[1] Raed's family held a three-day wake for him. Those who attended "celebrated" what they called his "martyrdom," as Jordanian newspapers reported. The Shias whom Raed had murdered drew no sympathy at the wake. For Raed to have been a martyr, those Shias by definition must have been infidels whose murder was justified. The tale of Hilla and Salt is emblematic of how Iraq has been changing the hearts and minds of some Sunnis in the region, and of the divide that now separates Shias and Sunnis, and of the bloodletting that will define the boundaries between the two.

The celebration in Salt brought retribution in Baghdad. Enraged by reports of the wake, a Shia mob attacked the Jordanian embassy on March 20. Iraq and Jordan exchanged strong words and withdrew their respective diplomats. Jordan, which had been Iraq's gateway to the world during the years of wars and sanctions, was now estranged from its neighbor. Sectarian tensions were driving old allies apart, replacing the filial bonds of Arab identity and longstanding ties of commerce with deep suspicions. For Iraq's Shias, Jordan was the country of Abu Musab al-Zarqawi and the haven for

Ba'thist exiles. For many in Jordan, Iraq was fast becoming a Shia country friendlier to Iran than to its Arab neighbors. Iraq would, however, be only a beginning.

The extremist narrative that combines anti-Shiism and anti-Americanism is especially resonant in the Arab countries surrounding Iraq, where the war and its violence have had the greatest impact. The ties that bind Iraq with its neighbors are old and deep, involving religion, ethnicity, ideology, and tribal affiliation. These ties also relate Sunni extremism in Iraq to developments elsewhere in the Middle East.

Al-Anbar and the Euphrates Valley, where the Sunni insurgency has based its war on America and the Shia, have close ties of trade, blood, and creed with Jordan, Syria, and Saudi Arabia. Some forty miles west of Baghdad astride the highway to Amman, in the Iraqi province of al-Anbar, Fallujah was once the crossroads of caravans going west from Baghdad to Salt and Amman and north from Riyadh and Nejd in today's Saudi Arabia to Mosul, Aleppo, and Damascus in Syria. Fallujans have been tied to Jordanians, Syrians, and Saudis by tribe, family, and marriage.[2] These relationships predate the post–World War I map of the Middle East. Fallujah was the first important stop for caravans moving north from Nejd, the seat of power in Saudi Arabia and the home of Wahhabism, and caravans from Nejd brought Wahhabi ideas to Fallujah, which were strengthened by tribal, commercial, and marital relations between Fallujans and Nejdis. These ties make the fate of Fallujah, and more broadly that of the Sunnis, so near and dear to Saudis.

Now this city of some 350,000 inhabitants has come to symbolize the Sunni resistance to U.S. occupation throughout the so-called Sunni Triangle. Until U.S. troops occupied Fallujah in November 2004, the city had served as the hotbed of the insurgency. But its tradition of Islamic resistance to occupation stretches back to before

Iraq existed. Not only did the insurgency focus on Fallujah, but Fallujah's legacy propped up the insurgency. Called "the city of minarets" for its more than two hundred mosques, Fallujah has long been an important center of Sunni Islam and its politics in Iraq. In 1920 a local leader named Sheikh al-Dhari rebelled against the British forces.[3] Then as now, Fallujah was subdued by force, and after much bloodshed. Sheikh al-Dhari's grandson, Sheikh Harith al-Dhari, is the secretary-general of the Association of Muslim Clerics and the imam of Umm al-Qora mosque, one of the most important in Baghdad, with ties to the insurgency.

It was during the decade of sanctions, as central power weakened, that the fundamentalism and Salafism associated with the insurgency grew roots in Iraq. The works of the Iraqi exile thinker Muhammad Ahmad al-Rashid on jihad and the Islamic state, which were smuggled from Egypt, gained a following, but more important, the tentacles of fundamentalist and Salafist trends popular elsewhere in the region began to penetrate the country.

The Muslim Brotherhood, with its strong presence in Jordan and Syria and affiliation with the Wahhabi establishment in Saudi Arabia, established itself in the Sunni regions of western Iraq that border on Jordan and Syria, and is today entrenched in the Iraqi Islamic Party. Firebrand preachers such as the Egyptian Hamid Kashk and the Syrian Mahmoud Qoul Aghassi (also known as Abu Qaqaa) were popular with Iraqi Sunnis even before the war, and copies of their sermons became ubiquitous in Sunni towns afterward. Throughout the decade of anti-Saddam sanctions, Jordanian mosques remained concerned with the plight of ordinary Iraqis and raised funds that were disbursed through mosque networks in Iraq.[4] Also active in Iraq were Islamic activists such as Laith Shubailath of Jordan and extremist Salafist activists—some with close ties to al-Qaeda—such as Muhammad al-Maqdisi, who is a friend and by some accounts one of Zarqawi's mentors. Before the war toppled the Saddam regime, extremists from everywhere would come to the Jordanian-Iraqi border towns to buy weapons smuggled out of Iraq.[5] Trade in weapons created ties that straddled boundaries and gave extremists contacts and allies inside Iraq, and in turn made it possible for the growing insurgency in that country to spread across the region.

Extremist activists had an incentive to move into Iraq. They were losing ground to the more moderate main body of the Muslim Brotherhood in Jordan and were often hounded by Jordanian or Syrian security forces. Their activism over the decade leading to the Iraq war not only introduced fundamentalist thinking in al-Anbar but also created organizational links that would facilitate the insurgency after the war. In fact, Zarqawi's emergence as a force so soon after the war reveals the extent of involvement of Jordanian Salafis in Iraq. Extremist ties between Jordan and Iraq ran in both directions. The flight of hundreds of thousands of Iraqi exiles and refugees to Jordan and Syria has only expanded the opportunity for building extremist networks that cut across national boundaries. The extremism that was exported to Iraq before and during the war, strengthened and radicalized, spread back into Jordan. The same ties also made developments in Iraq directly relevant to Islamic activism in Syria and Saudi Arabia.

Shias in Lebanon, Bahrain, and Saudi Arabia have all watched developments in Iraq with great interest. They all embraced Sistani's pragmatic approach to politics and were quick to echo his call for "one man, one vote." They all looked to gain from following in the footsteps of Iraqi Shias in adopting democracy to turn the tables on the Sunnis. Amal and Hezbollah leaders and preachers praised Sistani, hinting that once again Lebanon would look to Najaf rather than Qom for religious direction.

Hezbollah's endorsement of Sistani was less a spiritual matter than one of political self-interest. Hezbollah's leaders were noticeably cool toward Sistani's call for clerics to withdraw from politics but saw benefit in the symbolism of his leadership. Their initial reaction to developments in Iraq was quickly to adopt Sistani's political formula as their mantra. "One man, one vote" in Lebanon would mean that the Shia, who make up more than two fifths of the population, would dominate government. In the months after the January 2005 elections in Iraq, Hezbollah's television station, al-Manar, continually referred to the "one man, one vote" formula. Hezbollah's endorsement of Sistani and its power play in Lebanon raised the ire of the Sunnis, who had until then stood in awe of the party for its anti-Israeli posture but who saw Iraqi Shias as American stooges and expected Hezbollah to support the Sunni insurgency in Iraq. Hezbollah, however, saw benefits in touting the Iraqi example. When the United States called for Syrian withdrawal from Lebanon and democracy in that country, Hezbollah became more aggressive in its rhetoric, anticipating that just as Sistani had used Washington's call for democracy to force Bremer to concede on the "one man, one vote" formula, in Lebanon too Washington's enthusiasm for democracy would only pave the way for the Shias' rise to power, at the cost of Christians and Sunnis.

In February 2005, after Lebanon's Sunni ex-premier Rafiq Hariri was murdered by the blast of a huge road mine in Beirut, hundreds of thousands of mostly Christian and Sunni demonstrators took peacefully to the streets to denounce Syria's domination of Lebanon. Amal and Hezbollah joined hands to reply with a larger pro-Syrian crowd of their own. The issue of the day was Syrian presence in Lebanon, but the underlying message of these counterdemonstrations was to flaunt Shia power. Not to be outdone, the anti-Syrian crowds grew even larger. The demonstrations served as a prelude to elections in June 2005, in which the alliance of Amal and Hezbollah swept the Shia vote in the south to become a notable voice in the parliament. The Shias had demonstrated their power, but it was clear that it would not be easy to use that power to change the country. A new census (the last one had been in 1932) and changes in Lebanon's electoral map were unlikely to happen painlessly. So after the June elections Hezbollah had to work within the existing system and hope that as democracy gained momentum, political reform would follow. Given the Sunni anger at developments in Iraq, it was prudent for Hezbollah to downplay its approval of Shia empowerment there. Sunni approval of Hezbollah's politics was a great asset that the organization did not want to give up without the palpable promise of greater power in Lebanon. For now Hezbollah distanced itself from sectarian tensions in Iraq, joined the anti-Syrian government, and emphasized Lebanese nationalism (*al-wataniya*) rather than calling for Shia empowerment. That would have to wait for another day.

In doing all this, Hezbollah was following the Iraq model. Shias in Iraq had distanced themselves from Arab nationalism, instead defining themselves as Iraqi and Shia. But without the Sunni domination promoted by Saddam and his brand of Arab nationalism, Iraqi nationalism in a Shia-majority country would become the vehicle for Shia identity. Lebanese nationalism was once promoted by the country's Christian minority, but like the Iraqi Shias, Hezbollah has embraced Lebanese nationalism as defined by Shias, as a mix of Lebanese and Islamic and Arab identities. After resisting Israel, the Shias viewed themselves as defenders of Lebanon. Their Lebanon would continue to support Arab causes—fighting Israel, defending Palestinians, and resisting the occupation of Iraq—but the country's politics and nationalism would not be defined by those causes. In fact, other transnational ties, especially those to Shias beyond the Arab world, would also feature prominently in this new conception of national identity. Shia revival therefore did not mean pan-Shiism or a unitary Shia language of power, but anchoring Shia interests in national identities. In time, "Iraqi-ness" and "Bahraini-ness" and even "Lebanese-ness"—given the Shias' favorable numbers there—may come to mean forms of "Shia-ness" just as Iranian nationalism has long been entwined with Shia identity. For the time being, new conceptions of nationalism, divorced from the Sunni-dominated Arab identity of old, are a convenient way of breaking apart the old order. In time they may transcend sectarian identities as well.

Bahraini Shias reacted somewhat differently from their cousins in Iraq and Lebanon. They constitute more than 70 percent of their tiny island country's population of 700,000 and consider themselves to be the salt of the earth ruled by a minority of Sunni settlers who invaded from Qatar in the eighteenth century.[6] Since Bahrain gained its independence in 1970, Shias have been heavily involved in every coup attempt, street agitation, uprising, and reform movement in the Persian Gulf emirate. Trouble began in earnest in 1994 as the poor and politically marginalized Bahraini Shias protested their lack of jobs and rights. The government reacted brutally, jailing and exiling political and religious leaders and perpetuating the cycle of violence and repression.[7]

In 1999 the country's new ruler, Sheikh Hamad Bin Isa al-Khalifa, decided to open up the political system. This happened at a time of Shia agitation that led to the imprisonment of the Shia leader, Sheikh Abdul-Amir al-Jamri. Eager to consolidate his rule in the face of unrest, the emir called for elections to give the country's population a voice in governance. What he had in mind was not democracy but a parliament of notables that would allow him to control the population by coopting their leaders—"a cooptation of the effendis," as Bahrainis called it dismissively. Many Bahrainis boycotted the 2002 elections, especially the restless Shia youth and those Shia activists who were enamored of the Iranian revolution and followed religious parties such as the al-Wifaq (the Accord) movement and the Front for Islamic Revolution in Bahrain (Al-Jibha al-Islamiya li'l-Tahrir al-Bahrayn).[8] These voices instead called for a complete opening of the political system. Unhappy with limited access to power and the growing prominence of the Wahhabi brand of Islam and the Muslim Brotherhood among Sunnis, the more radical elements in al-Wifaq and the Front began to agitate. The boycott allowed the minority Sunnis to take twenty-seven of the forty seats in the parliament, which only aggravated the situation.

Thus when the second Gulf war came, Bahrain was already restless. The Shia youth, jobless and resentful, looked like the youth of Sadr City. What they lacked was a Bahraini Muqtada al-Sadr. Pictures of Iran's Ayatollah Khamenei and Lebanon's Ayatollah Muhammad Husayn Fadlallah adorned shops and homes. When a local newspaper printed an unflattering cartoon of Ayatollah Khamenei in July 2005, large crowds marched in the capital, Manama, chanting, *"Labeik* Khamenei" (we are responding to your call, Khamenei).[9] Bahraini young people were not keen to follow the leadership of their traditional elders, and less keen to heed their call for calmness and patience. Revolutionary fervor began to give place to democratic hope after Sistani began to clamor for "one person, one vote" and the Shia won the January 30 Iraq elections. As a measure of how closely Bahrainis now followed Iraq, in May 2004 large crowds protested the fighting between U.S. troops and the Mahdi Army in Najaf and Karbala. The mass of Bahraini Shias took the example of Iraq to heart and began to demand real democracy, which would mean a transfer of power to Shias and not just a "House of Lords" to legitimate the Sunni monarchy. In March and June 2005, thousands poured into the streets to ask for full-fledged democracy. They wanted what their numbers warranted, that is, to rule Bahrain just as their cosectarians were now ruling Iraq. Bahrain's sectarian troubles will bear directly on Shia-Sunni relations in the UAE, Kuwait, and, most important, Saudi Arabia, whose Eastern Province sits a stone's throw from the causeway that links Bahrain to the Arabian mainland.

Saudi Shias, unlike their Lebanese and Bahraini coreligionists, are only a minority of 10 to 15 percent, or some two million. Although some live in Mecca, Medina, and even Riyadh, the majority are concentrated in the oases of al-Hasa and Qatif in the oil-rich Eastern Province. Saudi Shias have for years faced religious and economic discrimination, especially after Khomeini locked horns with the Saudi monarchy. They were seen as an Iranian fifth column, and as the drumbeats of Sunni extremism grew louder in the 1990s were increasingly denounced as "Islamic heretics." They were accused of sabotage, most notably for bombing oil pipelines in 1988, which led to the execution of a number of them. Worse yet, the Saudi government responded to Khomeini's threat and militancy among some of its Shia citizens with a collective punishment of the community, restricting their freedoms and marginalizing them economically. Wahhabi ulama were given the green light to sanction violence against the Shia. Several fatwas by the country's leading cleric, Abdul-Aziz ibn Baz, denounced the Shias as apostates, and one by Abdul-Rahman al-Jibrin, a member of the Higher Council of Ulama, even sanctioned the killing of Shias—a call that was reiterated in Wahhabi religious literature as late as 2002.[10]

Unlike Iraq and Lebanon, Saudi Arabia has nothing resembling a Shia elite of any kind. There have been no Shia cabinet ministers. Shias are kept out of critical jobs in the armed forces and the security services. Only a few years ago, the Saudi monarchy made great stir of its decision to add two Shia members (the first ever) to the handpicked 120-member Majlis, which functions as the kingdom's royal council or parliament. Shias got two more members (for a total of four) when the council was expanded to 150 in 2005. There are no Shia mayors or police chiefs, and not one of the three hundred Shia girls' schools in the Eastern Province has a Shia principal. The government restricted the names that Shias could use for their children to discourage them from showing their identity. Meanwhile, Saudi textbooks, criticized for their anti-Semitism, are equally hostile to Shiism, characterizing the faith as a form of heresy and worse than Christianity and Judaism. Wahhabi teachers tell classrooms full of Shia schoolchildren that they are heretics.

In the town of Dammam, a quarter of whose 600,000 residents are Shia, Ashoura is banned, and so is the distinctly Shia call to prayer. There is no Shia cemetery, and there is only one mosque for the town's 150,000 Shias. Shia citizens of Qatif, a city of 900,000, have fared better in recent years. There they are the majority, and since the Iraq war they have been allowed to build new mosques and a seminary and to observe Ashoura in a limited fashion.

Saudi Shias' political leaders have mostly studied in Najaf. Until the 1940s Qatif housed a few seminaries and a small center of religious learning, nicknamed "Little Najaf." Unable to express their faith, let alone teach it, Saudi seminarians went to Iraq. In the 1970s, many prominent Shia leaders, such as Sheikh Hasan al-Saffar, left for Kuwait, where they organized the Islamic Reform Movement (al-Haraka al-Islahiya al-Islamiya) to demand religious and political freedoms. Al-Saffar, who is today the most prominent Saudi Shia leader, returned to Qatif in 1977 to lead the call for reform. The Iranian revolution soon followed, and the Saudi Shia demands for greater rights were swept into Khomeini's broader call for revolution and an end to the Saudi regime. Mass protests erupted in the kingdom in 1979 as Shias defied the government ban on celebrating Ashoura.[11] The Saudi National Guard suppressed the protests, and many activists, including al-Saffar, took refuge in Iran, where they transformed the Shia Reform Movement into the Organization for Islamic Revolution in the Arabian Peninsula (Munazammat al-Thawra al-Islamiya fi'l-Jazira al-Arabiya).[12] By the late 1980s it was evident that a Shia revolution on the Arabian Peninsula was a pipedream. Shia leaders backed away from uncompromising demands to ask for religious and political freedoms. In 1993 King Fahd responded positively to these entreaties by meeting some of al-Saffar's followers. Eager to end active Shia resistance to the Saudi regime, Fahd promised to improve the lot of the Shia, ordered the elimination of derogatory references in textbooks and other forms of explicit discrimination, and allowed many exiles to return.[13]

Continued tensions between Tehran and Riyadh were, however, instrumental in the turn to militancy among some Saudi Shias, who in 1987 formed the Saudi Hezbollah. The group was fingered for the bombing of the American military housing compound in al-Khobar, which killed 19 and wounded 350. The group remained small and did not attract much public support. On the eve of the Iraq war, relations between Shias and the Saudi state remained icy. Shias had for the most part abandoned revolutionary posturing, but discrimination continued, and as Saudi society witnessed an increase in extremism, Shias began to feel more pressure.

Saudi Arabia's Shias reacted to the fall of Saddam's Sunni dictatorship enthusiastically. Almost immediately they demanded rights from the monarchy: to be recognized as citizens of Saudi Arabia and also to be Shia—to call their mosques what they are and to celebrate Ashoura. They asked the House of Saud to formally declare Shiism to be a part of Islam and put an end to Wahhabi attacks on their faith as heresy. They did not seek to separate from the kingdom but asked for a seat at the table. In effect, they asked for what Afghan Shias got in the new post-Taliban constitution in that country.

Soon after the fall of Baghdad, eager to shield Saudi Arabia from the aftershocks of Shia revival in Iraq, Crown Prince Abdullah adopted a conciliatory posture toward Saudi Shias. He met with a delegation of Shia leaders, which presented him with a petition for equal rights signed by 450 Shia men and women, entitled "Partners in the Nation." The crown prince called for a better understanding between Sunnis and Shias and invited prominent Shias to a few sessions of the "national dialogue," a public forum where Saudis are allowed to discuss ways to combat religious extremism. This gesture of good will was followed by a relaxation of restrictions over Shias in Qatif, but not much else changed.

Yet the Shias of Saudi Arabia were not ready to be fobbed off in this way. Looking to the Iraqi model, they adopted the demand for democracy and political reform. Shia voters turned out for the limited local elections of February 2005, which coincided with Ashoura. In some areas Shias pushed the voter turnout up to 45 percent, far higher than the average 20 percent, which led worried Sunnis to urge their coreligionists by text-message and e-mail to show up at the ballot box to deny Shias victory at the polls.[14] Given the developments in Iraq, both Ashoura and the election found added significance: "'We are voting here to show we exist,' said a Shia electrical engineer near the end of a queue of 250 people waiting outside a converted primary school in the eastern city of Dammam."[15]

During the campaign period, Hasan al-Saffar, who had returned from fifteen years of exile, had urged Shia participation in the voting. He openly compared Saudi Arabia and Iraq, implying that democracy would be good for the Shia in both lands, and that just as Iraqi Shias had risked so much to cast their vote, so should their Saudi cousins. Muhammad Mahfouz, the editor of a Shia magazine in Qatif, put it this way: "What is happening today in Iraq raised the political ambitions of the Shi'ites that democracy and public participation are instruments capable of defusing internal disputes, so Shiites can attain their rights and aspirations."[16] The response of Wahhabi clerics to such talk was similar to the one aired by Sunni insurgents in Iraq: Elections will empower Shias and their heresy. Better not to have elections than to empower Shias. The Saudi clerics did not actually highlight this point with bombs, but the underlying sentiment was that of Sunni hegemonism.

In Qatif, Shias won city council seats that enable them to discuss openly the problems that they see facing the community. Given the legacy of relations between Wahhabis and Shias, which have only worsened owing to growing Salafi activism in the kingdom, the potential for sectarian conflict in Saudi Arabia is daunting. It was with Saudi Arabia in mind that in May 2005 Ayatollah Sistani strongly criticized the Yemeni government for its suppression of a rebellion by Zaydis (an offshoot of Shiism) in northwest Yemen.[17] This was a clear warning to the Saudi regime regarding the treatment of its Shia minority and an indication that transnational Shia ties and the Najaf establishment will challenge Sunni regimes, demanding greater rights for local Shia populations.

After he became king, in 2005, Abdullah took steps to defuse tensions. He relaxed some of the restrictions on the Shia. The government allowed the publication of forty works on Shia family law, including some by Hasan al-Saffar. Shias of Medina were allowed to build a larger place of worship to commemorate Imam Husayn (which will also cater to Shia pilgrims). Clashes between Saudi police and Iranian pilgrims who insist on chanting the names of imams during religious occasions in Mecca and Medina also declined.[18] Shias welcomed these improvements, but there is much more to done for them to experience equality and freedom in Saudi Arabia.

———————

What Iran's revolution had failed to do, the Shia revival in post-Saddam Iraq was set to achieve. The challenge that the Shia revival poses to the Sunni Arab domination of the Middle East and to the Sunni conception of political identity and authority is not substantially different from the threat that Khomeini posed. Iran's revolution also sought to break the hegemonic control of the Sunni Arab establishment. The only difference is that last time around the Shias were the more radical and anti-American force, and now the reverse seems to be true.

The same constellation of regional forces that resisted Khomeini's challenge will probably resist this one. Although the context and ideologies at play are different now, the national interests at stake are the same. The battle lines in Iraq today are essentially the same as the ones during the Iran-Iraq war; they have merely moved some two hundred miles to the west. They will likely rest on the line—more or less running through Baghdad, among other places—that separates the predominantly Shia from the predominantly Sunni regions of Iraq.

Iran's strategy in this conflict is the same as it was in the 1980s: to focus attention on anti-American and anti-Israeli issues, appropriate popular Islamic and Arab slogans, and avoid discussion of sectarian differences. This strategy worked for Hezbollah in Lebanon, and the Sadrists, inspired by Hezbollah, tried to implement it in Iraq as well. The Saudi and Jordanian strategy too will be the same as it was in the 1980s: to contain Iran by focusing on sectarian issues and rallying the Sunnis. Hence, while Iran complains about the U.S. and British "occupation" of Iraq, the Jordanian and Saudi monarchies lament sectarianism, the Shia revival, and growing Iranian influence in Iraq. During a visit to the United States in September 2005, a frustrated and uncharacteristically blunt Prince Saud al-Faysal, Saudi Arabia's foreign minister and the son of King Faysal, told his American audience that the potential for disintegration of Iraq was real and that that would "bring other countries in the region into the conflict."[19] Leaving little doubt as to who Saudi Arabia considered to be its greatest rival in that conflict, he chided the United States, saying that "we [Saudi Arabia and the U.S.] fought a war together to keep Iran out of Iraq after Iraq was driven out of Kuwait. Now we are handing the whole country over to Iran without reason."[20] The prince's refrain would soon become the mantra for leaders from Lebanon to Bahrain: warning of growing Iranian influence to gain international support for resisting Shia empowerment.

By seeking to rouse sectarian conflict, Sunni extremists are filling more or less the same role that the alliance between Iraq's Sunni-led Ba'thist regime, Saudi Arabia, Jordan, and Kuwait performed during the Iran-Iraq war, which was to prevent Shia Iran from becoming a regional power. In this sense, the violent Sunni extremists are also serving the national interests of those countries. Although ruling regimes in Riyadh, Amman, and Kuwait stand opposed to Sunni extremism and support the U.S.-led war on terror, their interests in Iraq are aligned with the insurgency and its goal of wrecking a new, Shia-led Iraqi state.

As the scope of the sectarian conflict in Iraq expands, the contours of the regional coalitions with stakes in the conflict will become clearer. As was the case during the Iran-Iraq war, the sectarian struggle in Iraq will metamorphose into a broader struggle for power between the Sunni Arab establishment of old and the emerging Shia power, and between Saudi Arabia and Iran as the natural heavyweights on each side. The extremist character of the insurgency for now has obfuscated the cold reality of this conflict. By the same token, the Shia-Sunni rivalry will also complicate the larger global battle against Sunni extremism.

The war in Iraq came at a time when Sunni extremism was on the rise in the Muslim world. The decade preceding the war had witnessed the growing influence of Wahhabi and Salafi trends in Sunni extremist circles and a turn to jihadi activism and violence after the events of 9/11. The Iraq war provided a new arena for this militancy to express itself. Abu Musab al-Zarqawi went to Iraq with the specific purpose of confronting the United States and providing al-Qaeda's global war against America with a new venue.[21] In Iraq's sectarian divide, Zarqawi and his extremist followers saw an opportunity. A Shia-Sunni civil war would destroy America's project in Iraq far more quickly and thoroughly than al-Qaeda's terrorism could by itself. Sectarian conflict could also make Iraq's conflict a regional one, providing al-Qaeda with a larger base of support and recruitment. Anti-Shia prejudice could be used to augment anti-Americanism, solidify Sunni public opinion, and expand the scope of al-Qaeda's influence to an extent not possible with anti-Americanism alone. After all, America's confrontation with al-Qaeda in Afghanistan never mobilized Arabs on the street. Sectarianism held that promise.

The specter of violence in Iraq feeding Sunni extremism and al-Qaeda's terrorism elsewhere became more real in October 2004, when Zarqawi and his group, Society of Unity of God and Jihad (Jamaat al-Tawhid wa al-Jihad), pledged allegiance (bay'a) to Osama bin Laden, who in turn appointed Zarqawi as his deputy. Zarqawi's operation then adopted the new name of al-Qaeda in Mesopotamia (Tanzim al-Qaeda wa'l-Jihad fi Balad al-Rafidayn). The endorsement of insurgency in Iraq by al-Qaeda also coincided with rise of al-Qaeda cells in Saudi Arabia, Lebanon, the Palestinian territories, and even Iran.

Iran pointed the finger at Iraq's Sunni insurgents in May 2005, when a spate of bombings killed ten people in two Iranian cities shortly before Iran's presidential election. In July 2005, a theretofore unknown group calling itself God's Soldiers of the Sunni Mujahedeen posted a video of the beheading of an Iranian security official.[22] The group is said to be a Salafi outfit, consisting of Sunnis from southeastern Iran with potential ties to insurgents in Iraq. It has been leading a miniature insurgency in Iran's southeastern Baluch region, causing fear that sectarian violence in Iraq is spreading into Iran and that Zarqawi and his allies in Saudi Arabia and elsewhere are intent on targeting Iran directly.[23]

In the months after receiving his bin Laden endorsement, Zarqawi continued to grow in strength. His military capabilities became more sophisticated, as he was able to tap into new sources of financial support and consult with Ba'thists and former Iraqi military officers to improve his arsenal. His followers' presence on the ground was increasingly that of a guerrilla army capable of establishing control over territories and towns across the Euphrates Valley. This made it easier for the United States to target his forces directly in places such as Tal Afar in the fall of 2005. Still, territorial control pointed to the growing breadth of Zarqawi's network. His improved capability also enabled him to operate outside Iraq, relying on a broader network of support, recruits, and resources both to sustain his efforts in the insurgency and to strike elsewhere, most notably in an unsuccessful attack on two U.S. warships in the port of Aqaba in Jordan in August 2005 and the bombing of three hotels in Amman in November 2005. The ultimate impact of Zarqawi's network will depend on the extent to which sectarianism resonates with the broader cross-section of Sunnis in the region and shapes their political attitudes.

In extremist Sunni circles, the Shia revival in Iraq is seen as a calamity, a monumental reversal in the fortunes of Islam. It is also further evidence of sinister U.S. intentions toward Islam after the events of September 11—the grand conspiracy to weaken and sub-jugate the faith. This has served as a new call to arms, expanding the scope of the confrontation with the United States Sectarian feelings now constitute an important dimension of the reaction in the Arab world and beyond to developments in Iraq, especially among the burgeoning extremist Sunni forces, which are growing in promi-nence. To extremists, Washington has snatched Iraq from the hands of "true" Islam and delivered it to "heretical" Shias. In fact, the weakening of the traditional bastions of Sunni Arab power, the regimes in Cairo, Amman, and Riyadh, owing to their failure to pre-vent this "calamity," has made the extremist voice more prominent. The conflict that mattered to the mobilization of extremists and support for them on the Arab and Pakistani streets was not the one Washington was focusing on—it was not the battle of liberty against oppression but rather the age-old battle of the two halves of Islam, Shias and Sunnis. This was the conflict that Iraq has rekindled and this is the conflict that will shape the future.

The fallout from Iraq is perhaps most readily evident in Saudi Arabia, a country that has a restless Shia minority and an ongoing Salafist insurgency with ideological and organizational ties to al-Qaeda and the insurgency in Iraq. Young Saudi men have gone to fight and die in Iraq by the thousands. According to one estimate, of the roughly 1200 foreign fighters captured in Syria between sum-mer 2003 and summer 2005, fully 85 percent were Saudis.[24] It is not clear who financed their recruitment, training, and travel from Saudi Arabia to Syria and on to Iraq. It is clear, however, that Wahhabi and Salafi clerics and activists in the kingdom encouraged them to join the anti-Shia, anti-American jihad in Iraq. The sermons that call the youth to jihad in Iraq reek of anti-Americanism, but just as important, if not more so, they echo the old Wahhabi hatred of the Shia. War on America is now war on Shiism, and war on Shiism is war on America.

Wahhabi fatwas continue to declare Shiism a heresy, but also portray Shiism as a "fifth column for the enemies of true Islam . . . The danger of the Shi'ite heretics to the region . . . is not less than the danger of the Jews and Christians."[25] The war in Iraq has been viewed as the proof of "the strength of the bond between America and the Shi'ite heretics."[26] The well-known Saudi Salafist cleric Saffar al-Hawali boycotted the national dialogue convened by Crown Prince Abdullah in 2003 to protest Shia participation in it.[27] Another Saudi cleric, Abu Abdullah Ahmad al-Imran, described an important objective of the Zarqawi group as attacking the "symbol of heresy of the sons of al-Alqami"—the same Abbasid-era Shia vizier whom Saddam had invoked in order to suggest that the Shia had betrayed Iraq and Islam in the spring of 2003, just as they allegedly had centuries earlier, when the Mongols had swept down on Baghdad.[28]

On March 2, 2004, when a series of bombs in Baghdad and Karbala killed some 143 Shias who were commemorating Ashoura, a Kuwaiti Wahhabi cleric used his website to condemn this cherished Shia holy day as "the biggest display of idolatry" and accused Shias of forming an "axis of evil linking Washington, Tel Aviv, and the Shia holy city of Najaf" to grab Persian Gulf oil and disenfranchise Sunnis.[29] These sentiments were echoed by the Saudi Wahhabi cleric Nasir al-Umar, who accused Iraqi Shias of close ties to the United States and argued that both were enemies of Muslims everywhere.[30] The language of Wahhabi ulama in Saudi Arabia echoes the anti-Shia vitriol of the Taliban in Afghanistan and extremist Sunni forces in Pakistan.

The extremists' commitment to the Sunni cause in Iraq will at some point prove dangerous to the Saudi regime. The current scale of al-Qaeda activism in the kingdom pales before what the full wrath of Wahhabism—filled with fear and rage by the Shia revival in Iraq, and possibly facing Shia demands for rights inside the kingdom—might unleash.

That Saudi Arabia's close ally, the United States, is viewed as complicit in the Shia revival further undermines the House of Saud. The Saudi monarchy's Islamic image has already been tarnished by events in Iraq. Since Riyadh can no longer claim to be sustaining Sunni dominance across the region, it witnessed a decline in its religious legitimacy within the kingdom as well as elsewhere. Al-Qaeda and the Iraqi resistance—jihadis who despise the House of Saud—are now trumpeting this decline. It is difficult for the Saudi monarchy to claim to be the defender of the Sunni prerogative to power in the region without directly supporting the insurgency in Iraq. The Shia revival in Iraq, perhaps more than democracy and prosperity there, may well lead to regime change in Saudi Arabia and elsewhere in the region.

The ripple effects of all this will touch Jordan as well. King Abdullah was correct to worry about a Shia crescent extending from Beirut to Tehran. Yet what should worry Amman is less the Shia power that such a crescent would represent and more the Sunni backlash that it will generate. Sunni extremism has been drawing strength from Iraq. What happened in Salt in March 2005 is emblematic of the mood in Jordan, where 95 percent of the population is Sunni.

Jordan is in many regards already deeply involved in the insurgency and the sectarian conflict in Iraq. The insurgency is at its core an alliance of Zarqawi's followers and Iraqi Ba'thists. Significantly, its power structure is replicated in Jordan, where extremist Sunni activists and Ba'thists meet, conspire, and organize support for the insurgency in Iraq.[31] This de facto base is critical both to the insurgency's operations in Iraq and to its spread across the Middle East. It is through Jordan that the two most intense insurgencies in the region, those in Iraq and in the Palestinian territories, could converge.

Iraq is radicalizing Jordan's fundamentalist debates, infusing them with anti-Shia attitudes. Jordanians sympathize with Iraqi Sunnis and support the cause of the insurgents. Saddam Hussein is popular with Jordan's large Palestinian population, who fondly remember his SCUD missile attack on Tel Aviv in 1990. All this poses a challenge to the Jordanian monarchy. Zarqawi and the Jordanian youth of cities like Zarqa and Salt, who are for now busy with the insurgency in Iraq, nurse a hostility toward the Hashemite dynasty in Amman very much like that which Osama bin Laden and his ilk harbor toward House of Saud. Just as the war in Afghanistan produced an al-Qaeda insurgency in Saudi Arabia, the war in Iraq may produce a similar extremist opposition to the monarchy in Jordan. Jordan has long been vulnerable to the radicalization of Palestinian politics in the West Bank; now it is vulnerable to the radicalization of Sunni politics in al-Anbar.

The deep divide between the Alawi regime in Syria and its largely Sunni population remains. Developments in Iraq have both fueled Sunni anger and raised Sunni expectations of empowerment. The Syrian regime will be threatened by both the example of a minority regime's having fallen just next door and the radicalization of that country's Sunnis.

Although by 2005 an American invasion of Syria no longer appeared likely, still Washington proved eager to reduce Damascus' regional influence. Following the murder of Rafiq Hariri in February 2005, Washington lost no time in supporting the popular anti-Syrian movement in Lebanon that led to Syria's withdrawal of its troops. The U.S. goal was not only to foster democracy in Lebanon but to weaken and possibly topple the Syrian regime by humiliating it.

Syria reacted to the American pressure by maintaining an ambivalent attitude toward the insurgency in Iraq. Although the Asad regime's interest obviously did not lie in the success of Sunni extremist movements at home or in a neighboring land, a too-quick or too-easy American success in Iraq would not benefit Damascus either. Much like Iran, therefore, Syria followed a sort of "controlled chaos" policy toward the situation in Iraq, doing some things at U.S. insistence to help suppress the insurgency (such as arresting some militants) but also quietly looking the other way or even giving some covert support to the insurgency in hopes of keeping the United States pinned down across the border.[32] None of these calibrations, however, obviated the Asad regime's potential vulnerability to the "blowback effect" that could come from growing Sunni extremism in Iraq.

In Lebanon, the opening of the political system and the prospects for democracy hinge on intersectarian harmony. Amal has joined Hezbollah in creating a Shia front that has participated in elections and now joined the government. Yet as Lebanon moves in the direction of democracy, it will have to confront the question of distributing power among its various communities in accord with their numbers. This will be more difficult to manage in an environment of heightened sectarian tensions in the region as a whole. Sunni extremism emanating from Iraq, which has been making headway in Lebanon, will make it more difficult for the country to conduct a new census and undertake constitutional reforms. It will become more difficult for Hezbollah to rise above the bloody legacy of Lebanon's sectarian divisions and to overcome resistance from Sunni and Christian populations in order to accomplish a peaceful transfer of power to the more numerous Shias. Iraq's sectarian pains are reminiscent of Lebanon's past but may also be a window on its future.

It is clear today that America cannot take comfort in an imagined future for the Middle East, and cannot force the realization of that future. Such an approach guided the path to war in Iraq and has proven to be unworkable. The lesson of Iraq is that trying to force a future of its liking will hasten the advent of those outcomes that the United States most wishes to avoid. Through occupation of Iraq, America has actually made the case for radical Islam—that ours is a war on Islam—encouraging anti-Americanism and fueling extremism and terrorism. The reality that will shape the future of the Middle East is not the debates over democracy or globalization that the Iraq war was supposed to have jump-started but the conflicts between Shias and Sunnis that it precipitated. In time we will come to see this as a central legacy of the Iraq war.

The task before America is now to take stock of the reality of the region after Iraq and to build its relations with the Middle East with that reality in mind. The first fact that confronts the United States is that the most salient threat from extremist interpretations of Islam now wears Sunni garb. It is Sunni militancy—al-Qaeda, Wahhabi and Salafi activists, and the network of Muslim Brotherhood organizations throughout the Middle East, North Africa, and Europe— that poses the greatest threat to U.S. interests. Religious and political ideology among Sunnis in the Middle East, unlike among Shias, is moving in the wrong direction, toward militancy and violence. If the Shias are emerging from their dark years of ideological posturing, revolution, and extremism, the Sunnis seem to be entering theirs, or at least passing into a darker phase.

A grassroots outpouring of sympathy for the victims of September 11 occurred on the streets in only two places in the Muslim world, both within days of the collapse of the twin towers and both among the Shia. The first was in Iran, where tens of thousands snubbed their government to go into the streets of Tehran and hold a candlelight vigil in solidarity with victims of the attacks. The second was in Karachi, where a local party that is closely associated with the city's Shia[33] broke with the public mood in Pakistan to gather thousands to denounce terrorism.[34] What followed September 11 in Afghanistan and Iraq has only strengthened these feelings. The Shia in Afghanistan, between 20 and 25 percent of the population, were brutalized by the Taliban. The constitution adopted in that country in 2003 has broken with tradition to allow a Shia to become president and to recognize Shia law. The Shia have come out from the margins to join the government and take their place in public life. The violent face of Sunni militancy in Iraq underscores the divergent paths that Sunni and Shia politics are taking.

The Shia revival constitutes the most powerful resistance and challenge to Sunni extremism and jihadi activism within the region. Shia revival is an anti-Wahhabi and anti-extremist force. Its objectives are served by change in the regional balance of power and democracy. In turn, democracy will unleash the full extent of the Shia challenge to Sunni extremism. Democracy will bring to power Shia majorities and give greater voice to Shia minorities, whose ideology and politics diverge from the extremist bent of Sunni radicalism.

The war in Iraq may take many directions. The country may split up or hold together; it may sink into civil war, or its competing communities may hammer out a power-sharing formula to make it work. Stability will require compromise among Shias, Sunnis, and Kurds, but it will still place Sunnis at the bottom of a power structure that they once ruled. This will not douse the flames of Sunni extremism that Iraq has stoked across the Middle East. The United States cannot decide what direction sectarian conflict will take. It will instead have to prepare for the unintended consequences of the Iraq war. A second explosion of Islamic extremism will come out of the Iraqi insurgency, whose force and tenacity will be entwined with the Shia-Sunni power balance across the Middle East, and which will seek to use sectarian conflicts to expand the scope of its jihad across the region.

There will also be new forces to contend with—the new Shia voices, separate from the old Arab order with which Washington is so familiar. When the dust settles, the center of gravity will no longer lie with the Arab Sunni countries but will be held by Shia ones. That center of gravity will move eastward, away from Egypt and the Levant to Iran, Iraq, and the Persian Gulf. The United States does not know the Shia well. That will have to change, if for no better reason than that the Shia live on top of some the richest oil fields in the region. It is in America's interest to take Shias and the Shia revival seriously. It will not be easy for the United States to balance the demands of Sunnis with those of Shias, or to hold the hands of the Sunni establishment as it contends with the Shia challenge and the Sunni backlash to it. It is a process that must begin with an understanding of the nature of the conflict and the future that it will shape.

Sectarian identities in the Middle East stretch back a millennium. They matter to society and politics, but the conflicts that they animate are due to the lopsided distribution of resources and power that have benefited one sect at the cost of the other. Over time the Shia-Sunni conflict can be brought under control only if the distribution of power and resources reflects the demographic realities of the region. Dictatorships have done a poor job of building such an order. They have used force to impose the will of the minority over that of the majority, which is a problem in the Middle East well beyond the borders of Iraq—but that is not a lasting formula nor one that will survive political openness. Nor will the messy processes of democratization and globalization immediately solve these problems: they will have winners and losers as well, and ignite new conflicts. As is the case with all disputes involving religion or ethnicity, loyalties die hard, but they are less likely to command bloodshed if they are divorced from social, economic, and political injustices.

The Middle East is bound to go through—indeed, is now going through—a period of violence as the old order gives place to a new one and Shias and Sunnis adjust to the new realities. In time, however, the region will arrive at a new status quo. Most Shias and Sunnis will look for ways to reach a state of peace, to live together and share political goals and aspirations. Democracy will be far more efficient than dictatorship at attaining that inclusive goal. Future stability must be based not on the hegemony of one sect over another but rather on an inclusive vision of Islam and the Arab world that will recognize the identity and beliefs of both Shias and Sunnis and distribute wealth and power in accordance to numbers.

Those forces that are most dangerous to Western interests and to the peace of the region are likely to thrive during this transition. It is in the interests of Shias, Sunnis, and the West to minimize the pains of transition and hasten its end. This means contending with the reality of sectarian rivalries and understanding what motivates them and how they play out socially and politically. As in all wars of religion and conflicts over identity, in the end, peace, like war, is a function first and foremost of recognizing the fact of differences, and only then going beyond them in the pursuit of common goals. It is not possible to tell how the sectarian struggle in Iraq will turn out, or when and where the next battle between Shias and Sunnis will be joined, or how many sectarian battles the Middle East must endure and for how long. What is clear is that the future for the Middle East will not be brighter than the past so long as the shadow of sectarian conflict hangs over it. This is the conflict that will shape the future.

ΠΟΤΕS

INTRODUCTION

1. Roschanak Shaery-Eisenlohr, "Constructing Lebanese Shi'ite Nationalism: Transnationalism, Shi'ism, and the Lebanese State," Ph.D. dissertation, Department of Near Eastern Languages and Civilizations, University of Chicago, 2005, pp. 48–58.

2. Graham E. Fuller and Rend Rahim Francke, *The Arab Shi'a: The Forgotten Muslims* (New York: St. Martin's, 1999), p. 20.

3. Doug Struck, "New Attacks Threaten Political Truce in Iraq," *Washington Post*, Dec. 4, 2005, p. A21.

4. Dexter Filkins, "Sunnis Accuse Iraqi Military of Executions," *New York Times*, Nov. 29, 2005, p. A1.

5. Mark Danner, "Taking Stock of the Forever War," *New York Times*, Sept. 11, 2005; www.nytimes.com/2005/09/11/magazine/11OSAMA.html?ex=1127534400 &en=5ac8138d02c3a89f&ei=5070&emc=etal.

6. Ellen Knickmeyer and Jonathan Finer, "Iraqi Sunnis Battle to Defend Shiites: Tribes Defy an Attempt by Zarqawi to Drive Residents from Western City," *Washington Post*, Aug. 14, 2005, p. A1.

7. Alissa J. Rubin, "Revenge Killings Fuel Fear of Escalation in Iraq," *Los Angeles*

Times, Sept. 11, 2005; www.latimes.com/news/printedition/front/la-fg-assassi-nate11sep11,1,5180083,full.story?coll=la-headlines-frontpage&ctrack =1&cset=true.

Chapter 1. THE OTHER ISLAM: WHO ARE THE SHIA?

1. Mahmoud Ayoub, *Redemptive Suffering in Islam: A Study of the Devotional Aspects of "Ashura" in Twelver Shi'ism* (The Hague: Mouton, 1978).

2. "Shiite," *Columbia Electronic Encyclopedia*, 6th ed. (New York: Columbia University Press., 2003); Answers.com, GuruNet Corp., Oct., 1 2005, www.answers.com/topic/shiite.

3. Ann K. S. Lambton, *State and Government in Medieval Islam: An Introduction to the Study of Islamic Political Theory: The Jurists* (New York: Oxford University Press, 1981).

4. Allamah Sayyid Muhammad Husayn Tabataba'i, *Shi'ite Islam*, Seyyed Hossein Nasr, trans. and ed. (Albany: SUNY Press, 1975), pp. 174–89.

5. Hamid Enayat, *Modern Islamic Political Thought* (Austin: University of Texas Press, 1982), pp. 32–34.

6. Reza Shah-Kazemi, *Justice and Remembrance: Introducing the Spirituality of Imam Ali* (London: I.B. Tauris, 2006).

7. Mahmud Shahabi, "Shi'a," in Kenneth Morgan, ed., *Islam: The Straight Path; Islam Interpreted by Muslims* (New York: Ronald Press, 1958), pp. 188–97.

8. Ayatollah Jafar Sobhani, *Doctrines of Shi'i Islam*, Reza Shah-Kazemi, trans. and ed. (London: I. B. Tauris, 2001), pp. 96–119.

9. Seyyed Hossein Nasr, *Ideals and Realities of Islam* (London: Allen & Unwin, 1966), pp. 160–61.

10. H. A. R. Gibb, *Studies on the Civilization of Islam*, Stanford J. Shaw and William R. Polk, eds. (Princeton, N.J.: Princeton University Press, 1962).

11. Kamran Scot Aghaie, ed. *Women of Karbala: Ritual Performance and Symbolic Discourses in Modern Shi'i Islam* (Austin: University of Texas Press, 2005); David Pinault, "Zaynab bint 'Ali and the Place of the Women of the Households of the First Imams in Shiite Devotional Literature," in Gavin Hambly, ed., *Women in the Medieval Islamic World* (New York: St. Martin's, 1998), pp. 69–98.

12. Shaykh Muhammad Mahdi Shams al-Din, *The Revolution of al-Husayn [a]: Its Impact on the Consciousness of Muslim Society*, I.K.A. Howard, trans. (London: Muhammadi Trust, 1985).

13. Mahmoud Ayoub, "The Excellence of the Imam Husayn in Sunni Hadith Tradition," *Alserat* (London), Imam Husayn Conference Number, 12, 2 (Spring/ Autumn 1986): 58–70.

14. Azim Nanji, "The Imam Husayn: His Role as a Paradigm," ibid. pp. 188–94.

15. David Pinault, *The Shiites: Ritual and Popular Piety in a Muslim Community* (New York: St. Martin's, 1992), pp. 66–72.

16. Rudyard Kipling, "On the City Wall," *Indian Tales* (London: Kessinger, 2004), pp. 135–36.

17. Ehsan Yarshater, "Ta'ziyeh and Pre-Islamic Mourning Rites in Iran," in Peter Chelkowski, ed., *Ta'ziyeh: Ritual and Drama in Iran* (New York: New York University Press, 1979), pp. 88–94; William O. Beeman, "Cultural Dimensions of Performance Conventions in Iranian Ta'ziyeh," ibid. pp. 24–31; Heinz Halm, *Shi'a Islam: From Religion to Revolution* (Princeton, N.J.: Markus Weiner, 1997), pp. 41–85.

18. David Pinault, *Horse of Karbala: Studies in South Asian Muslim Devotionalism* (New York: St. Martin's, 2000), pp. 14–21, 109–56.

19. Juan R. I. Cole, *Roots of North Indian Shi'ism in Iran and Iraq: Religion and State in Awadh, 1722–1859* (Berkeley: University of California Press, 1989), p. 117.

20. Pinault, *The Shiites*, pp. 161–62.

21. Vernon James Schubel, *Religious Performance in Contemporary Islam: Shi'i Devotional Rituals in South Asia* (Columbia: University of South Carolina Press, 1993), pp. 37–38.

22. See various essays in Chelkowski, *Ta'ziyeh*.

23. Enayat, *Modern Islamic Political Thought*, pp. 183–84.

24. Kamran Scot Aghaie, *The Martyrs of Karbala: Shi'i Symbols and Rituals in Modern Iran* (Seattle: University of Washington Press, 2004), pp. 92–93.

25. D. K. Crow, "The Death of Al-Husayn B. 'Ali and Early Shi'i Views of the Imamate," *Alserat* (London), Imam Husayn Conference Number, 12, 2 (Spring/ Autumn 1986): pp. 82–89.

26. Willian C. Chittick, trans. and ed., *A Shi'ite Anthology* (Albany: SUNY Press, 1981), pp. 93, 98.

27. Abbas Kadhim, "The Politics and Theology of Imami Shi'a in Iraq during the 5th/11th Century," Ph.D. dissertation, Near Eastern Studies Department, University of California, Berkeley, 2005, pp. 45–53.

28. Seyyed Nossein Nasr, *Ideals and Realities of Islam* (London: Allen & Unwin, 1966), pp. 121–46.

29. Martin Lings, *What Is Sufism?* (Berkeley: University of California Press,

1975); and Anne Marie Schimmel, *Mystical Dimensions of Islam* (Chapel Hill: University of North Carolina Press, 1975).

30. Javad Nurbakhsh, "The Nimatullahi," in Seyyed Hossein Nasr, ed., *Islamic Spirituality* (New York: Crossroad, 1991), vol. 2, pp. 144–61.

31. Quintan Wiktorowicz, "A Geneology of Radical Islam," *Studies in Conflict and Terrorism* 28, 2 (Mar.-Apr. 2005): pp. 75–97.

32. Edward Wong, "Sufis Under Attack as Sunni Rifts Widen," *New York Times,* Aug. 21, 2005, p. 10.

Chapter 2. THE MAKING OF SHIA POLITICS

1. Marshall Hodgson, *The Venture of Islam* (Chicago: University of Chicago Press, 1977), vol. 3, pp. 1–162.

2. Rula Jurdi Abisaab, *Converting Persia: Religion and Power in the Safavid Empire* (London: I. B. Taurus, 2004).

3. Jean Calmard, "Shi'i Rituals and Power II: The Consolidation of Safavid Shi'ism: Folklore and Popular Religion," in Charles Melville, ed., *Safavid Persia* (London: I. B. Tauris, 1996), pp. 139–90.

4. Abdulaziz A. Sachedina, *Islamic Messianism: The Idea of the Mahdi in Twelver Shi'ism* (Albany: SUNY Press, 1981).

5. Juan Cole, *Sacred Space and Holy War: The Politics, Culture and History of Shi'ite Islam* (London: I. B. Tauris, 2002), pp. 58–77.

6. Shahla Haeri, *Law of Desire: Temporary Marriage in Shi'i Iran* (Syracuse, N.Y.: Syracuse University Press, 1989).

7. William C. Chittick, trans. and ed., *A Shi'ite Anthology* (Albany: SUNY Press, 1981) pp. 68–69.

8. Said A. Arjomand, *The Turban for the Crown: The Islamic Revolution in Iran* (New York: Oxford University Press, 1988), pp. 177–88.

9. Valerie Hoffman-Ladd, "Devotion to the Prophet and His Family in Egyptian Sufism," *International Journal of Middle East Studies* 24, 4 (Nov. 1992): pp. 615–37.

10. Henry Corbin, *En Islam iranien: aspects spirituels et philosophiques; le Shi'isme duodémain* (Paris: Gallimard, 1991).

Chapter 3. THE FADING PROMISE OF ΠATIOΠALISΠ

1. The text of the speech was published in *Al-Quds al-Arabi* (London) under the title "A Letter from Saddam Hussein to the Iraqi People and the Arab Nation," Apr. 29, 2003. See www.al-bab.com/arab/docs/iraq/saddamtapes2.htm.

2. Augustus R. Norton, *Amal and the Shia: The Struggle for the Soul of Lebanon* (Austin: University of Texas Press, 1987).

3. Faleh Jabar, *The Shi'ite Movement in Iraq* (London: Saqi, 2004).

4. Graham E. Fuller and Rend Rahim Francke, *The Arab Shi'a: The Forgotten Muslims* (New York: St. Martin's, 1999), pp. 33–52.

5. Stanley Wolpert, *Jinnah of Pakistan* (New York: Oxford University Press, 1984).

6. Stanley Wolpert, *Zulfi Bhutto of Pakistan* (New York: Oxford University Press, 1993).

7. Elie Kedourie, "Anti-Shiism in Iraq under the Monarchy," *Middle Eastern Studies* 24 (Apr. 1988): 249–53.

8. Toby Dodge, *Inventing Iraq: The Failure of Nation-Building and a History Denied* (New York: Columbia University Press, 2003).

9. Ronald Nettler, "Ibn Taymiyah, Taqi al-Din Ahmad," in John L. Esposito, ed., *The Oxford Encyclopedia of the Modern Islamic World* (New York: Oxford University Press, 1995), vol. 4, pp. 165–66; Muhammad 'Abdul-Haqq Ansari, ed. and trans., *Ibn Taymiyyah Expounds on Islam: Selected Writings of Shaykh al-Islam Taqi ad-Din Ibn Taymiyyah on Islamic Faith, Life, and Society* (Riyadh: General Administration of Culture and Publication, 2000).

10. Taqi al-Din Ahmad Ibn Taymiya, *Minhaj al-Sunnah al-Nabawiya fi naqd al-Kalam al-Shia al-Qadariya (Path of the Prophetic Tradition in Analyzing the Theology of the Shia)* (Cairo, 1962), vol. 2, pp. 361–76.

11. Ibid, vol. 1, pp. 379–85.

12. Hamid Algar, *Wahhabism: A Critical Essay* (Oneonta, N.Y.: Islamic Publications International, 2002); Natana J. DeLong-Bas, *Wahhabi Islam: From Revival and Reform to Global Jihad* (New York: Oxford University Press, 2004).

13. Jacob Goldberg, "The Shi'i Minority in Saudi Arabia," in Juan R. I. Cole and Nikki R. Keddie, eds., *Shi'ism and Social Protest* (New Haven: Yale University Press, 1986), pp. 233–35.

14. Juan R. I. Cole, *Roots of North Indian Shi'ism in Iran and Iraq: Religion and State in Awadh, 1722–1859* (Berkeley: University of California Press, 1988).

15. Saiyid Athar Abbas Rizvi, *A Socio-Intellectual History of the Isna Ashari Shi'is in India* (Canberra: Ma'rifat, 1986), vol. 2, pp. 69–71.

16. Barbara D. Metcalf, *Islamic Revival in British India: Deoband, 1860–1900* (Princeton, N.J.: Princeton University Press, 1982), pp. 57–59.

17. Ibid, pp. 268–80.

18. Albert Hourani, *Arabic Thought in the Liberal Age, 1798–1939* (New York: Cambridge University Press, 1983).

19. Seyyed Vali Reza Nasr, "Religious Modernism in the Arab World, India and Iran: The Perils and Prospects of a Discourse," *Muslim World* 83, 1 (Jan. 1993): pp.20–47.

20. Nikki R. Keddie, *An Islamic Response to Imperialism* (Berkeley: University of California Press, 1983).

21. Karim D. Crow and Ahmad Kazemi Moussavi, *Facing One Qiblah: Legal and Doctrinal Aspects of Sunni and Shi'ah Muslims* (Singapore: Pustaka Nasional, 2005), pp. 16–22.

22. Yitzhak Nakash, *The Shi'is of Iraq* (Princeton: Princeton University Press, 1994).

23. Roschanack Shaery-Eisenlohr, "Ajamis in Lebanon: The Non-Arab Arabs?" *Middle East Report* 237 (Winter 2005): 40–41.

24. Interview of General Mansour Qadar with Gholam Reza Afkhami in the Oral History of Iran Program, Foundation for Iranian Studies, Bethesda, Md, 1986, pp. 40–56.

25. Fouad Ajami, *The Arab Predicament: Arab Political Thought and Practice since 1967*, 2d ed. (New York: Cambridge University Press, 1992); Fouad Ajami, *Vanished Imam: Musa Al-Sadr and the Shia of Lebanon* (Ithaca, N.Y.: Cornell University Press, 1986).

26. "Muhammad Husayn Fadlallah: The Palestinians, the Shi'a, and South Lebanon," *Journal of Palestine Studies* 6, 2 (Winter 1987): p. 3.

27. Silvya Naef, "Shi'i-Shuyu'i or: How to be a Communist in a Holy City," in Rainer Brunner and Werner Ende, eds., *The Twelver Shia in Modern Times* (Leiden: E. J. Brill, 2001), pp. 255–67.

28. Jabar, *The Shi'ite Movement in Iraq*, pp. 128–36, 199–215.

29. "The Shiite Question in Saudi Arabia," *Middle East Report* 45 (Brussels: International Crisis Group, 2005), p. 3.

Chapter 4. KHOMEINI'S MOMENT

1. Alexander Knysh, "*Irfan* Revisited: Khomeini and the Legacy of Islamic Mystical Philosophy," *Middle East Journal* 46, 4 (Autumn 1992): 631–53.

2. Said A. Arjomand, "Ideological Revolution in Shi'ism," in Said A. Arjomand, ed., *Authority and Political Culture in Shi'ism* (Albany: SUNY Press, 1988), pp. 178–209.

3. Mohammad H. Faghfoory, "The Impact of Modernization on the Ulama in Iran, 1925–1941," *Iranian Studies* 26, 3-4 (Summer/Fall 1993): 277–312.

4. Hamid Enayat, "Iran: Khumayni's Concept of the 'Guardianship of the Jurisconsult,'" in James Piscatori, ed., *Islam in the Political Process* (New York: Cambridge University Press, 1983), pp. 160–80.

5. Shahrough Akhavi, *Religion and Politics in Contemporary Iran: Clergy-State Relations in the Pahlavi Period* (Albany: SUNY Press, 1980), p. 165.

6. Interview with a senior aide to the Shah, Washington, D.C., 1989.

7. Hamid Dabashi, *Theology of Discontent: The Ideological Foundation of the Islamic Revolution in Iran* (New York: New York University Press, 1993), 216–72.

8. Ali Rahnema, *An Islamic Utopian: A Political Biography of Ali Shari'ati* (London: I. B. Tauris, 1998).

9. Laleh Bakhtiar, trans. and ed., *Shariati on Shariati and the Muslim Woman* (Chicago: Kazi, 1996), p. xvii.

10. A revolutionary view of Imam Husayn became a cornerstone of urban guerrilla movements that went to battle with the Shah's regime. A noted work in this regard was Ahmad Rezaie, *Nehzat-e Husayni* (*Husayn's Movement*) (Tehran: Sazman-e Mojahedin-e Khalq-e Iran, 1976).

11. An influential book in this regard was Nematollah Salehi Najafabadi, *Shahid-e Javid* (*Immortal Martyr*) (Tehran 1971).

12. Richard Ernsberger Jr., "Religion Versus Reality," *Newsweek International*, Dec. 12, 2005; www.msnbc.msn.com/id/10313618/site/newsweek/.

13. Kamal Tehrani, "Majera-e Shegeftangiz-e Nameh-e Moaven-e Aval-e Rais Jomhour be Imam Zaman" (The Vice President's Astonishing Letter to the Twelfth Imam), *Entekhab* Oct. 16, 2005; www.entekhab.ir/display/?ID=6760&PHPSES SID=b24d119ca808c4c1bfdb21b173a35df4.

14. Haggay Ram, *Myth and Mobilization in Revolutionary Iran: The Use of the Friday Congregational Sermon* (Washington, D.C.: American University Press, 1994).

15. Interview with former Pakistani foreign minister Agha Shahi, Lahore, 1989.

16. Interview with a senior advisor to the Shah, Washington, D.C., 1991.

17. Interview with members of the queen's entourage, Washington, D.C., 1991.

18. Interview with an Iranian exile who met with Saddam in summer 1980. Paris, 1987.

19. Interview with Niaz Naik, former Pakistan foreign secretary, who accompanied General Zia on that trip, Lahore 1990.

Chapter 5. THE BATTLE OF ISLAMIC FUNDAMENTALISMS

1. Michael Sells, trans., *Approaching the Qur'an: The Early Revelations* (Ashland, Ore.: White Cloud, 1999), p. 120.

2. Gilles Kepel, *Jihad: The Trail of Political Islam* (Cambridge: Harvard University Press, 2002).

3. *Herald* (Karachi), Sept. 1992, p. 34.

4. Steve Coll, *Ghost Wars: The Secret History of the CIA, Afghanistan, and Bin Laden, from the Soviet Invasion to September 10, 2001* (New York: Penguin, 2004), especially pp. 214–17.

5. Human Rights Watch Report: "Afghanistan: The Massacre in Mazar-i Sharif," 10, 7 (Nov. 1998); Ahmed Rashid, *Taliban: Militant Islam, Oil and Fundamentalism in Central Asia* (New Haven: Yale University Press, 2001), pp. 62–64, 74; Robert Canfield, "New Trends Among the Hazaras: From 'Amity of Wolves' to 'the Practice of Brotherhood,'" *Iranian Studies* 37, 2 (June 2004): 241–62.

6. Although the actual setting for James Hilton's novel has never been established, many have identified Hunza as a likely candidate; see, for instance, Michael Winn, "Hunza: Shangri La of Islam," *Saudi Aramco World* (Jan.-Feb. 1983); www.saudiaramcoworld.com/issue/198301/hunza-shangri-la.of.islam.htm.

7. Seyyed Vali Reza Nasr, "Islam, the State, and the Rise of Sectarian Militancy in Pakistan," in Christophe Jaffrelot, ed., *Pakistan: Nationalism Without a Nation* (London: Zed Books, 2001), pp. 87–90.

8. Interviews with Pakistani diplomats who accompanied Zia on this visit, Lahore, Pakistan, 1990.

9. Muhmmad Qasim Zaman, "Sectarianism in Pakistan: The Radicalization of Shi'i and Sunni Identities," *Modern Asian Studies* 32, 3 (1998): 687–716.

10. *Herald* (Karachi), May 1994, p. 46.

11. Seyyed Vali Reza Nasr, "The Rise of Sunni Militancy in Pakistan: The Changing Role of Islamism and the Ulama in Society and Politics," *Modern Asian Studies* 34, 1 (Jan. 2000): 162–63.

12. Mary Ann Weaver, "Children of Jihad," *The New Yorker*, June 12, 1995, p. 46.

13. Irfan Husain, "The Assassins at the Gate," *Dawn* (Karachi), June 5, 2004; www.dawn.com/weekly/mazdak/20040605.htm.

Chapter 6. THE TIDE TURNS

1. On controversies surrounding this fatwa see Charles Kurzman, "Pro-U.S. Fatwas," *Middle East Policy* 10, 3 (Fall 2003): 155–66.

2. Philip Kennicott, "The Religious Face of Iraq: Shiite Leader Ali Sistani's Edicts Illuminate the Gap with the West," *Washington Post*, Feb. 18, 2005, p. C1.

3. Cited in Reuel Marc Gerecht, "Ayatollah Democracy," *Atlantic Monthly*, Sept. 2004; www.theatlantic.com/doc/print/200409/gerech.

4. Andrew Cocburn, "Iraq's Oppressed Majority," *Smithsonian*, Dec. 2003, p. 105.

5. Amir Paivar, "Iran's Rafsanjani Praises Sadr's Shi'ite Uprising," *Reuters*, Apr. 10, 2004; http://iranfilter.com/link.php/933.

6. Rod Nordland and Babak Dehghanpisheh, "What Sistani Wants," *Newsweek*, Feb. 14, 2005; www.msnbc.msn.com/id/6920460/site/newsweek/.

7. Vali Nasr and Ali Gheissari, "The Democracy Debate in Iran," *Middle East Policy* 11, 2 (Summer 2004): 94–106

8. Helena Cobban, "Hezbollah's New Face," *Boston Review*, Apr.-May 2005; http://bostonreview.net/BR32.0/cobban.html.

9. Martin Kramer, "The Oracle of Hezbullah: Sayyid Muhammad Husayn Fadlallah," in R. Scott Appleby, ed., *Spokesmen of the Despised: Fundamentalist Leaders of the Middle East* (Chicago: University of Chicago Press, 1997), pp. 83–181.

10. Wilfried Buchta, "Die Islamische Republik Iran und die religiös-politische Kontroverse um die marja'iyat," *Orient* 36, 3 (1995): 459–60.

11. Nicholas Blanford, "Iran, Iraq, and Two Shiite Visions," *Christian Science Monitor*, Feb. 20, 2004; www.csmonitor.com/2004/0220/p01s02-woiq.html.

12. Anthony Shadid, *Night Draws Near: Iraq's People in the Shadow of America's War* (New York: Holt, 2005), pp. 364–65.

Chapter 7. IRAQ: THE FIRST ARAB SHIA STATE

1. Anthony Shadid, *Night Draws Near: Iraq's People in the Shadow of America's War* (New York: Holt, 2005), p. 164.

2. Jon Lee Anderson, "The Candidate," *The New Yorker*, Feb. 2, 2004, p. 63.

3. Rod Nordland, "The Cities Were Not Bathed in Blood" *Newsweek*, Feb. 9, 2005; www.msnbc.msn.com/id/6887461/site/newsweek.

4. Ahmed H. al-Rahim, "The Sistani Factor," *Journal of Democracy* 16, 3 (July 2005): 51.

5. Rod Nordland and Babak Dehghanpisheh, "What Sistani Wants," *Newsweek*, Feb. 14, 2005.; www.msnbc.com/id/6920460/site/newsweek.

6. Anderson, "The Candidate," pp. 51–63.

7. Steve Negus and Dhiya Rasan, "Pro-Iran Shia Group Ahead in Iraq Polls," *Financial Times*, Feb. 11, 2005; http://news.ft.com/cms/s/67b76a9c-7c5f-11d9-8992-00000e2511c8.html.

8. Steven Vincent, "Shiites Bring Rigid Piety to Iraq's South," *Christian Science Monitor*, July 13, 2005; http://search.csmonitor.com/2005/0713/p01s01-wome.htm

9. Andrew Cocburn, "Iraq's Oppressed Majority," *Smithsonian*, Dec. 2003, p. 99.

10. Cited in *Informed Comment*; www.juancole.com/2004/12/voter-registration-stations-attacked.html.

11. Borzou Dargahi, "Sunnis See Iran's Hand in Call for Federalism," *Los Angeles Times*, Aug. 21, 2005. p. A9.

12. For an illuminating reflection of these sentiments, see Shadid, *Night Draws Near.*

13. "Iran in Iraq: How Much Influence?," *Middle East Report* 38 (Brussels: International Crisis Group, 2005), p. 18.

14. Seymour Hersh, "Get Out the Vote," *The New Yorker*, July 25, 2005, www.newyorker.com/fact/content/articles/050725fa_fact.

15. Robin Wright and Peter Baker, "Iraq; Jordan Sees Threat to the Election from Iran," *Washington Post*, Dec. 8, 2004, p. A1.

16. "Badr Commander Killed in Baghdad," *Middle East Online*, July 6, 1005, www.middle-east-online.com/english/?id=13948.

17. Anthony Loyd, "Iraq's Relentless Tide of Murder," *Times* (London), Sept. 30, 2005; www.timesonline.co.uk/article/0,,7374-1804229,00.html.

18. Anthony H. Cordesman and Patrick Baetjer, *The Developing Iraqi Insurgency: Status at the End of 2004* (Washington, D.C.: Center for Strategic and International Studies, 2004); www.csis.org/features/iraq_devinsurgengy.pdf.

19. Ahmed Hashim, "Iraq's Chaos: Why the Insurgency Won't Go Away," *Boston Review*, Oct.–Nov. 2004); http://bostonreview.net/BR29.5/hashim.html.

20. Text available at U.S. Department of State website; www.state.gov/p/nea/rls/31694.htm.

21. Sabrina Tavernise and Robert F. Worth, "Relentless Rebel Attacks Test Shiite Endurance," *New York Times*, Sept. 19, 2005, p. 1.

22. Joe Klein, "Saddam's Revenge," *Time*, Sept. 18, 2005; www.time.com/time/magazine/printout/0,8816,1106307,00.html.

23. Anthony Shadid, "In Iraq: One Religion, Two Realities," *Washington Post*, Dec. 20, 2004, p. A1.

24. "Tosieh-e Ayatollah Safi be Ulama-e al-Azhar: Sokout Manfi ra Beshkanid" (Ayatollah Safi's Recommendation to Ulama of al-Azhar: Break the Negative Silence), *Baztab* (Tehran), Sept. 1, 2005; http://baztab.com/news/28494.php.

25. Abu Bashir Tartousi, "Hawl al-Harb al-Ta'ifiya fi al-Iraq" (About Sectarian War in Iraq), *Tajdid al-Islami*, Sept. 17, 2005; www.tajdeed.org.uk/forums/showthread.php?s=7db36a1f947c54c5884590786a626586&threadid=38120.

26. "Sunni Mufti Warns Against Iraq Civil War," *Middle East Times*, Sept. 18, 2005; www.metimes.com/articles/nrmal.php?Stroy1d=20050919-095301-2195r.

27. "Kalamat al-Shaykh Abu Musab al-Zarqawi wa Radd al Ulama al-Sunnah" (Speech of Sheikh Abu Musab Al-Zarqawi and His Response to the Sunni Ulama), *Tajdid al-Islami*, Sept. 19, 2005; www.tajdeed.org.uk/forums/showthread.php?s=7db36a1f947c54c5884590786a626586&threadid=38120.

28. "Bayan al-Jamaat al-Qaeda Fi Balad al-Rafidayn" (A Statement from al-Qaeda in Mesopotamia)," GoAfalaladyn.com, Sept. 20, 2005; www.goafalaladyn.com/vb/showthread.php?t=5756.

29. "Tawzih min Tanzim al-Qaeda fi Balad al-Rafidayn Hawl Maqif Ba'd Kalamat al-Shaikh Abu Musab Zarqawi" (Clarification from al-Qaeda in Mesopotamia on Its Stand after Sheikh Abu Musab al-Zarqawi's Statement)," GoAfalaladyn.com, Sept. 20 2005; www.goafalaladyn.com/vb/showthread.php?t=5726.

Chapter 8. THE RISE OF IRAΠ

1. John Burns, "Registering New Influence, Iran Sends a Top Aide to Iraq," *New York Times*, May 18, 2005, p. A10.

2. Vali Nasr, "Iran's Peculiar Election: The Conservative Wave Rolls On," *Journal of Democracy* 16, 4 (October 2005): 9–22.

3. Daniel Henninger, "Wonder Land: Here's One Use of U.S. Power Jacques Can't Stop," *Wall Street Journal*, Dec. 17, 2004; p. A14.

4. Ewen MacAskill and Ian Traynor, "Saudis Consider Nuclear Bomb," *Guardian*, Sept. 18, 2003; www.guardian.co.uk/international/story/0,,1044380,00.html.

5. Rober Baer, "The Devil You Think You Know," *Newsweek International*, Aug. 15, 2005; http://msnbc.msn.com/id/8853607/site/newsweek/.

6. Cited in *Informed Comment*, July 3, 2005; www.juancole.com/2005_07_01_juancole_archive.html.

7. Peter W. Galbraith, "Iraq: Bush's Islamic Republic," *New York Review of Books*, Aug. 11, 2005; www.nybooks.com/articles/18150.

8. "Shi'ite Supremacists Emerge from Iran's Shadows," *Asia Times*, Aug. 27, 2005; www.atimes.com/atimes/Middle_East/GI09Ak01.html.

Chapter 9. THE BATTLE FOR THE MIDDLE EAST

1. Sami Moubayed, "Terror Puts Jordan on the Map," *Asia Times*, Aug. 27, 2005); www.atimes.com/atimes/Middle_East/GH27Ak03.html.

2. Rashid Khalidi, "Fallujah 101: A History Lesson about the Town We Are Currently Destroying," *In These Times*, Nov. 12, 2004; www.inthesetimes.com/the ittlist/site/main/article/1683/.

3. Marc Lynch, "Beyond the Arab Street: Iraq and the Arab Public Sphere," *Politics and Society* 31, 1 (March 2003): 67–82.

4. Joseph Braude, *The New Iraq: Rebuilding the Country for Its People, the Middle East, and the World* (New York: Basic, 2003), p. 54.

5. Juan Cole, *Sacred Space and Holy War: The Politics, Culture and History of Shi'ite Islam* (London: I. B. Tauris, 2002), pp. 31–57.

6. Graham E. Fuller and Rend Rahim Francke, *The Arab Shi'a: The Forgotten Muslims* (New York: St. Martin's, 1999), pp. 119–54.

7. Laurence Louër, "Les aléas du compromis des élites au Bahreïn," *Maghreb-Machrek* 177 (Autumn 2003): 59–78.

8. "Bahrain's Sectarian Challenge" *Middle East Report* 40 (Brussels: International Crisis Group, 1005), p. 7.

9. Mazen Mahdi, "Bahraini Shiites Protest Al Ayan Cartoon," *Arab News*, July 3, 2005; www.arabnews.com/?page=4&section=0&article=66306&d=3&m=7&y=2005.

10. Toby Jones, "The Iraq Effect in Saudi Arabia," *Middle East Report* 237 (Winter 2005): 24.

11. Jacob Goldberg, "The Shi'i Minority in Saudi Arabia," in Juan R. I. Cole and Nikki R. Keddie, eds., *Shi'ism and Social Protest* (New Haven: Yale University Press, 1986), p. 239.

12. Madawi al-Rasheed, *A History of Saudi Arabia* (New York: Cambridge University Press, 2001), pp. 146–48.

13. Fuller and Francke, *The Arab Shi'a*, p. 190.

14. Gwenn Okruhlik, "The Irony of Islah (Reform)," *Washington Quarterly*, 28, 4 (Autumn 2005): 161.

15. "Saudi Shia Flock to Polls," *Aljazeera.net*, March 3, 2005; http://english .aljazeera.net/NR/exeres/84CBBC2F-11D0-4A59-BDE3-5B3EBFF104A3.htm.

16. Neil MacFarquhar, "Saudi Shiites, Long Kept Down, Look to Iraq and Assert Rights," *New York Times*, Mar. 2, 2005, p. A1.

17. Jane Novak, "Ayatollah Sistani and the War in Yemen," *Worldpress.org*, May 18, 2005; www.worldpress.org/Mideast/2083.cfm.

18. "Azadiha-ye Taze Rahbar Jadid Arabestan be Shiayan va Zanan" (New Saudi Leader Grants New Freedoms to Shias and Women), *Baztab* (Tehran), Sept. 17, 2005; http://baztab.com/news/29095.php.

19. Joel Brinkley, "Saudi Minister Warns U.S. Iraq May Face Disintegration," *New York Times*, Sept. 23, 2005, p. A6.

20. Richard Beeston, "Two Years On, Iran Is the Only Clear Winner of War on Saddam," *Times Magazine*, Sept. 23, 2005; www.timesonline.co.uk/article/0,,251-1793148_1,00.html. Also see "U.S. Policies Risk Sparking Civil War in Iraq: Saudi FM," *Islamonline*, Sept. 21, 2005; www.islamonline.net/English/News/2005-09/21/article02.shtml.

21. Mark Danner, "Taking Stock of the Forever War," *New York Times*, Sept. 11, 2005; www.nytimes.com/2005/09/11/magazine/11OSAMA.html?ex=1127534400&en=5ac8138d02c3a89f&ei=5070&emc=eta1.

22. "Fears Grow in Iran over Rise of Sunni Insurgency," *Jane's Intelligence Review*, Aug. 2, 2005; www.janes.com/security/international_security/news/jir/jir050804 _1_n.shtm.

23. Mostafa Badrosadat, "Az Ayatollah Sistani ta Mawlavi Abdol-Hamid" (From Ayatollah Sistani to Mawlvi Abdol-Hamid), *Baztab* (Tehran), July 12, 2005; http://baztab.com/news/26347.php.

24. Rober Baer, "The Devil You Think You Know," *Newsweek International*, Aug. 15, 2005; http://msnbc.msn.com/id/8853607/site/newsweek.

25. Michael Scott Doran, "The Saudi Paradox," *Foreign Affairs* 83, 1 (Jan.-Feb. 2004): 46.

26. Ibid, p. 49.

27. "The Shiite Question in Saudi Arabia," *Middle East Report* 45 (Brussels: International Crisis Group, 2005), p. 11.

28. Reuven Paz, "'Zarqawi's Strategy in Iraq'—Is There a New al-Qaeda?" *Occasional Papers* 3, 5 (Herzliya, Israel: Project for Research of Islamic Movements, 2005), p. 3.

29. *Economist*, Mar. 6, 2004, p. 41.

30. Jones, "The Iraq Effect," p. 24.

31. Lee Smith, "Jordan's Baathists Boom: The Economy Is Humming, Thanks to Iraqi Cash," *Weekly Standard*, Sept. 5, 2005; www.weeklystandard.com/Content/Protected/Articles/000/000/006/000vwbne.asp; "Former Regime Members Run Revolt from Jordan," *Reuters*, Aug. 21, 2005; www.alertnet.org/thenews/newsdesk/GEO151076.htm.

32. "Iran in Iraq: How Much Influence?" *Middle East Report* 38 (Brussels: International Crisis Group, 2005), p. ii.

33. The Ethnic party MQM has long been a vehicle for Shia politics, and many of its ward bosses are Shia; see Mumtaz Ahmad, "Shi'i Political Activism in Pakistan," *Studies in Contemporary Islam* 5, 1–2 (Spring–Fall, 2005): p. 59.

34. Cited in Oskar Verkaaik, *Migrants and Militants: Fun and Urban Violence in Pakistan* (Princeton, N.J.: Princeton University Press, 2004), pp. 2–3.

ACKNOWLEDGMENTS

I have incurred many debts in writing this book. Thanks to all the colleagues, statesmen, religious leaders, and average people across the Muslim world who over the years shared their wisdom and experiences with me and helped to shape my thinking on this topic. As I wrote this book, I benefited from the suggestions of several friends and colleagues. Some pointed me to new arguments and others to important facts and sources. I am grateful to Rula Abisaab, As'ad Abukhalil, Maryam Abou Zahab, Said A. Arjomand, Anne Marie Baylouni, Afshin Molavi, Ahmad Kazemi Moussavi, Augustus Richard Norton, and Glenn Robinson. Leila Fawaz and Abbas Kadhim deserve a special note of thanks for reading the early drafts of this book and giving it the full measure of their attention and erudition. Philip Costopoulos read what I wrote with great care and empathy, and honed my arguments in more ways than one.

My literary agent, Larry Weissman, was instrumental in getting this book off the ground, and it owes much to his enthusiasm and persistence. My editor at W. W. Norton, Alane Salierno Mason, took special interest in this book. She understood its importance and believed that it told a story that must be heard. She read the manuscript closely and made invaluable suggestions regarding its arguments, structure, and style. Her questions and comments were always thought-provoking, and the book owes much to her insight and guidance. The team at Norton was always a pleasure to work with. Thanks to my copy editor, Liz Duvall, for her meticulous work; and to Alane's editorial assistants, Vanessa Levine-Smith, Lydia-Winslow Fitzpatrick, and Alex Cuadros, for all their help.

Finally, my family deserves a special note of thanks. They patiently supported me during the months of intense writing. My wife, Darya, read the early drafts and made valuable comments. My two sons, Amir and Hossein, along with my little daughter, Donia, who was born at about the same time as the idea for this book, were always an inspiration. My sons' many questions about what I was writing, why, and for whom reminded me that if there is one overriding aim to telling this tale, it is to keep alive the hope for a better future—for them, and for that part of the world they come from.

INDEX

Vali Nasr teaches at the Naval Postgraduate School, where he is professor and associate chair of research at the Department of National Security Affairs. He is also Senior Adjunct Fellow on the Middle East at the Council on Foreign Relations. He was born in Iran and received his B.A. from Tufts University, his M.A.L.D. from the Fletcher School of Law and Diplomacy, and his Ph.D. from the Massachusetts Institute of Technology. He has written extensively on politics and religion in the Middle East and South Asia. His previous books include *Democracy in Iran: History and the Quest for Liberty*; *The Islamic Leviathan: Islam and the Making of State Power*; *Mawdudi and the Making of Islamic Revivalism*; *The Vanguard of the Islamic Revolution: The Jama'at-i Islami of Pakistan*; and *Expectation of the Millennium: Shi'ism in History*. He has also published numerous articles on political Islam and the history and politics of the Middle East and South Asia. He was an associate editor of *The Oxford Dictionary of Islam* and is the advisory editor of *The Oxford Encyclopedia of the Islamic World*. He has also written for the *New York Times, Time,* and the *Washington Post* and is a frequent commentator for CNN, BBC, National Public Radio, and *The Newshour with Jim Lehrer*. His works have been translated into several languages. He has received research awards from the John D. and Catherine T. MacArthur Foundation, the Harry Frank Guggenheim Foundation, and the Social Science Research Council; and is a recipient of the Carnegie Corporation Scholar Award of the Carnegie Corporation of New York. He lives in San Diego, California, with his wife, two sons, and daughter.